Jainism in Southern Karnataka

Jainism in Southern Karnataka
(up to AD 1565)

S.P. Chavan

D.K. Printworld (P) Ltd.
New Delhi

Cataloging in Publication Data — DK
[Courtesy: D.K. Agencies (P) Ltd. <docinfo@dkagencies.com>]

Chavan, S.P. (Shakuntala Prakash), 1962-
Jainism in southern Karnataka, up to AD 1565 / S.P. Chavan.
p. 23 cm.
Revision of the author's thesis (Ph. D.) — under the title: Development of Jainism in southern Karnataka.
Includes bibliographical references (p.)
Includes index.
ISBN 8124603154

1. Jainism — India — Karnataka — History. I. Title. II. Title: Development of Jainism in southern Karnataka.

DDC 294.409 548 7 21

ISBN 81-246-0315-4
First published in India in 2005

Published and Printed by:
D.K. Printworld (P) Ltd.
Regd. Office: 'Sri Kunj', F-52, Bali Nagar
New Delhi-110 015
Phones: (011) 2545-3975; 2546-6019; *Fax*: (011) 2546-5926
E-mail: dkprintworld@vsnl.net
Website: www.dkprintworld.com

Dedicated to

Late Bhupal Tatoba Chavan

&

Smt. Sushila B. Chavan,

My Father- and Mother-in-Law

Foreword

IT gives me a great pleasure to write foreword to this monumental work on Jainism which is one of the leading and minority religion of India. The author Dr. S.P. Chavan took much labour to present the systematic account on "Jainism in Southern Karnataka."

Jainism was born in north India, i.e., in Bihar but later on Karnataka became the second home of Jainism since fourth century BC. She has provided a good account for the development of Jain centres in south Karnataka like Śravaṇbeḷgoḷa, Humcha, Moodbidri, etc., which are the most important Jain Sacred places even today where number of devotees visits, every year.

The idol of Bāhubali installed by the Cāmuṇḍarāja in AD 981 at Śravaṇbeḷgoḷa is one of the wonders of the world and the author describes this in detail, which forms an interesting reading. The author makes use of epigraphical and archaeological evidences to trace the development of Jainism in south Karnataka, besides the works of B.L. Rice, R. Narasimhachar, H.K. Sastri, B.A. Saletore. The personal visit to the historically important places like Humcha, Moodbidri, Śravaṇbeḷgoḷa, etc., helped the researcher to get better insight into the problems dealt in this thesis. Thus it can be said that, she is familiar with the relevant sources both primary and secondary.

Author also narrated very nicely the role of Bhaṭṭārakas of south Karnataka in spreading and projecting Jainism in early medieval period. No doubt this book will be welcomed by academic world at a large scale and for everyone interested in religious history, this book is in the collectors segment as well as a must for the devoted and true institutions, college and public libraries engrossed in preserving the world religions chronically.

I wish a grand success to the author and this book.

Dr. B.D. Khane

Preface

THIS study focuses on Development of Jainism in Southern Karnataka up to AD 1565, with a special reference to the contribution of Śravaṇbeḷgoḷa, Humcha, Moodbidri and Venur along with the services rendered by Bhaṭṭārakas of these for promoting the course of Jainism in this area. Jainism first came into existence in northern India, but after fourth century BC, it penetrated into south Karnataka and Śravaṇbeḷgoḷa became the earliest Jain settlement in south Karnataka. From fourth century BC to AD 1565, i.e., at the end of Vijayanagara empire; Jainism received royal patronage from various royal dynasties like Rāṣṭrakūṭas, Gaṅgas and Vijayanagara empire in Karnataka. Therefore Jainism was a force which flourished for more than two thousand years in Karnataka.

Fortunately, there are a number of epigraphs, inscriptions and old historical monuments available to reconstruct the various stages of development of Jainism in this period.

Some earlier archaeologists, epigraphists and historians of south India like B.L. Rice, R. Narasimhacharya, K.A. Nilkanthasastri, H.K. Sastri, S. Setter, etc., have rendered great services by making all these inscriptions available in English. In addition to epigraphical sources, an abundant literary sources, produced by *paṇḍit*s and Jain *ācārya*s and other scholars during this period, are also important and useful to fill up the gaps. There is no systematic study of the role played by temple cities like Śravaṇbeḷgoḷa, Humcha, Moodbidri, Karkala and Venur in promoting Jainism in south Karnataka.

Personally I visited Śravaṇbeḷgoḷa, Humcha, Moodbidri, Karkala Venur and Mysore University library in order to collect the necessary source material for my research work.

This book is divided into the seven chapters. The first chapter is an introductory in which subject is introduced. Jainism even though first came into existence in north India but later on Karnataka became its second home. A brief survey of a development of Jainism has been taken along with the life and career of Ṛṣabhanātha, Pārśvanātha and Mahāvīra. Again how this religion penetrated into south Karnataka is also narrated.

In the second chapter an endeavour has been made to trace the development of Śravaṇbeḷgoḷa (first phase) which was the earliest Jain centre in Karnataka from fourth century BC to ninth century AD. This is earliest Jain centre responsible for the spread of Jainism and Jain culture in south India.

A number of Jain temples were erected subsequently by the nobles and royal families in and around Śravaṇbeḷgoḷa which developed into powerful centre of Jainism in south India. Again some archaeological evidences and inscriptions are available in large scale, which speak about the glory of Śravaṇbeḷgoḷa in the ancient and medieval period.

In the third chapter (second phase) the development of Śravaṇbeḷagoḷa has been discussed from AD 981 to AD 1565. Because the installation of idol of Bāhubali on the Indragiri hill by Cāmuṇḍarāya, general of Gaṅgarāja AD 981 was an outstanding event in the history of Jainism in south India in general, and Karnataka history in particular. Bāhubali's icon from Śravaṇbeḷgoḷa became one of the wonder of the world.

The fourth chapter deals with Humcha Dist., Śimogā as a Jain centre, which is important place in the religious history of Jains. Humcha is an abode of goddess Padmāvatī, Yakṣiṇī of Pārśvanātha. Moreover Humcha is a historical place where one can find old Jain temples built in eighth to twelfth century AD.

Humcha is famous for the temples of Padmāvatī and Pārśvanātha. There are some Jain temple complexes which speak about the past glory of the site. These temples are not only old but also have some 22 inscriptions.

In the fifth chapter the religious history of Karkala, Moodbidri and Venur as Jain centres since early medieval period has been narrated. The centre of Jain gravity shifted from Humcha to Karakala in the thirteenth century AD. Even today these places have religious importance and a number of pilgrims and tourists not only from India but all over the world visit these places. Venur is also another important Jain centre but it is neglected one. There also is an image of Bāhubali.

In the sixth chapter the role of Bhaṭṭārakas from Śravaṇbeḷgoḷa, Humcha, Moodbidri and Karkala is enumerated, which was important for promoting Jain culture in south Karnataka. Even the present Bhaṭṭārakas of these *pīṭha*s are playing vital role in protecting and spreading Jainism in their respective areas.

The history of Bhaṭṭāraka institutions is interesting and fascinating. Bhaṭṭāraka is regarded as religious ruler of Jain community. The creation, development and reservation of sacred task were notable achievements of Bhaṭṭārakas.

In the last, seventh chapter, conclusions are drawn. To save human race on this globe, peace is required. To maintain peace, *ahiṁsā*, the cardinal principles of Jainism is a must to follow. So study of the development of Jainism in southern Karnataka, no doubt, is useful to the modern student of history.

The present work will open a new dawn to the study of the contribution of other Jain centres in other parts of India and will be useful to the students of history.

Kolhapur **S.P. Chavan**

List of Illustrations

Contents

Acknowledgements

I would like to pay my gratitude to all of them who have helped me in various ways in the completion of my this research work.

I take this opportunity to express heartful reverence to my guide and mentor *guruvarya* Dr. B.D. Khane, Reader, Department of History, Shivaji University, Kolhapur; for his continuous encouragement and guidance that served as a beacon in my research work.

It is a duty of pleasure and privilege to express my sense of gratitue to various writers, authors and archaeologists, whose scholarly works, I have referred to and even incorporated (cited) some relevant portions in support of my research work.

I have been blessed by His Holiness Bhaṭṭāraka Swamijis of Śravaṇbeḷgoḷa, Humcha, Moodbidri, Karkala & Elacharya Rastra Saint 108 Vidhyanand Muniji who has always remained my guide.

I thank the library staff members of Humcha, Śravaṇbeḷgoḷa, Moodbidri, Deccan College, Poona, Mysore University, Karnataka University, Dharawad, where I persued different and important materials for my research work.

Particularly I would like to convey my warm gratitute to my husband Shri Prakash B. Chavan, for his encouragement and co-operation without which this work would not have been completed I also admire son Master Padmaraj & daughter Priti who showed great patience during my research work for past so many years. Besides I am greatful to my parents, mother Menaka and father Dhanapat Talandage and my maternal uncle Neminath Magadum.

I must express my deep appreciation and warm thanks to Susheel Kumar Mittal, Director, D.K. Printworld (P) Ltd., New Delhi for kindly undertaking my this research, for publication and for the generous courtesy, patience and promptitude displayed in the execution and completion of the work within a short span of time.

Dr. S.P. Chavan

List of Abbreviations

ARIE	: *Annual Reports of Indian Epigraphy*
ARSIE	: *Annual Reports of South Indian Epigraphy*
ASI, AR	: *Archaeological Survey of India, Annual Reports*
ASM, AR	: *Archaeological Survey of Mysore, Annual Reports,* Bangalore
ASR	: Archaeological Survey of India, Reports
CHI	: *Comprehensive History of India*, ed., K.A.N. Sastri
EB	: *Encyclopaedia Britannica*
EHD	: *The Early History of the Deccan*
EC	: *Epigraphia Carnatica*
EI	: *Epigraphia Indica*
EJ	: *Epigraphia Janica*
IA	: *Indian Antiquary*
IHQ	: *Indian Historical Quarterly*, Calcutta
Introd	: Introduction
JA	: *Jaina Antiquary*, Arrah
JG	: *Jaina Gazetteer*
JBORS	: *Journal of the Bihar and Orissa Research Society*
JIH	: *Journal of Indian History*
JSB	: *Jaina Sidāhānta Bhāskar*, Arrah (Hindi)
KI	: *Karnataka Inscription*, Dharwar
KSG	: Karnataka Inscription, Dharwar
MAR	: *Mysore Archaeological Reports*

MCg	:	Mysore and Coorg
MJ	:	Medieval Jainism
QJMS	:	*Quarterly Journal of the Mythic Society*
SBJ	:	Sacred Books of the Jains (Series)
SII	:	*South Indian Inscription*
SIR	:	*South Indian Research*, Vepery Madras

Abbreviated Names of Different Tālukas

BL	:	Belūr
Ch	:	Chamrājnagar
Hg	:	Heggadadevankoṭe
HI	:	Holakere
Kp	:	Koppa
Mg	:	Mudgere
Nr	:	Nagar
SB	:	Sorab
SB	:	Śravaṇbeḷgoḷa
Sh	:	Śimogā
Sk	:	Śikārpur
SP	:	Śrīnivāspur
TL	:	Tīrthahallī

Jain's Sacred Places in Karnataka
कर्नाटक के जैन तीर्थस्थान

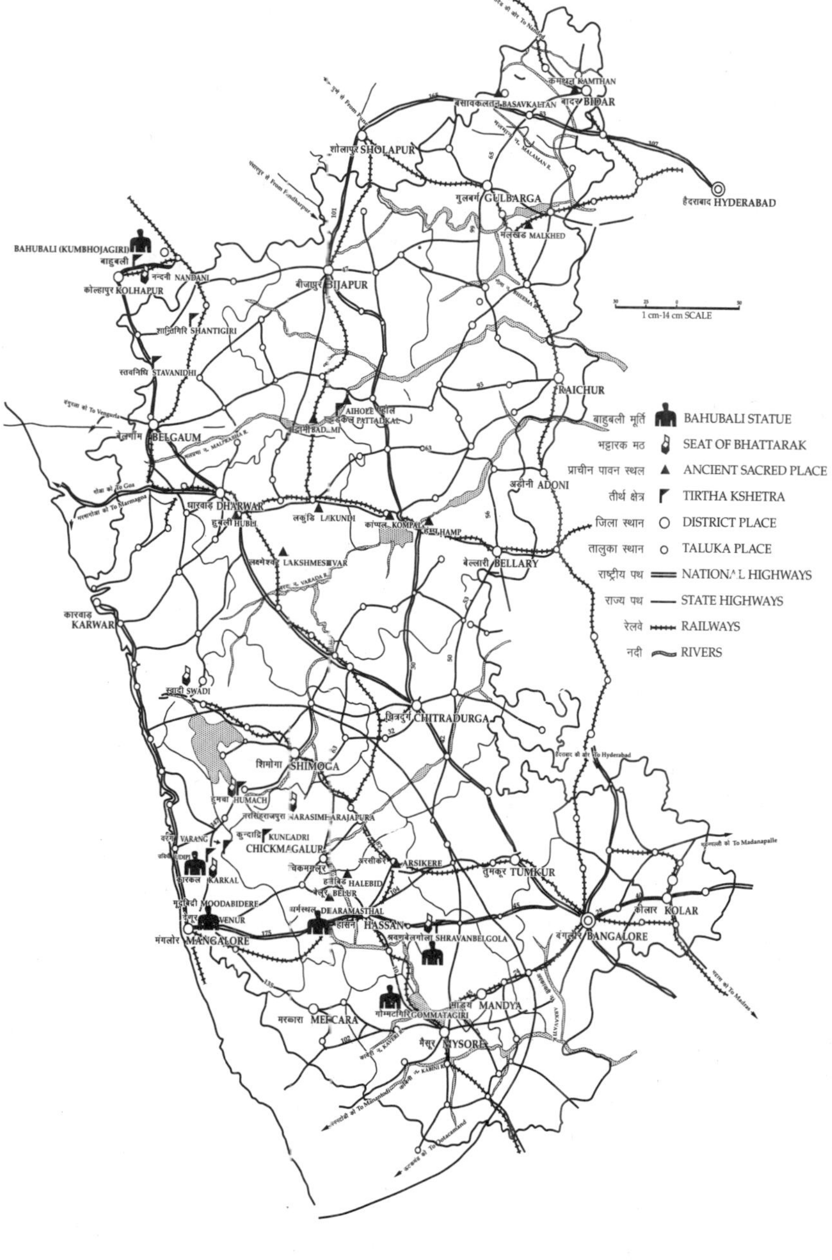

Key to Transliteration

अ *a* (but)	आ *ā* (palm)	इ *i* (it)
ई *ī* (beet)	उ *u* (put)	ऊ *ū* (pool)
ऋ *ṛ* (rhythm)	ए *e* (play)	ऐ *ai* (air)
ओ *o* (toe)	औ *au* (loud)	ळ* *ḷ*
क *ka* (skate)[1]	ख* *kha* (blockhead)[1]	ग *ga* (gate)[1]
घ *gha* (ghost)[1]	ङ *ṅa* (sing)[1]	
च *ca* (chunk)[2]	छ* *cha* (catch him)[2]	ज *ja* (john)[2]
झ *jha* (hedgehog)[2]	ञ *ña* (bunch)[2]	
ट *ṭa* (start)[3]	ठ* *ṭha* (anthill)[3]	ड *ḍa* (dart)[3]
ढ* *ḍha* (godhead)[3]	ण* *ṇa* (under)[3]	
त *ta* (path)[4]	थ *tha* (thunder)[4]	द *da* (that)[4]
ध* *dha* (breathe)[4]	न *na* (numb)[4]	
प *pa* (spin)[5]	फ* *pha* (philosophy)[5]	ब *ba* (bin)[5]
भ *bha* (abhor)[5]	म *ma* (much)[5]	
य *ya* (young)	र *ra* (drama)	ल *la* (luck)
व *va* (vile)	श *śa* (shove)	ष *ṣa* (bushel)
स *sa* (so)	ह *ha* (hum)	क्ष *kṣa* (*kṣatriya*)
त्र *tra* (*trishūl*)	ज्ञ *jña* (*jñāni*)	

अं (˙)*ṁ* (*saṁskṛti*) *ṁ anusvāra* (nasalisation of preceding vowel)

अः *ḥ* (*prātaḥ*) *ḥ visarga* (aspiration of preceding vowel)

* No exact English equivalents for these letters.

[1] guttural [2] palatal [3] lingual [4] dental [5] labial

1

Introductory

JAINISM is one of the prominent religions in India. Though now in minority, it has been one of the oldest religions of India. *Ahiṁsā*, vegetarianism, controlled way of life and the concept of *aparigraha* constitute the main tenets of Jainism. These doctrines emphasize the importance of simplicity, charity and service in life. Jainism has played an important role in shaping the human life and in maintaining balance in environment.

Philosophy apart, Jain monks and their followers have also contributed handsomely to the literature, art, architecture and culture of India. The Jain *grantha bhaṇḍāra*s are recognized as a part of our proud heritage. The Jain temples have attracted people for their sculpturesque beauty.

*Tīrthaṅkara*s and Jain *muni*s have preached love, non-violence and renunciation of *tṛṣṇā* (passion). The fundamental concept underlying the doctrines of Jainism is *LIVE AND LET LIVE.*

Since the times of Bhagwan Ṛṣabhadeva this religion has spread over the different parts of the country. Although the *tīrthaṅkara*s of Jainism were born in Bihar and in the northern provinces of the country, the religion preached by them has also blossomed and flowered in Karnataka as well.

Jainism was founded by 24 *tīrthaṅkara*s from Ṛṣabhanātha, also known as Ādinātha, to Vardhamāna Mahāvīra. All these *tīrthaṅkara*s flourished in north India and due to their endeavour Jainism as a heterodox religion came into existence. Last two of the 24 *tīrthaṅkara*s, namely, Pārśvanātha of eight century BC and

Mahāvīra of the sixth century BC are regarded respectively, as historical personalities.

In the fourth century BC, during the period of Candragupta Maurya, Jainism penetrated into the south and Karnataka became the second home of Jainism. Fortunately, Jainism received royal patronage from Royal dynasties like Kadambas, Cālukyas, Rāṣṭrakūṭas, Gaṅgas, Hoyasalas, and Vijaynagara rulers who ruled Karnataka area from time to time. Even today, there are a number of sacred Jain places like Śravaṇbeḷgoḷa, Humcha, Moodbidri, Karkala, which are located in southern Karnataka. Rich archaeological and literary sources are available to study the spread of Jainism in South Karnataka.

Therefore, sincere attempts have been made in this research work, to study the development of Jainism in southern Karnataka upto AD 1565.

Here it would be quite apt to include a brief physiography and formation of modern Karnataka State which would be of great help in understanding the sites of southern Karnataka and the Jain centres which played a vital role in the development and spread of Jainism in south Karnataka, upto AD 1565.

Formation of Karnataka State

Karnataka is the land of primeval forests, lovely cities, ornate shrines and scenery abounding with all charms of the tropics. Situated between 2000 to 3000 ft above the sea level, it has a mild and salubrious[1] climate attracting and appealing a great number of tourists.

EXTENT, LOCATION AND BOUNDARY

Karnataka may be broadly described as the region inhabited by the Kannaḍa-speaking people in south India. It extends over 1,91,756,97 sq. kms. Situated between longitudes 14º12' E and

1. B.C. Nagaraja, *Jain Temples and Tourist Places of Karnataka*, Bangalore, 1993, p. 1.

78º30' E and latitudes 11º30' N and 18º45' N, Karnataka occupies an important position in the middle of the western half of the south Indian peninsula. Maharashtra to the north, Andhra Pradesh in the east, Tamil Nadu and Kerala in the south and Arabian sea on the west form the boundaries of the present Karnataka State.[2]

The States' Reorganization

The Government of India set-up the States Reorganization Commission (SRC) in 1953 with Syed Fazl Ali as its Chairman and Sardar K.M. Panikar and Pandit H.N. Kunzru as members. They toured the country and submitted their report in 1955. This Commission recommended the division of the whole of the country into fourteen major States and a few strategic States. The SRC enumerated linguistic and cultural homo-geneity as one of the principles.

The SRC favoured the creation of a Karnataka State comprising the Kannaḍa-speaking areas of Bidar, Raichur and Gulbarga districts of the former Hyderabad State and Bijapur, Belgaum, Dhārwāḍ and North Kanara Districts of the former Bombay state. It included the whole of the then part B state of Mysore, the then part C state of Kodagu and South Kanara district and Kasaragod Tāluka of the former Madras State, excluding the Kasaragod Tāluka of the South Kanara district.[3]

Thus, the new Mysore state came into existence on 1 November, 1956 with the Mahārājā of Mysore as its Governor. 17 years later, the state was renamed as Karnataka on 1 November, 1973.[4]

The name of the state was officially changed with effect from 1st November, 1973 with the passing of a resolution, moved

---

2. B.V. Shetty, *Studies in Karnataka History*, New Delhi, 1984, p. 1.
3. I.M. Muthanna, *History of Modern Karnataka*, Bangalore, 1980, p. 89.
4. B.V. Shetty, *op. cit.*, p. 118.

by the State Chief Minister D. Devaraj Urs and unanimously adopted by both the Houses of the State Legislature.[5]

Since 1973, Karnataka State consists of the following districts:

1. Bangalore city (State capital)
2. Bangalore — Rural district
3. Kolar
4. Tumkur
5. Māṇḍya
6. Mysore
7. Koḍagu
8. Hassan
9. Chickmangalur
10. South Kanara
11. Śimogā
12. Citradurga
13. Bellāry
14. Rāicūr
15. Dhārwāḍ
16. Uttara Kannaḍa
17. Belgaum
18. Bījāpur
19. Gulbarga
20. Bidār

Out of these districts, Hassan, Bangalore, Mysore, Śimogā and South Kanara, located in the South Karnataka, are rich for the Jain monuments and sacred places.

Therefore, the study of Śravaṇbeḷgoḷa (Hassan district) Humcha (Śimogā district) — Moodbidri, Karkala, etc., (South Kanara) is important because these centres played vital role in the spread of Jain religion in Karnataka which later became the second home of Jainism.

Before we see the development of Jainism in South Karnataka, it is essential to take a brief survey of Jainism right from its inception and spread in the north India to south India especially in South Karnataka, where, even today, this religion is markedly influential. The cultural contribution of Jainism in south India is also note-worthy. Therefore, the following pages are devoted to study the history of Jainism from its birth to the third century BC, when Candragupta Maurya along with Bhadrabāhu and his 12,000 Jain followers migrated to the South

5. B.V. Shetty, *op. cit.*, p. 118.

Karnataka from Pāṭaliputra and spent his last days at Śravaṇbeḷgoḷa which was the earliest Jain settlement in South Karnataka.

Nature of Jain Religion

It is interesting to see the nature of Jain religion. Jainism is a monastic religion which like Buddhism denies the authority of the Veda, and is therefore regarded by the *Brāhmaṇa*s as heretical.[6]

Jainism has many distinct features of its own. Historically, it occupies a place mid-way between Brāhmaṇism on the one hand and Buddhism on other. The Jain motto of life is ascetic or stoic. The path to happiness and prosperity lies through self-denial, self-abnegation and self-mortification.[7] Again Jainism is a religion of strength, believing that man is spirit and his supreme goal in life or *uttama puruṣārtha* is the attainment of Godhood or arhathood. Jainism, as a system of philosophy, has made substantial contribution to the under-standing of the nature of the world and the problems of life.[8] The Jain faith prescribes its followers a moral system which believes in non-injury (*ahiṁsā*), non-thieving, truthfulness, chastity and detachment from temptations.

Though both Jainism and Buddhism believe in *ahiṁsā*, the concept of final release *mokṣa* differs from *nirvāṇa* in Buddhism. *Mokṣa* is not a mere extinction but an absolute purity and freedom from *karma*. The Buddhist idea of *ahiṁsā* consists in showing mercy to animals, etc., while the Jains carry it to an extreme point since it insists on desisting from hurting even the smallest insect.[9]

---

6. A.K. Jain, *Lord Mahāvīra in the Eyes of Foreigners*, New Delhi, 1975, p. 14.
7. B.C. Law, "A few thoughts on Jainism," in *Journal of Indian History*, vol. XXXIX, Trivandrum, 1961.
8. T.G. Kalaghatgi, *Jainism — A Study*, Mysore, 1976, p. ix.
9. N. Nagaraj, *Śravaṇbeḷgoḷa*, Bangalore, 1980, p. 9.

The Jains believe in the existence of twenty-four *tīrthaṅkara*s and they are accorded the highest position. The *tīrthaṅkara*s are those who attained enlightenment by performing severe austerities and practise of *ahiṁsā* for the benefit of mankind. They are free from the cycle of the life and death. Ṛṣabhanātha was the first *tīrthaṅkara* and the last two being Pārśvanātha and Mahāvīra, who were historical figures. Pārśvanātha prescribed four vows namely non-violence, truthfulness, non-thieving and detachment while the Mahāvīra added chastity as the fifth.[10]

What is Religion?

There is no unanimity regarding the definition of the term religion. Generally it is believed that a religion is a code of devotional and festival rules. Religion is an eternal reality, most pure and sacred. Indeed, religion is meant to show the way to attain salvation or the final beatitude, or freedom from the misery of births and deaths.

One of the remarkable features of our country is that our people regard religion as a beginningless and endless basic of life. Like universe, it is an eternal process in human life. Religion is a thing of soul and it can shine only from within.

The belief of the Jains that religion is a science of soul, and of culture, holds good. Its theory is based on reason and it works on the natural law of cause and effect. The Jains believe that it equips man befittingly to live a righteous life in order to attain its sovereign purpose, the outwardly freedom and freedom within.[11]

As a science, religion is *dharma* which deals with the ways of life for the attainment of the highest aspirations of man. Those who have vanquished all the evil *karma*s and conquered attachment, and aversion and have attained the infinite knowledge of a *kevalī* (omniscient being), are called *jin*s (the

10. N. Nagaraj, *Śravaṇbeḷgoḷa*, Bangalore, 1980, p. 10.
11. K.P. Jain, *The Religion of Tīrthaṅkaras*, U.P., India, 1964, p. 6.

spiritual conquerors) and their followers are called as Jains or Jinists.

It is a fact that eternal science of religion or reality, which omniscient teachers reveal from time to time is named differently after these various epithets of its propounders.

Hence the true eternal religion has been called by different names. The religion which is called Jainism today was known in the past also as the religion of *arhats* or *vrātyas*, *śramaṇas* or *nirgranthas*, though the *tīrthaṅkaras* gave it no particular name. They simply called it *dharma* or *mārga* (the way).[12]

Some Important Concepts of Jainism

Scholars have expressed their views regarding the concept of Jainism in their own way. Dr. J.F. Kohl remarks:

> The Jaina religion is based on pre-Aryan ideas and one of this is animism. It is the source of respect to all living beings and we can learn that *ahiṁsā* is not only the greatest conception, but also one of the most ancient in the world.[13]

Another scholar, Dr. Hermann Jacobi declared that:

> There is nothing to prove that Pārśva was the founder of Jainism. Jain tradition is unanimous in making Ṛṣabha, the first *tīrthaṅkara* (as its founder). . . . There may be something historical in the tradition which makes him the first *tīrthaṅkara*.[14]

Nudity has been the hall-mark of a primitive religion and in Jainism it has been a fundamental principle of asceticism in its highest form.

Dr. Heinrich Zimmer was emphatic on the point when he remarked that:

> Jainism does not drive from the Brāhmaṇa-Āryan sources but

12. K.P. Jain, *The Religion of Tīrthaṅkaras*, U.P., India, 1964, p. 7.
13. K.P. Jain, *op. cit.*, p. 19.
14. *Ibid.*, p. 23.

> reflects the cosmology and anthropology of a much older, pre-Āryan upper class of the north-eastern India.[15]

Jainism is a very old religion, for a scholar can hardly deny eternity of any religion, the roots of which reach back to very remote times of the pre-Āryan races in India.[16]

Jainism: An Independent Pre-Historical Religion of Ancient India

Dr. Hermann Jacobi said:

> Jainism is an original system quite distinct and independent from all others; and that therefore, it is of great importance for the study of philosophical and religious life in an ancient India.[17]

Jainism being the religion of the omniscient *tīrthaṅkara*s, is independent and a practical religion of living truth.[18]

According to Swami Shastri, the modern researches have shown that Jains are not Hindu dissenters but that Jainism and history are long anterior to the *Smṛti*s and Commentaries which are recognized authorities in Hindu law and usage. In fact, Mahāvīra, the last of the Jain Tīrthaṅkara, was contem-porary of Buddha and died about 527 BC. The Jain religion refers to a number of previous *tīrthaṅkara*s which definitely indicates that Jainism as a distinct religion had flourished several centuries before Christ.

It is well known that Jainism rejects authority of the Vedas which form the bedrock of Hinduism and denies the efficacy of various ceremonies which the Hindus consider essential.[19]

These aforesaid interesting concepts of Jainism in which

---

15. K.P. Jain, *op. cit.*, p. 22.
16. *Ibid.*, p. 24.
17. K.P. Jain, *The Religion of Tīrthaṅkara*s, U.P., India, 1964, p. 26.
18. *Ibid.*, p. 27
19. *Ibid.*, p. 25.

many align as well as agree that Jainism is pre-Vedic religion and denies the authority of Vedas.

Jainism as a Pre-Vedic Religion

Some scholars pointed that Jainism is a pre-Vedic religion. Jainism represents a continuation of this pre-Vedic stream. Some of the relics, recovered from the excavations of Mohenjo-Dāro and Harappā, are related to *śramaṇa* or Jain tradition.

Kāyotsarga is generally supposed to belong to the Jain tradition. There are some idols even in *padmāsana* pose. A few others, found at Mohenjo-Dāro, have heads of serpents. They probably belonged to the pre-Vedic *nāga* tribe. The image of the seventh *tīrthaṅkara,* Lord Supārśva has a canopy of serpent heads.[20]

In the Vedic period there existed two distinct religious cultural traditions — the strictly orthodox and Āryan tradition of the Brāhmaṇas and the straggling culture of the *muni*s and *śramaṇa*s, most probably going back to pre-Vedic and pre-Āryan times.[21]

During the later Vedic period, the two streams tended to mingle, and the result was the great religious ferment from which Jainism appears to have originated. Jainism and other *śramika* religious sects grew up among the imperfectly Āryanized communities of the east in response to the cultural atmosphere and social needs. These sects spread out, flourished and became highly popular there. On the other hand, Brāhmaṇical religion had its strong hold in the north and the west.[22]

Further, the existence of Jain religion can be traced not only to Vedic period but even to the Indus valley period of Indian history. The names of Jain *tīrthaṅkara*s are mentioned in the Vedas and there are evidences which show that the Indus valley people

20. K.C. Jain, *Lord Mahāvīra and his Times*, Bihar, 1974, p. 8.
21. *Ibid.*, p. 10.
22. *Ibid.*, p. 11.

must be worshipping Ṛṣabhadeva, the first *tīrthaṅkara* of the Jains along with their deities.[23]

Jainism and Buddhism

Jainism has a little concern with Buddhism, yet it looks strange to find such scholars who have stated that Jainism was an offshoot of Buddhism and some people still think that both the religions are identical.

Prof. Hermann Jacobi, who has established the independence of Jainism on the testimony of the Buddhist scriptures which refer to Jñātṛputra Mahāvīra and his followers by the name of *nirgrantha*s is of opinion that if there was any borrowing between Jainism and Buddhism, it was not on the side of Jainism.[24] In brief Jainism is not an offshoot of Buddhism.

Dr. Heinrich Zimmer has remarked in this context:

> The Buddhist historical records, then would seem to support the traditional Jain representation of Mahāvīra as the last — not the first, as Western scholar until recently have insisted — of the Jain "crossing-makers through the torrent of rebirth to the yonder shore."[25]

As such Jainism and Buddhism are certainly two distinct religions. Although their propounders, Mahāvīra and Buddha were contemporaries, but the concepts and antiquity of Jainism are quiet different and more remote than those of Buddhism. Yet, it is a fact that Mahāvīra and Buddha both laid great stress on the principle of *ahiṁsā*.[26]

Mahāvīra was senior in age to Buddha, the former preceding the latter by a few years. When they had started their career as religious teachers and the reformers Śreṇika, Bimbisāra and Ajātaśatru were powerful kings of Magadha and the Vṛjjī,

---

23. V.A. Sangave, *Jaina Society Through the Ages*, New Delhi, 1992, p. 1.
24. *Jaina Sūtras, SBE*, vol. XXII & XLV, Introduction.
25. K.P. Jain, *The Religion of Tīrthaṅkaras*, p. 32.
26. *Ibid.*, p. 32.

while the Licchavis of Vaiśālī and the Mallas of Kuśinara and Pāvā formed two powerful confederacies.[27]

Thus, the age of Mahāvīra in the sixth century BC is marked by outstanding achievements in different spheres — political, religious, social, economic, artistic and literary. It saw the beginning of the political unification of India under the hegemony of Magadha and the propagation of Buddhism, Jainism and other heterodox religious sects.[28]

The history of Jainism before Lord Mahāvīra is shrouded in considerable obscurity. Evidences which can reconstruct it are scanty, dubious and subject to different interpretations. Scholars have, therefore, come to widely divergent conclusions. The Jains themselves believe that their religion is eternal and that before Mahāvīra (600 BC), there lived 23 *tīrthaṅkara*s who appeared at certain intervals to propagate true religion for the salvation of the world.[29]

Some scholars hold that there are traces of existence of *śramaṇa* culture even in the pre-Vedic times. H. Jacobi tried to prove through both the Buddhist and the Jain records that Pārśvanātha, the immediate predecessor of Mahāvīra who is said to have flourished some 250 years before him, is a historical personality.[30]

The Meaning of Tīrthaṅkara

There are 24 *tīrthaṅkara*s in Jain canon who have been worshipped by Jains since the establishment of Jainism and its practice is observed even today. So it would be worth to know the meaning of *tīrthaṅkara*. The great Ācārya Sāmantabhadra Svāmī declares:

> *yena praṇītam prathu dharma*
> *tīrtham jyeṣṭam janaḥ prāpya jayanti-dukkham.*

---

27. K.C. Jain, *Lord Mahāvīra and his Times,* p. 72.
28. *Ibid.,* Introduction.
29. H. Zimmer, *Philosophies of India,* pp. 217-27.
30. K.C. Jain, *op. cit.,* p. 1.

> A *tīrthaṅkara* is one who creates a great formidable place of *dharma* of the best kind by whose help people conquer their sorrows.

In fact, a *tīrthaṅkara* is an ideal man of perfection, who by pursuing a righteous path based on *ahiṁsā* and truth through-out his life of a layman as well as that of an ascetic obtains perfect knowledge and absolute freedom from *karma*s, which alone keep a man in *saṁsāra* (cycle of existence). Such a perfect and ideal free man was Ṛṣabha and therefore he was called a *tīrthaṅkara*.[31]

He was followed by no less than 23 *tīrthaṅkara*s who were also absolutely perfect and omniscient teachers like him. They all preached and propagated by their ideal life that natural and scientific religion of truth and *ahiṁsā*, which today is known as Jainism.[32]

All *tīrthaṅkara*s were kṣatriyas, Munīsuvrata and Nami belonged to Harivaṁśa, and the remaining 22 to the Ikṣvāku race. The 23rd *tīrthaṅkara*, Pārśva, is said to have lived only for a hundred years and died 250 years before his celebrated successor Mahāvīra, who lived only for 72 years.[33] The tradition of 24 *tīrthaṅkara*s became well established among the Jains in about the first or second century AD.[34]

It is also interesting and fascinating to study the life and work of some important *tīrthaṅkara*s who were responsible to spread Jain Gospel and tenets among their followers. Here is a short sketch of their life.

Ṛṣabha as Founder of Jainism

According to the Jain tradition, Lord Ṛṣabha who belonged to the Ikṣvāku family of Ayodhyā, was the founder of Jainism. His parents were Nābhirāja and Marudevī. The son's name was

31. K.P. Jain, *op. cit.*, p. 43.
32. *Ibid.*
33. *Ibid.*, p. 3.
34. *Ibid.*, p. 5.

Bharata, after whom India is said to be named. We may thus look upon him as a great pioneer in the history of human progress.[35]

It is often said that there is a reference to Lord Ṛṣabha in the Vedic literature. Some Vedic preceptors paid reverence to Lord Ṛṣabha and regarded him as the Lord of Lords.[36] From this it is argued that Ṛṣabha lived before the Vedic times and was the first fountainhead of *śramaṇa* culture. From about the fourth and third centuries BC, it seems that Ṛṣabha became popular as the first *jina*, the *tīrthaṅkara* and the founder of Jainism. Manu and Brāhmaṇical literature has been described as the first ruler and the founder of the new social order.[37]

According to the Jain traditions the following are the *tirthaṅkaras* from 1st to 24th:

1.	Ṛṣabha	2.	Ajit
3.	Sambhav	4.	Abhinandan
5.	Sumati	6.	Padmaprabhu
7.	Supārśva	8.	Candraprabhu
9.	Puṣpa	10.	Śītal
11.	Śreyāṁśa	12.	Vāsupūjya
13.	Vimal	14.	Ananta
15.	Dharma	16.	Śānti
17.	Kunthu	18.	Arrha
19.	Malli	20.	Munisuvrat
21.	Nami	22.	Nemi
23.	Pārśva	24.	Mahāvīra

Among these *tīrthaṅkaras*, Ṛṣabha, Nemināth, Parśvanātha and Mahāvīra are the historical *tīrthaṅkaras*.

---

35. K.P. Jain, *op. cit.*, p. 6
36. *Ibid.*
37. *Ibid.*

Tīrthaṅkara Neminātha or Ariṣṭanemi and His Historicity

Ariṣṭanemi or Neminātha has been mentioned as the *tīrthaṅkara* of the Jains in the *Kalpasūtra*. He was the 22nd *tīrthaṅkara*. He was the son of a king named Samudravijaya of Śauripura, a big town on the bank of the river Yamunā. He was named Ariṣṭanemi because his mother saw in a dream a *nemi*. Giranāra or Raivataka hill is considered to be his *nirvāṇa*-place.[38]

Neminātha has been mentioned in the legend of Śrī Kṛṣṇa as his relative. According to the *Triṣaṣṭiśalākāpuruṣa-Carita*, he was cousin of Lord Kṛṣṇa, who negotiated his marriage with Rājamati, daughter of Ugrasena, ruler of Dvārikā, but Neminātha taking compassion on the animals which were to be slaughtered in connection with the marriage feast left the marriage procession suddenly and renounced the world.[39]

As Jain tradition makes Vāsudeva Kṛṣṇa a contemporary of Tīrthaṅkara Ariṣṭanemi who preceded Pārśvanātha, some scholars identify Ghora Aṅgirasa with Neminātha. Dr. Fuherer declared on the basis of Mathurā Jain antiquities that Neminātha was surely a historical personage.[40] Besides the above literary evidence, there are several ancient inscriptions which mention Lord Nemi as a great *tīrthaṅkara*. These and many other inscriptions corroborate the historicity of Tīrthaṅkara Neminātha.

Lord Pārśvanātha

Lord Pārśvanātha was the 23rd *tīrthaṅkara* born about 250 years before the last Tīrthaṅkara Mahāvīra in 775 BC at Varanasi in the royal house of King Aśvasena of Kāśī. Vāmā was the name of his benevolent mother.

He was a scion of the kṣatriya clan of the *nāga*s called Ugravaṁśī. His royal emblem was a hooded cobra. In the light of the new researches, Lord Pārśva is now being regarded as a

---

38. K.P. Jain, *op. cit.*, p. 77.
39. K.C. Jain, *op. cit.*, p. 7.
40. B.L. Rice, *Epigraphia Indica*, vol. I, p. 389.

historical personage by almost all the modern scholars of history. Though he was not the founder of the Jainism but he was a great reformer.

Lord Pārśva was a historical personality and a renowned teacher of ancient India.[41] The people worship this *tīrthaṅkara* since the eighth century BC. The parents of Mahāvīra, father Siddhārtha and mother Triśalā were also among the followers of Lord Pārśva.

Pārśvanātha as a Historical Figure

H. Jacobi and others have tried to prove on the basis of the authentic Jain and Buddhist records that Pārśva was a historical personage. Their arguments are as follows:

1. In the Buddhist scriptures, there is a reference to the four vows (*cāturyāma dharma*) of Pārśva in contradiction to the five vows of Mahāvīra.
2. The *nirgrantha* was an important sect at the time of the rise of Buddhism.
3. The *Majjhima Nikāya* records a dispute between Buddha Sakdal, the son of a *nirgrantha*. Sakdal was not himself a *nirgrantha*.
4. The existence of Pārśva in Mahāvīra's time is proved by the reported disputes between the followers of Pārśva and those of Mahāvīra.[42]

These arguments clearly show that Pārśvanātha was a real historical figure. As Pārśva (877-777 BC) was probably the first historical Jain, he had a large number of followers in and around Magadha. During those days, as said earlier, Mahāvīra's parents also worshipped Pārśvanātha.[43]

---

41. K.C. Jain, *op. cit.*, p. 87.
42. *Ibid.*, pp. 11-12.
43. *Ibid.*, p. 16.

Prof. Jaichandra Vidyalankara writes:

> *Tīrthaṅkara* Pārśva flourished in the ninth-eighth century BC. The Jains believe that their religion is very ancient and the 23 other *tīrthaṅkaras* existed even before Mahāvīra. It is not just and proper to regard this belief as quite erroneous and baseless, and to regard all-previous *tīrthaṅkaras* as imaginary beings and unhistorical would also be improper. There is nothing unbelievable about it. The early history of India is as much Jainistic as it is of those who profess the *vedas* . . . for the present the modern critics have accepted the historicity of Tīrthaṅakara Pārśva.

These are definite proofs of the fact that there existed in India sects different from the Vedic faith even before Mahāvīra.[44]

Lord Mahāvīra

The age of Lord Mahāvīra may be said to have marked a new epoch in Indian history. Also known as "The historic period," it provides a firm basis for the reconstruction of Indian chronology by furnishing dates of the death of Mahāvīra and Buddha.[45]

Lord Mahāvīra, the last *tīrthaṅkara* of the Jains, is described as a supreme personality and acknowledged as a great brāhmaṇa, a great guardian, a great guide, a great preacher, a great pilot and a great recluse. There gathered a large number of men and women belonging to different castes and classes around his personality. His disciples and followers sincerely believed that their Master was, whether walking or sitting, gifted with a supreme knowledge and vision of the *summun bonum*.

It is this earnest belief in the greatness of the teacher that induced them to repose their trust in him and in his words. To them, he stood as a living example of highest human virtue and perfection. His life was to them a perennial source of light and

44. K.P. Jain, *op. cit.*, p. 86.
45. K.C. Jain, *op. cit.*, p. 18.

inspiration. His sufferings and forbearance kept them steady in all their trials and tribulations. And his teachings and instructions were for them not ordinary words but utterances of one who saw the light of truth and was able to lead others along with the path to enlightenment.[46]

His Clan

"Mahāvīra" or the great hero was not the personal name of the religious teacher. He was better known to his contemporaries as *nirgrantha*, Nāta-Putta-Nigantha of the Nāta or Nāya clan. This name is composed of two separate epithets, *nigrantha* and *nātaputta*, the former implying religious and the latter secular. He was Nigrantha (*nirgrantha*) in a literal as well as in a figurative sense — unclothed and free from all worldly bonds and ties. He was called *Nātaputta* because he was a scion of the Nāya, Nāta or Jñātr̥ clan of the kṣatriyas.[47]

The Jain tradition places the birth of Mahāvīra in the year 599 BC. He belonged to Kaśyapa *gotra*. He was a son of kṣatriya Siddhārtha, also known as Śreyāṁśa and Yaśāṁśa, and kṣatriyāṇī Triśalā, also known as Videhadatta and Priyakarṇī of the Vāṣiṣṭha *gotra*. His mother was a sister of Ceṭaka, one of the king of Vaiśālī. His parents, both lay followers of Pārśva, were pious and chaste, virtuous and strict. They rigorously observed the principles of Jainism.[48] Such statement is found in the *Ācārāṅga*, one of the oldest texts of the Jains.

Mahāvīra was a native of Kundagrāma, a suburb of the town Vaiśālī (the modern Basārh), some 27 miles north of Patna. He was the second son of his parents. The Śvetāmbaras maintained and stated in the *Ācārāṅga-Sūtra, Kalpa-Sūtra*, etc., that the soul of Tīrthaṅkara Mahāvīra first descended into the womb of a brāhmaṇī, Devanandā, and was by the order of Indra, removed

46. K.C. Jain, *op. cit.*, p. 31.
47. *Ibid.*
48. *Ibid.*, p. 32.

thence to the womb of Triśalā. But, the Digambaras reject this story.

Mahāvīra's parents who were Jains and worshippers of Pārśva, gave him the name Vardhamāna (*vīra* of Mahāvīra is an epithet like *arhat bhagavat, jin,* etc., are titles common to all *tīrthaṅkaras*). He married Yaśodā and by her had daughter Annojjā. His parents died when he was 30 years old and his elder brother Nandīvardhana succeeded his father. With the permission of his brother and the other authorities, he carried out a long cherished resolve and became a monk with the usual Jain rites. Then followed the 12 years of self-mortification. Mahāvīra wandered about as a mendi, frian, bearing all kinds of hardship; after the first 13 months he even discarded clothes. At the end of this period dedicated to meditation, he reached the state of omniscience (*kevala*) corresponding to the *Bohi* of the Buddhists. He lived for 42 years, preaching law and instructing his 11 disciples (*gaṇadhara*) throughout his life. In the 72nd year of his life, he died at Pāvā and reached *nirvāṇa* (*mokṣa*).[49]

This event took place, as stated above, some years before Buddha's death, and may therefore, be attributed to about 480 BC. The Śvetāmbaras, however, place the *nirvāṇa* of Mahāvīra, which is the initial point of their era, 470 years before the beginning of the Vikrama era, or in 527 BC. The Digambaras place the same event 18 years later.[50]

Thus after Pārśvanātha, Mahāvīra became the leader of the Jain church. The religion preached by Mahāvīra was substantially the same as preached by his predecessor Pārśvanātha. It is said that Mahāvīra added *brahmacarya* (i.e., chastity), perhaps already included in *aparigraha*, as the fifth great vow to the four great

49. James Hasting, *Encyclopaedia of Religion and Ethics,* vol. VII, Hymns, Liberty, pp. 466-67.

50. *Ibid.,* p. 467.

vows, already preached by Pārśvanātha.[51] Mahāvīra continued further the practice of four-fold divisions of the community and it is stated that at the time of his death there were 1400 *yatis*, 36,000 *sādhvīs*, 1,59,000 *śrāvakas* and 3,18,000 *śrāvikās*.[52] Mahāvīra had in all eleven *gaṇadharas*. They were all religious teachers well-versed in Jain scriptures. After the *nirvāṇa* of Mahāvīra, the fifth *gaṇadhara* Sudharman became the head of the Jain church, others either having attained salvation or *kevalajñāna* (i.e., omniscience) before the death of Mahāvīra. Sudharman is said to have narrated the Jain canon to his disciple Jambūswāmī in the manner, that he had heared from his Master. The *nirgrantha śramaṇas* of the present time are all spiritual descendants of the monk Ārya Sudharman; the rest of the *gaṇadharas* having no descendants.[53] The next important event in Mahāvīra's life was his renunciation which took place on his attaining the age of thirty. Siddhārtha and Triśalā lived no longer then and Mahavira's elder brother and sister did not try to prevent him from embracing an entirely new life. The *Kalpasūtra* informs us that Mahāvīra retained his clothes for 13 months and then wandered about naked.[54]

The original canon gives us some references of Mahāvīra's wandering during his 12 years of pre-*kevala jñāna* period. The *Ācārāṅga* mentions a few places where he visited after his departure from home. The later texts, mention his visit to various places.[55] Both the works, *Ācārāṅga* and *Kalpasūtra*, have described in identical language, the story of his final enligh-tenment. The most important phase of Mahāvīra's life has been that of a teacher

---

51. A.C. Sen, *Schools and Sects in Jain literature*, Calcutta, 1931, p. 43.
52. U.D. Barodia, *History and Literature of Jainism*, Bombay, 1909, p. 40.
53. V.A. Sangave, *Jaina Community — A Social Survey*, Bombay, 1959, p. 47.
54. A.K. Chatterjee, *Comprehensive History of Jainism (up to* AD *1000)*, Calcutta, 1978, p. 24.
55. *Ibid*., p. 24.

and a path-finder. Some scholars observe that as a teacher Mahāvīra probably visited only a few places of Bihar and Bengal. But the general acceptance is that he mainly wandered between the age of 30 and 72.[56]

The Upalisutta of the *Majjhima Nikāya* refers to Nātaputta's visit to Nālandā along with a large company of Jain monks. According to the *Kalpasūtra* the teacher spent 14 rainy seasons at Rājagṛha and Nālandā. It was at Nālandā that Mahāvīra had met Goṣāla for the first time. Rājagṛha was a popular centre of the Jains.

Mahāvīra's Missionary Activities

The combined evidence of the Jain and Buddhist texts leaves no room to doubt the great success of Mahāvīra's missionary activities. The *nirgrantha* religion was founded by Pārśva around 800 BC. Slowly yet surely Jainism became a major religion of eastern India during the Mahāvīra's lifetime. Lord Mahavira's influence was tremendous in Bihar; however, other places like Śrāvastī region and western Bengal also came increasingly under the influence of the Jain religion.[57]

Royal Patronage

Let us now take a brief notice of Mahāvīra's relation with the contemporary political figures. Not only the rich bankers and merchants but even the kings, queens, princes, and ministers became lay disciples of the Jain Tīrthaṅkara Mahāvīra. His personal connections with the various rulers were through his mother Triśalā, the Licchavi Princess, and maternal uncle, Ceṭaka, the king of Vaiśālī.

According to the Jain tradition, kings like Śreṇika, Kuṇika Ceṭaka, Pradyota, Śatanīka, Dadhivāhana, Udayana, Viangoye, Vīrāgasa, Sañjaya Śaṅkha and many others and also the queens

56. *Ibid.*, p. 25.
57. *Ibid.*, p. 26.

like Prabhāvatī of Udayana, Mṛgavatī of Jayantī of Kośāmbī, the daughter of the king of Campā, followed Jainism. Princess called Atimukhā, Padmā, grandson of Śreṇika are said to have joined the order of Jainism. The Royal patronage must have facilitated the spread of Jainism.[58]

The Jain *Harivaṁśa Purāṇa* informs us that Lord Mahāvīra had preached his doctrine in Kaliṅga. The reference to Nandarāja as having taken away the image of Jin from the inscription of Khāravela in Kaliṅga is very interesting as it proves the existence of image-worship among the Jains even in the fifth century BC.[59] There are mentions of Mahāvīra's visit even to south India. From the *Jīvanadhara-Carita* of Bhāskara, it is known that Jīvanadhara, who was the ruling chief of his region at this time, was a Jain. Not only the rulers but also several contemporary clans were the followers of the religion of Mahāvīra. There are many references in the Jain *sūtras* which prove that Licchavis followed the Jain faith. The capital, Vaiśālī formed one of the headquarters of the Jain community during the days of Mahāvīra.[60]

It is clear from the above discussion that though only a few of these kings can definitely be identified, the late tradition without much historical support brings nearly all the kings of north India in those days under the influence of Mahāvīra in one way or the other.[61] While some of the names of these rulers seem to be imaginary, others might have flourished long after Mahāvīra.

Thus Jainism spread in different parts of India and received royal patronage. During the period of Mahāvīra, its influence seems to have been confined only to the modern States of Bihar, some parts of Bengal and U.P. It is probable that most of the ruling chiefs of this area patronized Jainism.

---

58. K.C. Jain, *op. cit.*, p. 64.
59. K.C. Jain, *op. cit.*, p. 69.
60. K.C. Jain, *op. cit.*, p. 70.
61. *Ibid.*, p. 71.

Jainism: Post-Mahāvīra Period

COUNCIL OF PĀṬALIPUTRA

The religious teaching of Mahāvīra were memorized by his immediate successors and they were thus handed down from one generation to another till they were canonized at the council of Pāṭaliputra in the early third century BC.

The First Jain Council and the Great Schism

The fourteen *parva*s of the textbooks of the old Jain scriptures which Mahāvīra himself had taught to his *gaṇadhara*s were perfected by Sambhūtavijaya and Bhadrabāhu. Sambhūtavijaya is said to have died in the same year in which emperor Candragupta Maurya ascended his throne. Towards the close of the fourth century BC, a terrible famine lasting for twelve years, broke out in south Bihar which led to the exodus of an important section of the Jains, headed by Bhadrabāhu, to the Mysore region in the south. Many Jains remained in Magadha under Sthūlabhadra, a disciple of Sambhūtavijaya. They summoned a Council of Elders of Jainism at Pāṭaliputra about 300 BC to collect and revive the knowledge of the sacred texts which was passing into oblivion. The result was the compilation of the twelve *aṅga*s that are considered as the most important parts of the Jain canon.[62]

After the first council of elders, later additions were also made to Jain canon (*aṅga*s) by learned monks like Samārya, Āryarakṣita, Vibhadra, etc. A collection of commentaries explaining parts of the canon were called *Niryukti*s. They are ten and were composed in the first or second century AD. The followers of Bhadrabāhu on their return to Magadha refused to acknowledge the canon as drawn up by their co-religionists in Bihar holding that 14 *parva*s were the ultimate one. Moreover, the gulf widened between those who had emigrated and those

62. B.N. Luniya, *Life and Culture in Ancient India, from the earliest times to AD 1000,* Agra, 1978, p. 166.

who stayed in Magadha. The latter had become accustomed to wearing white garments and discarded Mahāvīra's teachings whereas the former still continued going naked and strictly followed the teachings of Mahāvīra. This is how the first schism split the Jain church into the Digambaras (skyclad or naked) and Śvetāmbaras (clad in white). The followers of Bhadrabāhu were Digambaras, and those of Sthūlabhadra were known as Śvetāmbaras.[63]

Spread of Jainism

It is extremely difficult to trace the progress of Jain religion during the centuries preceding the Christian era in different parts of India. The available inscriptions, however, give us some help regarding the prevalence of Jain religion in some parts of India. Pārśva, as the evidences show, was successful in popularizing the *nirgrantha* religion in different parts of Uttar Pradesh. He personally visited places like Kauśāmbī, Sāketa Kāmpilyapura, Amalakappā, Mathurā and few other cities. Jain religion became one of the major religious sects of eastern India under Mahāvīra. Mahāvīra's preachings were highly appreciated in Bengal and as such the State came under the influence of Jainism.[64]

It is not easy to trace the history of the spread of Jainism after the death of Mahāvīra. But a careful study of the relevant portions of the *Therāvalī*, which is a part of the *Kalpasūtra*, give us some relevant idea about the history of the gradual spread of Jainism in different parts of India.[65]

Among the four *śakhās*, Godāsa, a disciple of Bhadrabāhu, flourished in the fourth century BC. We have already noticed that Mahāvīra himself visited some of the places of Bengal during

63. B.N. Luniya, *Life and Culture in Ancient India, from the earliest times to AD 1000,* Agra, 1978, p. 166.

64. A.K. Chatterjee, *op. cit.*, pp. 35-36.

65. *Ibid., op. cit.*, p. 37.

his missionary career.[66] That is why, Jainism flourished after his death in the regions where he taught his doctrine.

The great saint Bhadrabāhu, according to the *Bṛhatkathākoṣa* of Harisena (AD 931), was born in the town of Devakoṭṭa situated in the Puṇḍravardhana country.[67] Therefore, the *śakhā*s founded by Godāsa should be connected with Bengal. There is no doubt that by the time this *śakhā* originated (250 BC), Jainism was firmly established in Punjab.[68]

Ṛṣigupta originated a number of *śakhā*s among which the most significant name is that of Saurāṣṭrika. This shows that before the end of the third century BC Jainism reached the State of Gujarat, and as evidences prove, it has maintained its glorious existence even today. The Digambara traditions, both literary and epigraphic, delineate this celebrated royal personality as a Jain devotee.[69]

Jinadasagaṇi informs us that Samprati constructed the Jain shrines in countries like Andhra, Damila, Marahaṭṭa, etc. Jain tradition regarding Samprati's leaving the *nirgrantha* religion is based essentially on facts.[70]

Jainism in North India

The Jain monks of Bengal were mainly responsible for the early popularity of Jainism in Orissa. Archaeological and epigraphic sources give us some idea about the state of Jainism in places like Kauśāmbī, Śrāvastī, Rājagṛha, Ahicchatra, Takṣaśilā Siṁhapura and a few places of western India. The Jain literary evidences suggest the existence of Jain temples in almost all principal cities of north India.

Kauśāmbī like Sāketa was one of the early centres of Jainism.

66. *Ibid.*
67. A.K. Chatterjee, *op. cit.*, pp. 35-36.
68. *Ibid.*, pp. 37-38.
69. *Ibid.*, p. 39.
70. *Ibid.*, pp. 41-42.

Sāketa was connected with Munisuvrata is also proved by the evidences of the *Vividhatīrthakalpa* of Jinaprabha. The temple of Suvrata at Sāketa was built before 300 BC. It is quite natural for the Jains to be eager to build shrines in famous cities connected with the Brāhmaṇical culture and religion. Jainism spread in Varanasi in 800 BC during the time of Mahāvīra and also became popular in few other towns.[71]

The great city of Śrāvastī was associated with Jainism from pretty early times. It is believed to be the birth-place of Sambhavanātha, the third *tīrthaṅkara*. This city was very intimately associated with the life and activities of Mahāvīra and Buddha. Śrāvastī was the capital of Pasenadi (Prasenajit) of Kośala, a prominent figure in the Pāli texts. The Jains, however, ignore this royal personality.[72] Śrāvastī later became a famous centre of Digambara religion. It is evident from the *Bṛhatkathākoṣa* of Harisena, a text composed in AD 931.

Ahicchatra, the ancient capital of North Pañcāla, was certainly an important seat of early religion. According to the Śvetāmbara Jain tradition, Ahicchatra was sacred to Pārśvanatha and there was also a shrine dedicated to this *tīrthaṅkara* in Sri Lanka. This *tīrthaṅkara* flourished in the second half of the ninth century AD. A number of Jain inscriptions of the Kuṣāṇa period have also been discovered from the place and at least one of them refers to the city of Ahicchatra.[73]

Takṣaśilā was another important city of Jainism in early days. The Jain literary tradition associates Taxila with Bāhubali, a son of Ṛṣabha, who was believed to be a Jain *sādhu*.[74]

Great importance was attributed to the Jains for their wealth and education. The Digambaras, though found chiefly in southern India viz. Karnataka, Tamil Nadu and south Maharashtra, also

---

71. A.K. Chatterjee, *op. cit.*, p. 91.
72. *Ibid.*, p. 93.
73. R.D. Banerji, *Epigraphica Indica*, vol. X, p. 120.
74. A.K. Chatterjee, *op. cit.*, p. 97.

inhabited the north and the north-western provinces viz. U.P., eastern Rājpūtānā and Punjab. At present, it seems, from the evidence of the inscriptions, to have prevailed ever since the fourth century BC. Splendid temples bear testimony to the wealth and zeal of the sect. Some of which rank among the architectural wonders of India, which is on the hills of Girnār, Śatruñjaya, Mount Ābu, Ellorā and elsewhere.

Furthermore, a detailed list of patriarchs shows that after the sixth patriarchs, a great expansion of Jainism took place in the north and north-west of India.

The first patron king of the Jains was Samprati, a grandson of the great emperor Aśoka. A historical fact of the greatest importance for the history of Jainism was conversion of Kumārapāla, king of Gujarat, by Hemacandra.[75]

Advent of Jainism in South India

Jainism was a powerful influence that moulded the religious and cultural life of south India during the early and medieval epochs of its history. Jainism is an important religion in south India for over two thousand years now and has survived the ravages of time. There is a legend as mentioned in an eleventh-century Sanskrit work that Mahāvīra himself came to the south, to a Kannaḍa country (known at that time as Hemāṅgadadeśa) during the reign of King Jīvanadhara whom Mahāvīra met and admitted into the ascetic fold.

There are traditions even on Mahāvīra's visit to south India from the *Jīvanadhara-Carita* of Bhāskara. It is known that Jīvanadhara, who was the ruling chief of this region at this time, was a Jain. He cordially received Mahāvīra and became an ascetic after obtaining *dīkṣā* from him. Jīvanadhara seems to be an imaginary name, as there was no such ruler whose

75. A.K. Jain, *Lord Mahāvīra in the Eyes of Foreigners*, New Delhi, 1975, pp. 40-45.

kingdom extended to and comprised southern India during this period.[76]

The above account is also published in the *Karnataka State Gazetteer*, Vol. 1, as follows.

> Jainism in Karnataka is believed to go back to the days of Bhagwan Mahāvīra. Jivanadhara a prince from Karnataka is described as having been initiated by Mahāvīra himself.

There is a belief that even during the days of the very first *tīrthaṅkara* Ṛṣabha, presumably several thousand years before the arrival of the 24th *tīrthaṅkara* Mahāvīra in 599 BC, there were south Indian princes in his entourage who finally retired to the Śatruñjaya hills in Palitānā Sauraśtra.[77] But this account is not proved by any concrete evidence.

Migration of Candragupta and Bhadrabāhu to South

Legends and beliefs apart, the earliest historical evidence for the advent of Jainism in south India is the visit of the Saint Bhadrabāhu, the eighth teacher in succession after Mahāvīra along with the Magadhan monarch, Candragupta Maurya, to Śravaṇbeḷgoḷa in Mysore State. This event forms the subject-matter of a persistent legend in the Kannaḍa country and the southern sects of Jainism invariably trace their descent from Bhadrabāhu.

The event is recorded in an inscription of about AD 650. There is a cave named after Bhadrabāhu on the hill of Candragiri in Śravaṇbeḷgoḷa. It is said that the great saint lived and died there on the same hill where a shrine named after Candragupta is found which is said to be the oldest of the structures on the hill and the pierced screens contain an excellent sculptured relief relating the story of this visit.

---

76. K.C. Jain, *op. cit.*, p. 69.
77. Rajamal Jain and Laxmichandra Jain, Karnataka State Gazetteer, *Bharat Ke Digambara Jain Tirtha*, vol. V, Karnataka, vol. I, p. 14.

An inscription in Siddharabasadi and another in "Maranavami-mantapa" have preserved for us the memory of Candragupta, who was disciple of Bhadrabāhu. V.A. Smith, who doubted the authenticity of the legend, later admitted after much consideration that it had a "solid foundation in fact."[78]

Jain tradition affirms that when Bhadrabāhu, the last of the saints called *śrutakevalins*, forefold a famine of twelve years duration, the Mauryan Emperor Candragupta abdicated the throne and migrated to the south with the saint and his pupils. The emperor is said to have lived for many years as a Jain ascetic in Śravaṇbeḷgoḷa in Mysore State and ultimately committed suicide by *sallekhana*, or starvation, serving his teacher for twelve years. Inscriptions from Śravaṇbeḷgoḷa and its neighbourhood, which is held as old as AD 600 mentioned Bhadrabāhu and Candragupta Munīndra. It also mentions the pair (*yugma*) and says that there prevailed a state faith (*dharma*) and another shrine of even earlier date, probably not later than the fifth century, contains all the elements of the story given above.

After the forecast about the aforesaid famine, as mentioned above, the whole of the Jain *saṁgha* thereupon migrated from north to the south under the leadership of Bhadrabāhu. When they arrived at a mountain named Katavapra (i.e., Candragiri) in a populous and prosperous country (Mysore), an *ācārya*, Prabhacandra by name, knowing he had but a short time to live, sent away the entire *saṁgha* and with only one disciple attending on him, performed penance and gained emancipation from his body.

Two inscriptions of about AD 900 from the neighbourhood of Śrīraṅgapaṭan describe the summit of the lower hill, Candragiri, in Śravaṇbeḷgoḷa as having the footprints of both, Bhadrabāhu and Candragupta Munipati.

Later inscriptions at Śravaṇbeḷgoḷa bearing dates in the twelfth and fifteenth centuries repeat this tradition with

78. S.K. Ramchandra Rao, *Jainism in South India*, Madras, 1970, pp. 3-4.

variations. Similar attestation also comes from literary sources, of which the earliest seems to be the *Bṛhatkathākoṣa* of Harisena (AD 931). The absence of any clear evidence about the actual end of Candragupta Maurya lends some plausibility to this legend but it is improbable in itself, and the identity of the Candragupta Muni of the inscriptions is by no means beyond doubt.[79]

Bhadrabāhu's name is in all accounts associated with the spread of Jainism in south of the Vindhyas. In the lists of succession of the Digambara as well as the Śvetāmbara sects of the Jains, his name occurs as the eighth master after the passing away of Mahāvīra in 527 BC. The first master was Gautama who administered the community for twelve years and was succeeded by Sudharma (who was head for 12 years — according to the Digambara lists and 8 according to the Śvetāmbara); the latter was succeeded by Jambūsvāmī (whose period was according to Digambaras 38 years and according to the Śvetāmbaras 42). These three were styled as *kevalins*, the perfected and omniscient saints whose spiritual accomplish-ment were of the highest standard, after they led the community for a total period of 62 years (527-465 BC). They were succeeded by a line of five saints whose spiritual perfection was not so complete. They were called *śrutakevalins*, master of the 14 ancient texts belonging to *dṛṣṭivāda*, possessed of complete knowledge of scriptures but spiritually incapable of attaining to perfection; Bhadrabāhu was the last in the line of these *śrutakevalins*.[80]

According to Hemacandra, Bhadrabāhu passed away 170 years after the demise of Mahāvīra (527 BC) and this year would correspond to 357 BC. He is said to have lived for 76 years. The date of Bhadrabāhu appears bound up with that of Candragupta Maurya, the Magadhan king who is believed to have taken *dīkṣā* from Bhadrabāhu and came with him to the south. Hemacandra

---

79. K.A. Nilakanthasastri, *A History of South India*, Oxford, 1966, pp. 83-84.

80. S.K. Ramchandra Rao, *op. cit.*, pp. 4-5.

mentions that Candragupta became king 155 years after the passing away of Mahāvīra, i.e., 372 BC.

Candragupta ascended the throne in 313 BC. One of the beliefs is that the king died in 297 BC, which is held as the year of Bhadrabāhu's death by an another belief. Candragupta is supposed to have ruled for 24 years before he abdicated the throne in favour of his son Siṁhasena: This event is of about 289 BC if 313 BC is taken as the date of his ascension. This would agree with the Digambara tradition that Candragupta joined Bhadrabāhu in 288 BC.[81] This date may also be taken as the date of advent of the Jain community in the south.

A group of about 12,000 monks, led by Bhadrabāhu, left Magadha and moved southwards. This was one section of the Jain community, while the other section continued to stay in Magadha under Sthūlabhadra, a disciple of Bhadrabāhu. This latter section was known as the *ardhaphalaka*s, who later became the Śvetāmbaras.[82]

The Great Division

Since it is not possible here to deal in detail the great division of the Jain community into the Digambara and Śvetāmbara sects, it may be briefly mentioned that this division was of utmost importance to the development of Jainism in south India. One may say, although with reservation, that the Digambaras mainly dwelled in the south while the Śvetāmbaras in the north. The southern tradition attributed the division to around AD 79. The northern tradition, on the other hand, held it as an event of AD 82. Bhadrabāhu's visit to the south is considered by the former as the main cause responsible for this split. When Bhadrabāhu migrated out of Magadha with a large entourage of monks, the monks that remained in Magadha under the guidance of Sthūlabhadra were styled as *ardhaphalaka*s, having a peculiar

81. S.K. Ramchandra Rao, *op. cit.*, p. 6.

82. *Ibid.*, p. 9.

headdress. Bhadrabāhu passed away in Śravaṇbeḷgoḷa and his disciple Viśākha returned to Magadha after twelve years along with the group that had accompanied Bhadrabāhu. Viśākha found the differences between his own community and Sthūlabhadra's community sharp and beyond rapprochement. This is the Digambara version about the division.[83]

Jainism and Samprati 220-211 BC

One early migration led the community to the south-east, the country of Kaliṅga, as can be seen from the famous inscription of Khāravela. A similar extension or migration of the Jain community to the west must have brought Jainism to Mathurā.

Further south, the country around Ujjayinī was also a stronghold of Jainism. The evidence for this centre of Jain culture is mostly found in the later traditions. If the story of Aśoka, a grandson of king Samprati, and his conversion to Jainism by Suhastin is believed, then the spread to Mālwā must be held as early as the second century BC. We are further told that Samprati initiated his grandfather in sending religious missionaries to the countries of Āndhras and Dramilas to propagate the religion. The famous story of Kālakācārya, the Jain saint, implies the spread of Jainism in Mālwā in the first century BC.[84]

Samprati, the grandson of Aśoka, is generally accepted to have been a Jain, being converted to the Śvetāmbara creed by Suhastin. It appears that he had sent Jain missionaries on the latter's persuasion to south India. Though we do not know how far they penetrated into Karnataka, but this is the first available reference to the Śvetāmbaras in the south.[85]

To sum up, Jainism is a distinct and old religion founded by Ṛṣabha, also called Ādināth, and carried over further by 23

83. S.K. Ramchandra Rao, *op. cit.*, pp. 10-11.
84. R.C. Majumdar, *The Age of Imperial Unity*, Bombay, 1951, p. 418.
85. S.R. Sharma, *Jainism and Karnataka Culture*, Dharwar, 1940, p. 7.

tīrthaṅkaras. Pārśvanāth and Mahāvīra, the last two *tīrthaṅkaras*, were historic persons. Jainism was popular in north India, especially in Bihar, during Mahāvīra's period, i.e., sixth century BC. Jainism received royal patronage through Candragupta Maurya who flourished in the fourth century BC. He was a devout Jain and ended his life at Śravaṇbeḷgoḷa in Hassan District of Karnataka which became the second home of Jainism since the fourth century BC onwards. Subsequent second and third chapters deal with the rise and development of Śravaṇbeḷgoḷa as a leading Jain centre from the fourth century BC to the sixteenth century AD.

2

Śravaṇbeḷgoḷa as a Jain Centre (First Phase)

It is unanimously accepted by all historians of the north as well as south India that Candragupta Maurya along with his preceptor Bhadrabāhu migrated to Śravaṇbeḷgoḷa from Pāṭaliputra, the capital of Mauryan empire. There is no evidence in north India about the last days of Candragupta Maurya but fortunately we have ample evidence from Śravaṇbeḷgoḷa (i.e., from south India) which shed light on the end of Candragupta Maurya at Śravaṇbeḷgoḷa, a sacred place in Hassan District of Karnataka. It is also said by some historians like, K.S. Aiyyangar and Prof. N. Sastri that Śravaṇbeḷgoḷa was the earliest Jain colony in south India prior to Candragupta Maurya and Bhadrabāhu's arrival. Some inscriptions belonging to the sixth century AD and also the literary sources corroborate that Candragupta Maurya had observed *sallekhana* (i.e., fast unto death). There is even one Jain temple at Śravaṇbeḷgoḷa named after Candragupta Maurya called as Candragupta basadi.

Therefore, it would not be wrong to accept Śravaṇbeḷgoḷa as an earliest centre of Jain culture since at least the fourth century BC. A great number of Jain temples have been erected later by the nobles and royal families in and around Śravaṇbeḷgoḷa which developed as a powerful centre of Jainism in south India. Again some archaeological evidences and inscriptions are available which speak about the antiquity and glory of Śravaṇbeḷgoḷa in the ancient and medieval period.

Śravaṇbeḷgoḷa, the most ancient and prominent sacred place of the Jains in south India, has got a unique combination of many distinctive features which are rarely found elsewhere in the world. Śravaṇbeḷgoḷa is the most important *tīrtha* (sacred place) of the Jains in south India and at the same time it is held as a place of the great cultural significance in south Indian history. The holy place with a continuous and glorious tradition of several centuries occupies a unique position among the innumerable sacred places of the Jains practically in all parts of India from very ancient times. Such holiness is rarely seen attached to a similar religious place in different parts of the world. Śravaṇbeḷgoḷa is famous in the world not only for its religious sanctity but also for its natural beauty, historical antiquity and architectural superiority.

Moreover, Śravaṇbeḷgoḷa received royal patronage from Maurya, Kadambas, early Rāṣṭrakūṭas, Cāḷukyas of Bādāmī, Gaṅgas of Talakaḍ, Hoyasala and Vijayanagra rulers. Therefore, an endeavour has been made in this second chapter to study the development of Śravaṇbeḷgoḷa as a prominent Jain centre since the fourth century BC to the ninth century AD.

Derivation of the Name

It is interesting to see the origin of the name, Śravaṇbeḷgoḷa, and also Candragiri and Vindhyagiri (hills). The prefix a *sravan* in the name Śravaṇbeḷgoḷa refers to a Jain monk and *beḷgoḷa* to a white pond. The place is so named probably because of its colossal Jain image and a beautiful pond in the middle of the village. The derivation of the word "Beḷgoḷa" appears to have been from the two Kannaḍa words *beḷ* (white) and *koḷa* (pond). The Sanskrit equivalents *Śveta-Sarovara, Dhavala-*

Sarovara and *Dhavala-Saras* used in the inscriptions support the derivation of this word from the two Kannaḍa words.[1]

The name Yeḷgoḷa occurs in an inscription of about AD 650 and Beḷgoḷa in another inscription of about AD 800. Some later inscriptions have mentioned the name of the same place as Beḷguḷa, Beḷḷuguḷa, Beḷaguḷa, which have given rise to another derivation. According to this derivation, *guila* refers to a plant *Solanunn ferox* and a belief attached to it is that a pious old woman completely anointed the colossal image with the milk brought by her in a *gullakayi* or *gulla* fruit.[2] The place is also designated as Devara Beḷgoḷa (Beḷgoḷa of the God) and Gommaṭapura (the city of Gommaṭa, the name of the colossus) in some epigraphs.[3] Further, the epithet Dakṣiṇakāśī or Southern Kāśī is also applied to it in some modern inscriptions.[4]

On the same lines the Jains, especially from north India, frequently refer to Śravaṇbeḷgoḷa as *Jain Badri*, the *badri* is referred to the most holy place of the Jains. Furthermore, in modern Jain literature, the village Śravaṇbeḷgoḷa is sometimes respectfully described as "Abhinava Podanapura," i.e., modern Podanapura, the capital of Bāhubali during his career as a king.[5]

Name Vindhyagiri

The word Vindhyagiri like Śravaṇbeḷgoḷa also denotes a spiritual meaning. The word Vindhyagiri is derived from the three words, *vim* meaning soul, *dhya* meaning meditation, and

---

1. R. Narasimhachari, *Epigraphica Carnatica, Inscription of Śravaṇbeḷgoḷa*, vol. II, Bangalore, 1923, Introduction, p. 1.
2. K.A. Nilakanthasastri, *A Guide to Śravaṇbeḷgoḷa*, Mysore, 1981, p. 3.
3. R. Narasimhachari, *op. cit.*, p. 2.
4. *Ibid.*
5. V.P. Sangave, *The Sacred Śravaṇbeḷgoḷa* (*A Socio-Religious study*), New Delhi, 1981, p. 10.

giri meaning hill. Thus the word *vindhyagiri* denotes "hill for the meditation of soul." Since many Jain saints practised penance here in the form of meditation or contemplation, the word Vindhyagiri came to be associated with the hill.[6] Further, Vindhyagiri is also sometimes designated as Indragiri, i.e., the hill of God Indra.

Name Candragiri

The word *candragiri,* i.e., the hill of Candragupta, implies historical in the sense that it signifies the most important events in the life of Emperor Candragupta Maurya (297 BC) i.e., his arrival, his long stay, his practice of penance as a Jain ascetic and of his ultimate death according to the Jain rite of *sallekhana* (Candragupta Maurya, founder of the Maurya Dynasty, in the third century BC). In the old inscriptions, Candragiri is designated as *Katavapragiri* or *Katavapra* in Sanskrit and as *Kalvappu* or *Kalbappu* in Kannaḍa.[7]

Further a portion of the hill Candragiri has been referred to as *Tīrthagiri,* i.e., the sacred hill, in the inscription no. 76 and as *R̥ṣigiri,* i.e., the hill of the sages, in the inscription no. 84. Moreover, Candragiri is commonly termed in the local Kannaḍa language as *Cikka-beṭṭa* (i.e., the smaller hill) distinguishing it from the other larger hill known as *Dodda-beṭṭa*.

Thus the name given to the village as "Śravaṇbeḷgoḷa" and also the name of its hills Vindhyagiri and Candragiri are very appropriate as they correctly convey the spiritual significance and historical association of the Jains over several long centuries.

Religious or Ecclesiastical Importance of Śravaṇbeḷgoḷa

From the point of view of religion, Śravaṇbeḷgoḷa is regarded

6. *Ibid.*
7. *Ibid.*, pp. 10-11.

as a significant sacred place and prominent centre of spiritual activities of Jain *sādhus*, ascetics, in particular and of Jain *śrāvakas*, lay followers, in general.

In fact, the close association of the Jain ascetics with this place is clearly enshrined in the very name of this place, viz., Śravaṇbeḷgoḷa. The prefix *Śravaṇa* attached to the name of the place is derived from the Sanskrit word *śramaṇa* meaning a Jain ascetic. Hence the term Śravaṇbeḷgoḷa signifies Beḷgoḷa of *śramaṇas*, i.e., Jain ascetics. This is testified by the fact that from very ancient times many Jain ascetics used to practice penance here for long periods and ultimately lay down their lives in accordance with the rule of *sallekhana*, i.e., willing submission to inevitable death, prescribed by the Jain scriptures.[8]

In view of this fact, it is recorded in history that the great Jain sage Bhadrabāhu, the last of *śruta-kevalins*, i.e., masters of knowledge, and the eighth master in succession to Lord Mahāvīra, migrated alongwith his *saṁgha*, i.e., group of 12,000 Jain ascetics, to Śravaṇbeḷgoḷa from Magadha, i.e., Bihar in north India in the third century BC. Bhadrabāhu was followed by his disciple, Emperor Candragupta Maurya, who spent the rest of his life as a Jain ascetic practising penance at Śravaṇbeḷgoḷa.

This prevalent atmosphere of serene religious sanctity surrounding Śravaṇbeḷgoḷa was greatly enhanced by the installation of the imposing statue of Bhagavān Bāhubali on the top of the Vindhyagiri hill of Śravaṇbeḷgoḷa in the year AD 981 by Cāmuṇḍarāya, the renowned Military General and Prime Minister of Gaṅga monarch Rājamalla IV.[9]

This was the beginning of the influence of Jainism at Śravaṇbeḷgoḷa in south Karnataka. Samprati (220-211 BC), the

8. *Ibid.*, p. 2.
9. *Ibid.*, pp. 2-3.

grandson of Aśoka, whose capital was Ujjain, presently in M.P., who himself was a Jain in his earlier days sent missionaries to the south.[10]

In the long history of religious practices connected with Jainism, it is pertinent to note that the usual practice among the Jains from the ancient times was to construct temples only in honour of one or more of the 24 *tīrthaṅkara*s.

A new addition was made to this practice by setting at Śravaṇbeḷgoḷa an image of Bhagavāna Bāhubali who was not a *tīrthaṅkara*. Naturally, it greatly increased the religious importance of Śravaṇbeḷgoḷa in the minds of the Jains.[11]

Situation and Routes

Śravaṇbeḷgoḷa is situated at 12º 51' north latitude, and 76º 29' east longitude, about eight miles to the south of Cennarāyapāṭna in the Cennarāyapāṭna Tāluka of the Hassan district of the present Karnataka. It lies picturesquely between two rocky hills, one larger than the other, which stand up boldly from the plain and are covered with huge boulders. "In the whole beautiful state of Karnataka it would be hard to find a spot where the historic and the picturesque clasp hands so firmly as here."[12]

There are regular bus services from Arsikere, Hassan, Mysore and Bangalore to Śravaṇbeḷgoḷa. The distance from Hassan is 31 miles and that from Mysore is 62 miles, while the distance from Bangalore is 99 miles. There are District Board roads leading from the following railway stations to Śravaṇbeḷgoḷa and the distance from each station is noted against it in brackets:

---

10. T.G. Kalghatgi, *Gommateshvara Commemoration Volume* (AD *981-1981*), *Jainism Karnataka* (*Śravaṇbeḷgoḷa-Karnataka*) 1981, p. 15.
11. V.A. Sangave, *op. cit.*, p. 2.
12. K.A. Nilakanthasastri, *op. cit.*, p. 1.

(1) Hole-Narasipura (22 miles)
(2) Tiptur (40 miles)
(3) Arsikere (42 miles)
(4) Pāṇḍavapura (48 miles)

All roads to Śravaṇbeḷgoḷa pass through Cennarāyapāṭna and as the traveller drives through this place, he observes a conspicuous hill at a few miles to the south-east bearing on its summit which at first sight appears to be a column, but on drawing nearer it proves to be a colossal statue in the human form. This striking and unusual object is the image of Gommaṭeśvara, which is visible from miles around. This image marks the site of Śravaṇbeḷgoḷa, the chief seat of the Jains in south India, probably from the earliest authentic period of Indian history. There is a second class Travellers Bungalow for the use of visitors in the village. It is plainly furnished and has kitchens in Indian style. There are also vegetarian hotels in the village.[13]

Site of Śravaṇbeḷgoḷa

As a *tīrtha*, Śravaṇbeḷgoḷa has been the ancient and prominent centre of spiritual activities, the hallowed centre of attraction for the emperors, kings, queens, ministers, generals and other dignitaries, the sacred centre of meditation for the *ācāryas*, *sādhus* and other members of the ascetic order, the encouraging centre of inspiration for literary and cultural activities, the major seat of Bhaṭṭāraka and the most popular place of pilgrimage of the common people in south India. It has got a large number of shrines or sacred structures of different kinds, specially designed and constructed on the two hills, in the viillage and in the neighbouring villages.

A larger hill known as Dodda-beṭṭa or Vindhyagiri, situated towards the south, has on it a colossal image of

---

13. *Ibid.*, p. 2.

Gommaṭeśvara and a few *basadi*s or Jina temples, while a smaller hill, known as Cikka-beṭṭa or Candragiri, situated towards the north has on it the oldest inscriptions and a large number of basadis. It would be convenient to deal here with the historical monuments of Śravaṇbeḷgoḷa which are located in the following four centres:

(1) Cikka-beṭṭa (small hill or Candragiri).

(2) Dodda-beṭṭa (large hill or Vindhyagiri).

(3) The village.

(4) The adjacent village.

According to inscription no. 354, of AD 1830, the number of basadis in Śravaṇbeḷgoḷa is thirty-two, eight on the larger hill including the statue of Gommaṭeśvara, sixteen on the smaller hill, and eight in the village but unfortunately the names are not given.[14]

Cikka-Beṭṭa

The smaller hill or Cikka-beṭṭa, also known as Candragiri, is 3,052 ft above the level of the sea and rises about 175 ft above the plain. In old inscriptions, it is designated *katavapra* in Sanskrit and *kalvappu* or *kalbappu* in Kannaḍa. A portion of this hill is known as Tīrthagiri and R̥ṣigiri. All the basadis on this hill, except one shrine, stand in a walled area measuring about 500 ft, in its greatest length by about 225 ft, where it is widest. Almost all the temples are built in the Draviḍian style of architecture, the oldest of them going back probably to the eighth century AD.[15]

Altogether the number of temples in the walled area is thirteen and their plans are mostly similar to one another: a *garbhagr̥ha* or *adytum*, a *sukhanāsī* or vestibule, either open or

---

14. R. Narasimhachar, *op. cit.*, p. 2.
15. K.A. Nilakanthasastri, *op. cit.*, p. 23.

enclosed, and a *navaraṅga* or middle hall with or without a porch.

West Side of the Temple Sector (Two Temples)

ŚĀNTINĀTHA-BASADI

Its walls and ceiling were originally adorned with paintings, of which only a few traces are now left. An image of Śāntinātha, the 16th *tiīrthaṅkara,* to whom the shrine is dedicated, is a standing figure about 11 ft high.[16]

SUPĀRŚVANĀTHA-BASADI

It is a small temple. It enshrines a seated figure, about 3 ft. high of Supārśvanātha, the seventh *tīrthaṅkara,* canopied by a seven- hooded serpent.[17]

Middle of the Temple Sector (Seven Temples)

PĀRŚVANĀTHA-BASADI

It is a large structure of architectural merit. The tallest icon on the hill, about 15 ft. in height and canopied by a seven-hooded serpent, is the image of Pārśvanāth, the 23rd *tīrthaṅkar*. The outer walls are decorated with pilasters and miniature turrents. A lofty and elegant *mānastambha* stands in the front. *Mānastambha*s are pillars having a pavilion at the top containing four standing or seated *jina* figures facing the four directions. According to a Kannaḍa poem of about AD 1780, the pillar was set-up by a Jain merchant named Puttaiya during the rule of Mysore king Cikka-Deva-Rāja-Oḍeyar (1672-1704).[18]

KATTALE-BASADI

It is the largest temple on the hill, measuring about 124 ft. by

---

16. V.A. Sangave, *op. cit.*, p. 14.
17. *Ibid.*, p. 15.
18. Rajamala Jain and Laxmicandra Jain, *Bhārat Ke Digambara Jain Tīrtha* (Hindi), vol. V, Karnataka, Bombay, 1988, p. 265.

40 ft. It consists of a *garbhagṛha*, a *pradakṣiṇā* passage around it, an open *sukhanāsī* with the *navaraṅga* attached to it, a *mukhamaṇḍapa* or front hall and an outer veranda.

Ādinātha, the first *tīrthaṅkara*, to whom the temple is dedicated, is a fine seated figure about 6 ft. high. It is known as Kattale Basadi, i.e., temple of darkness, since it has no other opening for light than the single door in the front. It also seems to be called Padmāvatī Basadi, probably from the image of that goddess found in the veranda. The temple was erected by minister Gaṅgarāja in AD 1118 for his mother Pochavve.[19]

CANDRAGUPTA-BASADI

This *basadi* is the smallest on the hill, measuring about 22 ft. by 16 ft. It consists of three cells standing in a line with a narrow veranda in front. The cells on either side have small towers upon them resembling the Coḷa type. The middle cell has a figure of Pārśvanātha, the 23rd *tīrthaṅkara*, on the right of which is a figure of Padmāvatī and on the left a figure of Kuṣmāṇḍinī. All the figures are in a seated posture. There are standing figures of *yakṣa* and *yakṣīṇī* in the veranda. Such was the temple when it was originally built. The temple has been named so because, according to tradition, it was erected at the discretion of Emperor Candragupta Maurya. At the front of the temple, there is an ornamental doorway with perforated stone screens at the side. The doorway is beautifully executed, each architrave consisting of five fascias of elegant workmanship. The screens are pierced with square openings in ten regular rows and the interspaces, forty-five on each, are carved with mintue sculptures representing scenes from the lives of the Śrutakevali Bhadrabāhu and the Mauryan Emperor Candragupta. The label Dasoja occurring on one of the screens is undoubtedly the name of the sculptor who made the screens and the doorway. It is very probably

19. V.A. Sangave, *op. cit.*, p. 15.

identical with the sculptor who carved some of the fine branket images of the Cennakeśava temple at Belūr and therefore the period of the screens and the doorway would be about the middle of the twelfth century AD. The outer walls are decorated with pilasters and above them with two fine friezes, one of ornamental niches and the other of the heads and trunks of lions mostly in pains facing each other. It is, no doubt, one of the oldest building on the hill, probably going back to the eighth or ninth century.[20]

CANDRAPRABHU-BASADI

The Candraprabhu Basadi, which is to the west of Śāsana Basadi, consists of an open *garbhagṛha, sukhanāsī*, a *navaraṅga* and a porch and enshrines a seated figure of Candraprabha, the eighth *tīrthaṅkara*. In the *sukhanāsī* are placed the images of Śyāma and Jvālāmālinī, *yakṣa* and *yakṣī* of the *jina*. The pedestal of Jvālāmālinī shows a lion with riders seated one behind the other, though the usual cognizance is a bull. The images have no *prabhāvalī* and appear to be belonging to a period earlier than the Hoyasala.

The inscription on the rock close to the outer wall of the *navaraṅga* states that a basadi was built by Śivamāra and it may be concluded from its paleography that it refers to the Gaṅga king Śivamāra II. This basadi, also referred as the Candraprabha Basadi, is perhaps one of the oldest on the hill and is attributed to about AD 800.[21]

CĀMUṆḌARĀYA-BASADI

The Cāmuṇḍarāya Basadi is the finest and one of the largest temples on the hill. It is a homogeneous structure consisting of a *garbhagṛha* with an upper storey and a tower over it, an

20. K.A. Nilakanthasastri, *op. cit.*, p. 30 and *Archa. Report*, Bangalore, 1923, p. 67.

21. Rajamala Jain and Laxmicandra Jain, *op. cit.*, p. 262, and R.S. Sastri, *Archa. Report*, Bangalore, 1923.

open *sukhanāsī*, a *navaraṅga* and a porch with verandahs at the sides, all built of fine grained hard granite. It is dedicated to Neminātha, the 22nd *tīrthaṅkara*. The *sukhanāsī* consists of good figures of Sarvahana and Kuṣmāṇḍinī, the *yakṣa* and *yakṣī* of Neminātha.[22]

The inscription regarding the construction of this temple clearly states that it was built by Cāmuṇḍarāya and hence its date may probably be AD 982. But the inscription of about AD 1138, on the pedestal of the image of Neminātha in the *garbhagṛha*, says that, Echana, son of General Gaṅgarāja, built the *jina* temple, Trailokyarañjana, which was also known as Boppana Caityālaya. It is, therefore, clear that the image of Neminātha or at least the pedestal did not originally belong to this basadi and must have been brought here at some subsequent period from the temple founded by Echana which must have later ruined. The upper storey enshrines the figure of Pārśvanātha and an inscription on its pedestal says that Jinadeva, son of the Minister Cāmuṇḍarāya, built a Jain temple at Beḷgoḷa. It is highly probable that the construction of the temple started in about AD 982 and was perhaps completed in AD 995. Cāmuṇḍarāya, after whom the *basadi* is named, also set-up the colossus on the larger hill.[23]

ŚĀSANA-BASADI

The Śāsana Basadi is called so for the *śāsana* or the inscription set-up conspicuously at its entrance. The temple consists of a *garbhagṛha* and an open *sukhanāsī* or *antarāla* with the *navaraṅga* attached to it. The cell is dedicated to Ādinātha, the first *tīrthaṅkara*, whose image is flanked by male *cāmara*-bearers. The figure of Gomukha and Cakreśvarī, the *yakṣa* and *yakṣī* of this *jina*, are placed in the *navaraṅga*.

---

22. *Ibid.*, p. 262.
23. Kalghatgi Articles (Jain Bhagachandra), *op. cit.*, "Antiquity of Bāhubali and his monuments at Śravaṇbeḷgoḷa," p. 118.

The inscription on the pedestal of the image states that the temple was erected by the General of Gaṅgarāja, named Indirākulagṛha. He was granted the village of Parama by the king Viṣṇuvardhana in AD 1118 as a reward for the valour he had shown in the battle fought at Kannegal against the Cāḷukya emperor Tribhuvanamallapermadi and the twelve *sāmantas*. The basadi was probably built in AD 1117.[24]

MAJJIGANNA-BASADI

The Majjiganna Basadi is a small *basadi* enshrining the figure of Anantanātha, the 14th *tīrthaṅkara*. The outer walls have a row of flowers in separate panels. The *navaraṅga* has the round lathe turned pillars and the name on the *basadi* probably indicates its donor. It was founded by a man named Maggigan, and perhaps belonged to the later Gaṅga or early Hoyasala period. There are no inscriptions available to prove when it was built.[25]

East Side of the Temple Sector (Four Temples)

ERADUKAṬṬE-BASADI

The temple to the east of Cāmuṇḍarāya Basadi is dedicated to the God Ādinātha. It is called Eradukaṭṭe Basadi on account of the two stairs one on the east and another on the west of the approach to it. The main image has a Prabhāvalī and has male *cāmara*-bearers at its side. The figures of the *yakṣa* and *yakṣī* of the *jina* are found in the *sukhanāsī*.

The inscription on the pedestal of the image states that the temple was built by Lakṣmī, the wife of the Hoyasala General Gaṅgarāja. It dates back to about AD 1118.[26]

---

24. S. Setter, *Śravaṇbeḷgoḷa*, Dharwad, 1981, p. 21.
25. K.A. Nilakanthasastri, *op. cit.*, pp. 32-33.
26. Rajamala Jain and Laxmichandra Jain, *op. cit.*, p. 263.

SAVATIGANDHAVARAṆA-BASADI

The Savatigandhavaraṇa Basadi, usually known as the Gandhavaraṇa Basadi, is to the right of the Eradukaṭṭe Basadi. It is a fairly large structure consisting of a *garbhagṛha*, a *sukhanāsī*, and a *navaraṅga*. The temple is named after the epithet *Savatigandhavaraṇa*, a rutting elephant to co-wives, a peculiar title of Śāntaladevī, the Piriyarāśi or chief queen of the Hoyasala king Viṣṇuvardhana. The temple is dedicated to Śāntinātha, the 16th *tīrthaṅkara*, whose image has an ornamental *Prabhāvalī* and is flanked by male *cāmara*-bearers. The figures of Kiṁpuruṣa and Mahāmānasī, the *yakṣa* and *yakṣī* of this *jina*, are placed in the vestibul. The outer walls are decorated with pilasters and the *garbhagṛha* is surrounded by a large tower. This tower is an interesting example of a Hoyasala brick tower constructed in imitation of Gaṅga towers. As known from the inscription on the pedestal near the entrance to the Śāntinātha, it was built by Queen Śāntaladevī in AD 1123.[27]

TERINA-BASADI

On account of the car-like structure standing in front of it, the next temple is called Terina Basadi. It is also known as Bāhubali Basadi on account of an image of Bāhubali or Gommaṭa enshrined in it. The car-like structure known as *mandāra*, is sculptured on all the four sides with *jina* figures. The inscription on it records that Machikabbe and Shantikabbe, the mothers of Poyasalaseṭṭi and Nemiseṭṭi respectively, the royal merchants of king Viṣṇuvardhana, built the temple and the *mandāra* in AD 1117.[28]

ŚĀNTĪŚVARA-BASADI

The Śāntīśvara Basadi or Śāntinātha Basadi is another

27. *Ibid.*, p. 264, N. Lakshminarayan Rao, *Eminent Women of Karnataka* and *QJMS* (vol. 45), Bangalore, 1954, p. 12.

28. S. Setter, *op. cit.*, p. 30.

Hoyasala brick structure on the hill with round pillars in the *navaraṅga*. The temple stands on a high platform and has an ornamental masonry tower. It is not known when or by whom this temple was built.[29]

The Open Sector

There are some objects of interest too in the open sector on the Candragiri hill.

KUGE-BRAHMADEVA PILLAR

The lofty pillar standing at the south entrance of the enclosure with a small seated figure of Brahmadeva on the top is called the Kuge-Brahmadeva pillar. The figure of Brahmadeva is facing east. The pillar originally appears to have had eight elephants supporting its pedestal in the eight directions, but only a few of them are left now.

An inscription on the pillar commemorates the death of the Gaṅga king Mārasiṁha II which took place in AD 974 and hence the period of the pillar cannot be ascertained to a period later than the aforesaid date.[30]

MAHĀNAVAMĪ-MAṆḌAPA

To the east of the Bharateśvara image stand two *maṇḍapa*s, side by side, which are called the Mahānavamī Maṇḍapas. The four pillars of each *maṇḍapa* are cylindrical in shape and are of granite. The inscribed pillars set-up in the middle of these *maṇḍapa*s are beautifully executed with elegant towers at their tops. They are square in shape and have inscriptions on all the four faces and are made of pot stone. The inscription on one of the pillars is an epitaph of a Jain teacher named

---

29. V.A. Sangave, *op. cit.*, p. 17.
30. K.A. Nilakanthasastri, *op cit.*, p. 25 and *Archa. Report*, Bangalore, 1923, p. 72.

Nayakīrti who died in AD 1176. It was set-up by the minister Nāgadeva, the disciple of Nayakīrti.[31]

BHARATEŚVARA

To the north of Śāntinātha Basadi is the image of Bharateśvara, the brother of Bāhubali or Gommaṭa. It is 9 ft. high and carved out of a soft variety of soap-stone. It is half-built, being complete only to the knees. The pitted marks on several parts of the figure have been caused by the ignorant visitors who out of curosity to hear the metallic sound produced on hitting of the image with stones; such act is certainly a sign of vandalism. The period of the inscription seems to be about AD 900, nearly a century before the colossus on the large hill came into existence.[32]

IRUVE BRAHMADEVA TEMPLE

To the north of the north entrance to the enclosure is a solitary shrine known as the Iruve Brahmadeva temple. It consists only of a *garbhagṛha* enshrined with a low relief figure of Brahmadeva. The inscription on the doorway of this temple ascribes it to about AD 950.[33]

KANCHINA DONE

Kanchina done or bell metal pond is found to the north-west of the Iruve Brahmadeva temple. It is not known why this pond is known as Kanchina done. One of the inscriptions found there says that the pond was caused to be made by Manabha probably in the year AD 1194.[34]

LAKKI-DONE

There is another natural pond to the east of the walled area

31. S. Setter, *op. cit.*, p. 13.
32. K.A. Nilakanthasastri, *op. cit.*, p. 27.
33. *Ibid.*, p. 38.
34 *Ibid.*

known as Lakki-done. The very name suggests that the donor was a woman named Lakki. The rock to the west of this pond contains several epigraphs of about the ninth and tenth centuries AD. They mostly record the names of visitors to the place, some of the visitors being Jain *gurus*, poets, officers and other high personages.[35]

BHADRABĀHU-CAVE

Outside the walled area, on the south-east, there is a cave with a recently erected portico known as the Bhadrabāhu cave. According to a tradition, the *Śrutakevali* Bhadrabāhu came to Śravaṇabeḷgoḷa and lived in the cave. The cave enshrines the engraved footprint of this *Śrutakevali* who died here. The footprints are worshipped even now. It is also stated that the Maurya Emperor Candragupta came here on a pilgrimage and after having received *dīkṣā* or initiation from Dakṣiṇācārya had worshipped the footprints until his death. The event regarding the migration of *Śrutakevali* Bhadrabāhu to Śravaṇa-beḷgoḷa along with his disciple Candragupta, the Mauryan Emperor, which has already been described in detail, may be here referred to in brief:

Bhadrabāhu, the last *Śrutakevali,* had predicted at Ujjain a twelve years drought and famine in the north, whereupon the Jain community had migrated to the south under his leadership. Candragupta abdicated and accompanied Bhadrabāhu. On reaching Śravaṇabeḷgoḷa, Bhadrabāhu perceived the approach of his last moments, and hence ordered the community to proceed on their journey and he himself remained there until his death with his disciple Candragupta. Candragupta also lived there for some years as an ascetic, worshipping the footprints of his *guru* and ultimately died practising the Jain rite of *sallekhana* or starvation.

---

35. R. Narasimhachar, *Epigraphia Carnatica,* vol. II, S.B., p. 9.

The evidence of the local history, literature and inscriptions, of about the seventh century AD and later times, supports this event. The literary works which give varying accounts of it are the Sanskrit works *Bṛhatkathākośa* of AD 931 and the *Bhadrabāhucarita* of the fifteenth century, the Kannaḍa works *Munivaṁśābhyudaya* of AD 1680 and the *Rājāvali Kathe* of Devacandra. In front of the cave, another pair of foot-prints and some relievo images of *tīrthaṅkara* with his disciple are seen engraved. The inscription found below the images is an epitaph of Mallisenadeva.[36]

CĀMUṆḌARĀYA'S ROCK

An inscribed boulder near the foot of the hill is known as Cāmuṇḍarāya's rock. It is held that Cāmuṇḍarāya shooted an arrow from this rock directed towards the larger hill. He was directed to do so in a dream and as he followed the directions an image of Gommaṭa, which was then concealed by stones, bushes, etc., became instantly visible. The rock bears figures of some Jain saints with labels below giving their names.[37]

A full view of Jinanāthapura with its pot-stone temple of Śāntinātha is obtained from the north slope of Candragiri.

Dodda-Beṭṭa

The entire area of the Vindhyagiri hill has been divided into two parts by a heavy wall at some distance around the colossal image of Gommaṭeśvara. This long, high and solid wall was erected in AD 1117 by the able minister Gaṅgarāja with a view to protect the image from all possible injuries. The wall has thus made the area around the image into a compact enclosure.

---

36. K.A. Nilakanthasastri, *op. cit.*, pp. 24-25.
37. V.A. Sangave, *op. cit.*, p. 10.

(A) *In the enclosure*: The religious structures in the enclosure are as follows:

(1) A colossal image of the Gommaṭeśvara facing the north is in the centre of the western enclosure (wall).

(2) In all there are 43 images in cloisters around the image of the Gommaṭeśvara. Of these images, two are of *yakṣī* Kusmāṇḍinī, one of Bāhubali and forty of *tīrthaṅkaras*. The distribution of these 43 images is as under:

(a) Cloister on eastern side : is enshrouded with 14 images among which one is of Kuṣmāṇḍinī and 13 of *tīrthaṅkaras*.

(b) Cloister on the southern side : is enshrouded with the 16 images of *tīrthaṅkaras*.

(c) Cloister on the western side : has 13 images, among which one is of Kuṣmāṇḍinī, one of Bāhubali (high) and 11 of *tīrthaṅkaras*.

(3) Two images of *dvārapālakas*, i.e., doorkeepers, about 6 ft. in height, are seen erected at the sides of the entrance to the enclosure.

(4) One pillar, about 6 ft. above the ground level, enshrine a seated figure of Brahmadeva. It is erected just near the enclosure and was built by Cāmuṇḍarāya.

(5) One figure of Gullakayaji.

(B) *Outside the enclosure*:

(1) Siddhara Basadi

(2) Akhaṇḍa-Bagilu

(3) Tyagada Brahmadeva pillar

(4) Cennanna Basadi

(5) Odegal Basadi

(6) Caturviṁśati-Tīrthaṅkara Basadi

(7) Brahmadeva Mandira

(8) Siddhara Guṇḍu.[38]

The larger hill known as Indragiri or Dodda Beṭṭa rises about 470 ft. above the plain at its foot and is 3,347 ft. above the level of the sea. It is ovoid in shape, its longer diameter being perhaps a quarter of a mile. It is also sometimes designated Vindhyagiri. A flight of about 500 steps cut in the granite rock leads up to the summit. The antiquities are described below in the order in which they occur as one goes up the hill.[39]

SIDDHARA-BASADI

Immediately to the right of the entrance leading into the outer enclosure around the Gommaṭeśvara image is a small shrine, facing west, known as Siddhara Basadi. This shrine has only a *garbhagṛha* and a *sukhanāsī*. It is enshrining a seated figure of a *siddha*. On both sides of the *garbhagṛha*, doorway, stand two fine inscribed pillars which show elegant workmanship. Their tops are in the form of beautiful towers. The inscriptions are the epitaphs of two Jain teachers named Paṇḍitarāya who died in AD 1398 and Śrutamuni, who died in AD 1432.[40]

AKHAṆḌA-BAGILU

The entrace to the court of the colossal image is called *akhaṇḍadvāra* or *bagilu* since a good part of the doorway is carved out of a single rock. The well-carved architrave consists of a seated figure of Lakṣmī bathed by elephants standing on either side. The Gajalakṣmī group is under an ornamental arch carved in low relief. On both sides of this entrance are two small shrines, the one to the right containing the figure of Bāhubali and the left one enshrining a figure of

38. *Ibid.*, pp. 12-14.

39. R. Narasimhachar, *op. cit.*, p. 10.

40. S. Setter, *op. cit.*, p. 46.

his brother Bharata. Both the figures are carved in high relief out of the natural boulders. According to tradition, this doorway was caused to be made by Cāmuṇḍarāya. The image on either side of this entrance and also the flight of steps leading to this doorway were built by the General Bharateśvara in about AD 1130. To the right of this doorway stands a big boulder known as the Siddharaguṇḍa on which are carved numerous *siddha* relievos and some inscriptions. At a little distance, there is another entrance known as the Gullakayajji-Bagilu or doorway.[41]

TYAGADA BRAHMADEVA PILLAR

Opposite to Gommaṭa and outside the enclosure around Gommaṭa is a very elegantly carved pillar known as the Tyagada Brahmadeva pillar. Four creepers are shown on this pillar in bold relief as emerging out from the top corners of the cubical base intertwining all around the cylindrical shaft and each convolution having a beautifully designed flower or leaf in the centre. This beautiful work of art is said to have been supported from above in such a way that a handkerchief be passed under it. But the pavillion, which supports the pillar at present, appears to have been put up at a much later date.

The inscription on the north base which gives a glowing account of Cāmuṇḍarāya's expeditions confirms the traditional account of attributing the erection of this pillar to Cāmuṇḍarāya himself. Unfortunately the inscription has ruined on the three sides of the base leaving only a portion on the fourth side intact. Among the figures sculptured on the southern base of the pillar, the one flanked by *cāmara*-bearers is said to represent Cāmuṇḍarāya. Another figure in the same group is said to represent his *guru* Nemicandra,

---

41. R.S. Shastri, *Arch. Report*, Bangalore, 1923, pp. 75-85.
Report, Bangalore, 1923, pp. 75-85.

who is said to be the author of the work *Gommaṭeśvara*, written by him for the instruction of his disciple, Cāmuṇḍarāya, the great minister of the Gaṅga king Rājamalla. The name Chagada Kamba or Tyagada pillar accounted for the place by the statement where gifts were distributed.

However, the open *maṇḍapa*s adjoining the two cells were added, probably after the fourteenth century.[42]

CHENNANNA-BASADI

At some distance to the south-west of the Cauvīsa-Tīrthaṅkara Basadi is a *done* or natural pond. This *done* is the chief source of water supply on the hill at present. Near the *done* to its west stands a temple known as the Chennanna Basadi. It consists of a *garbhagṛha*, a porch and a verandah. The temple is built for Candranātha, the eighth *tīrthaṅkara*. A *mānastambha* or pillar stands in front of it.

From an inscription discovered recently on the same boulder on which the image is carved it is gathered that this temple was built by two brothers Chikkanna and Chennanna in AD 1667 and the two figures, one male and the other female, facing each other with folded hands, carved on the pillars of the verandah, probably represent Puṭṭasāmi Seṭṭi and Devīrammā, the parents of Chikkanna and Chennanna. To the north-east of the *basadi* is a *maṇḍapa* or pillared hall situated between the two *done*s or natural ponds. It can be surmised with the evidence of another inscription found near them that Chennanna might have constructed these *done*s.[43]

ODEGAL BASADI

The temples which stands on a lofty terrace with a high flight of steps leading up to it is called Odegal Basadi because of

---

42. S. Setter, *Śravaṇbeḷgoḷa*, p. 44.
43. K.A. Nilakanthasastri, *op. cit.*, pp. 7-8.

the *odegals* or stone props that have been used for strengthening the basement walls. This basadi is also known as Trikūṭa Basadi by reason of its having three cells facing different directions. It is a fine granite structure of the Hoyasala period with a plain exterior. It consists of three cells and three open *sukhanāsī*s with a common *navaraṅga* and *mukhamaṇḍapa*. The *navaraṅga* pillars are cylindrical in shape and the central ceiling has a lotus pendant. The main cell contains a fine figure of Ādinātha with a well carved *prabhāvalī*, flanked by male *cāmara*-bearers; the left cell has a figure of Neminātha and on its right a figure of Śāntinātha. Ādinātha or Vṛṣabhanātha was the first among the 24 *jinas*. He is also known as Purudeva. He was the father of Gommaṭa. All the three images are seated on the rock. To the west of the temple are engraved nearly 30 Mārvāḍī inscriptions in Nāgarī characters, running in date from AD 1645 to AD 1841, which are the records of the visits of pilgrims from northern India.[44]

CAUVĪSA-TĪRTHAṄKARA BASADI

The top of Indragiri has a defensive wall made of stone, inside which are most of the ancient structures. The first object inside this wall is the Cauvīsa-Tīrthaṅkara Basadi. It is a small shrine consisting of a *garbhagṛha*, a *sukhanāsī* and a porch. The object of figures stand in a line at the bottom and above them, in the shape of a *prabhāvalī*, are arranged small seated figures of *tīrthaṅkara*s numbering 24. These figures were set-up in AD 1648 by Cārukīrti Paṇḍita, Dharmacandra and others.[45]

BRAHMADEVA TEMPLE

Brahmadeva temple is a small shrine at the foot of the hill near the beginning of the ascent containing a shapeless flat stone daubed with red ochre which the people call Brahmā

44. B.L. Rice, *Epigraphia Carnatica*, vol. II, *SB*, p. 25.
45. K.A. Nilakanthasastri, *SB*, p. 7.

or Jaruguppe Appā. This temple was erected by Rangaiya, the younger brother of Girigauḍa of Hirisali, probably in AD 1679.[46]

SIDDHARA-GUṆḌU

It is a big boulder of stone (named after *siddhas*, i.e., liberated souls), on which are inscribed several inscriptions, the top portion being sculptured with rows after rows of seated figures representing the Jain *gurus* (i.e., ascetic teachers).[47]

GULLAKAYAJJI

Directly to the west of the Siddhara Basadi, and opposite to the Gommaṭa is a Brahmadeva pillar with a pavilion at the top enshrining a seated figure of Brahmadeva. Below this pavilion stands the figure of a woman called (Gullakayajji), about 5 ft high, facing the Gommaṭa and holding a *gullakayi* in her hands. There is a belief that when Cāmuṇḍarāya made elaborate arrangements for performing the *abhiṣeka* of Gommaṭa, the milk did not descend lower than the thighs. But when the *guru* directed him to use for anointment the little milk brought by a pious old woman in a *gullakayi,* it instantly ran down all over the statue in streams and covered the hill. It is said that Gullakayajji or granny was the Goddess Padmāvatī who, in order to break the pride of Cāmuṇḍarāya at his great accomplishment, appeared at the time of the anointment in the guise of a poor old woman. According to another tradition, she was the mythological Kuṣmāṇḍinī. It is said that Cāmuṇḍarāya got this image of Gullakayajji erected here and, as mentioned above, the village is also said to have been named after it, as it is attributed so by some.[48]

---

46. R. Narasimhachar, *op. cit.*, p. 25.
47. V.A. Sangave, *op. cit.*, p. 14.
48. K.A. Nilakanthasastri, *op. cit.*, pp. 11-12.

GOMMAṬEŚVARA IMAGE

On the summit of the hill stands the image of Gommaṭeśvara in an open court surrounded by a battlemuted verandah enshrining the images of Jain saints. This enclosure is again surrounded at stone distance by a heavy wall, a good part of which is picturesquely formed by boulders in their natural position.[49]

THE VILLAGE

As stated before, the village of Śravaṇabeḷgoḷa lies picturesquely between the two hills Indragiri and Candragiri. The village is well known for the manufacture of copper and brass vessels. Here a continuous din caused by the hammers of the coppersmiths could be heard throughout the day. The position of the important buildings, etc., exhibits the south view of the Kalyāṇī or pond in the middle of the village.

BHAṆḌĀRĪ BASADI

The largest structure in the village is the Bhaṇḍārī Basadi consisting of a *garbhagṛha*, a *sukhanāsī*, a *navaraṅga*, a porch, a *mukhamaṇḍapa* and *prākāra* or enclosure, all of large dimensions.

Since this *basadi* is dedicated to the 24 *tīrthaṅkaras*, it is alternatively known as Caturviṁśati-Tīrthaṅkara Basadi. The *garbhagṛha* has three doorways and the middle one opposite to the image of the 12th *jina* Vāsupūjya is well carved with perforated screens at its sides. The *sukhanāsī* has to its left the figures of Padmāvatī and Brahmā.

A noteworthy feature of this temple is the use of gigantic granite slabs for paving the floor. A verandah runs round the main building. The *mānastambha* in front of the *basadi* is a fine monolith. The temple is popularly known as Bhaṇḍārī Basadi, since it was erected by Hulla, the *bhaṇḍārī* or the

---

49. *Ibid.*, p. 12.

treasurer of the Hoyasala king Narasiṁha I (AD 1141-73). This *basadi* was built in AD 1159 and the king Narasiṁha named it Bhavyacūḍāmaṇi and granted the village Savaneru for its upkeep.[50]

AKKANA BASADI

The only temple built in the Hoyasala style of architecture in this village is the Akkana Basadi consisting of a *garbhagṛha*, a *sukhanāsī*, a *navaraṅga* and a porch, dedicated to the Pārśvanātha, whose image is sheltered by a seven-hooded serpent. Fine seated figures of Dharaṇendra and Padmāvatī, the *yakṣa* and *yakṣī* of this *jina*, are placed in the *sukhanāsī*. The panel has a seated *jina* figure under a triple umbrella in the centre, flanked on either side by a male *cāmara*-bearer a standing *jina*, *yakṣa* and *yakṣī*. The pedestal is flanked by elephants and the embankment has at its sides figures of Sarasvatī. The temple was erected in AD 1181 by the Jain lady, Aciyakkā, wife of Candramauli, the brāhmaṇa minister of the Hoyasala king Ballāla II, who granted the Bammeyanahalli village for its upkeep. The temple is called Akkana Basadi which is an abbreviation of Aciyakkana Basadi.[51]

SIDDHANĀTHA BASADI

In the west of the *prākāra* or enclosure of the Akkana Basadi is situated a temple known as Siddhanātha Basadi, so called because all the books bearing on the Jain *siddhānta* were once secured in a dark room of this basadi. This temple has an inscribed marble *caturviṁaśati-tīrthaṅkara* image, about 3 ft. high, with Pārśvanātha standing in the middle and other *jina*s seated around.

---

50. R. Narasimhachar, *op. cit.*, p. 26.
51. K.A. Nilakanthasastri, and S. Setter, *op cit.*, pp. 40-41, *op. cit.*, p. 66.

This temple has a *caturviṁśati-tīrthaṅkara* group set-up by a pilgrim in about AD 1700.[52]

DANASALE-BASADI

The Danasale Basadi near the entrance to Akkana Basadi, enshrines the *pañca-parameṣṭhi* group. The *parameṣṭhis* are the *jinas*, *siddhas*, *ācāryas*, *upādhyāyas* and the *sādhus*. According to the *Munivaṁśābhyudaya* of Cidānandakavi (AD 1680) Cikka-Deva-Rāja-Oḍeyar, *Mahārājā* of Mysore, visited Beḷgoḷa during the rule of his predecessor Dodda-Deva-Rāja-Oḍeyar in AD 1659-72 and saw the Dansale and got the village Madaneya granted by the king for its upkeep.[53]

NAGARA-JINĀLAYA

The Nagara-Jinālaya temple dedicated to Ādinātha, is a small building, consisting of a *garbhagṛha*, *sukhanāsī*, and a *navaraṅga*. The Brahmadeva image placed in one of the cells of the *navaraṅga* holds a fruit in the left hand and something that looks like a whip in the other hand.

The temple was erected in AD 1195 by the minister Nāgadeva, a lay disciple of Nayakīrti-Siddhānta-Cakravartī and Paṭṭanasvāmī of the Hoyasala king Ballāla II (AD 1173-1220). The temple was named Nagara-Jinālaya because the *nagara* or merchants were its supporters. It also appears to have borne another name "Śrī-nilaya."[54]

KALAMMĀ TEMPLE

The Kalammā temple near Akkana Basadi is a solitary Hindu temple. It is a small structure, dedicated to the goddess Kālī or Kalammā. Its only *garbhagṛha* is built of stone with a mortar over it. The goddess having four hands is in a seated posture

52. R. Narasimhachar, *op. cit.*, pp. 27-28.

53. *Ibid.*, p. 28.

54. V.A. Sangave, *op. cit.*, p. 20.

and is about 2.5 ft. in height. There is also a *liṅga* in front of the image. It is interesting to note that rice is received from the Jain *maṭha* for the offerings of this goddess.[55]

MANGAYI-BASADI

This plain temple is dedicated to Śāntinātha, the 16th *tīrthaṅkara*. In front of the temple there are two well-carved elephants. Inscription nos. 339 and 341 states that, the temple was built by Mangayi of Beḷaguḷa, a disciple of Abhinava-Cārukīrti-Paṇḍitācārya and a Crest Jewel of Royal dancing girls, and that it was named Tribhuvana-Cūḍāmaṇi temple. It was built in AD 1325. Further, the inscription no. 337 on the pedestal states that the statue was built by Bhīmā-Devī, a lay disciple of Cārukīrti Paṇḍitācārya and the queen of Devarāya-Mahārāya. This Devarāya was most probably the renowned Vijayanagar king Devarāya I (AD 1406-16).[56]

KALYĀṆĪ

The Kalyāṇī pond is a beautiful lake between Candragiri and Vindhyagiri. It has steps on all sides and is surrounded by a wall with gates surmounted by towers. There is a large pillared hall to the north with an inscription on one of its many pillars stating that the pond was constructed by Cikkadevarājendra. The latter was a king of Mysore who ruled from AD 1672 to 1704. The ceilings and the beams of the *maṇḍapa* appear to have once been decorated with paintings, of which only the traces can now be seen here and there. *Gommaṭeśvara-carita* of Anantakavi states that, Cikkadevarāja, who ordered the construction of the Kalyāṇī at the request of Annayya, his mint-master, died before its completion and that Annayya completed the construction of the pond during the rule of the king's grandson Kṛṣṇarāja Oḍeyar I (AD 1713-

55. R. Narasimhachar, *op. cit.*, p. 28.
56. S. Setter and V.A. Sangave, *op. cit.*, p. 66 and p. 20.

31). It is said that that this village derived its name from this pond. But since the name occurs even in inscriptions of the seventh century AD, we have to conclude that the pond which was in existence for ages in a natural condition was provided with steps, towers, etc., on the order of Cikkadevarāja.[57]

JAKKIKAṬṬE

This is a small tank to the south of the Bhaṇḍārī Basadi. The inscriptions seen below the *jina* figures on the two boulders near the tank nos. 367 and 368, states that Jakkimavve, a lay disciple of Subhacandra Siddhārthadeva and the wife of the elder brother of General Gaṅgarāja and the mother of General Boppadeva, caused the tank and the *jina* figures to be constructed.

As we know that Gaṅgarāja was the general of the Hoyasala-king Viṣṇuvardhana, the inscriptions hence seems to belong to AD 1120 and Jakkikaṭṭe, so named after the builder Jakkimavve, must be nearly 800 years old.[58]

CENNANNA'S POND

There is a small pond known as Cennanna at some distance to the south of the village. Cennanna is the same man who built the Cennanna Basadi on the larger hill. He got the making of this pond as also of a grove and a *maṇḍapa* recorded in a good number of inscriptions namely no. 369-375 and 480-490. From the inscription no. 390, we learn that the pond, grove etc., were built in about AD 1673.[59]

ADJACENT VILLAGES

There are several Jain temples like Haḷebeḷgoḷa in some other villages in the neighbourhood of Śravaṇbeḷgoḷa. Among these

---

57. K.A. Nilakanthasastri, *op. cit.*, pp. 5-6.
58. R. Narasimhachar, *op. cit.*, p. 32.
59. *Ibid.*, p. 32.

villages, the prominent villages are those of Jinanāthapura and Kambadahalli where exists Jain monuments of considerable antiquity. Jinanāthapura is about a mile to the north of Śravaṇbeḷgoḷa.

Jinanāthapura

The village was founded by Gaṅgarāja, the general of the Hoyasala king Viṣṇuvardhana in about AD 1117. The chief temple of this place is the Śāntinātha Basadi built by Rechimayya who made it for the worship of Sāgaranandī-Siddhāntadeva in about AD 1200. This temple is a fine specimen of the Hoyasala style of architecture consisting of a cell, a vestibul and a hall. The well-carved image of Śāntinātha is seated on a lion pedestal. The *garbhagṛha* is guarded by two *dvārapālas*.[60]

The village has also an inscribed Jain tomb generally known as the *samādhi maṇḍapa* but designated in the inscription as Śilākūṭa or stone house erected to commemorate the death of Bālacandradeva's son, a disciple of royal *guru* Nemicandra Paṇḍita of Belikumbha. The deceased had suffered a severe fever. The inscription states that the Śilākūṭa was built by Bairoja on the spot where the body was cremated in AD 1213.[61]

Kambadahalli

The name of the village Kambadahalli is derived from the lofty Jain pillar that stands near its north-west corner. The pillar is one of the most elegant in the state and has an image of seated Brahmā on its top. To the west of the pillar stands a group of seven shrines which are perhaps some of the oldest Jain monuments of importance in the state.

The earliest structure, which may be called the Ādinātha

---

60. *Ibid.*, p. 33.
61. K.A. Nilakanthasastri, *op. cit.*, pp. 46-47.

temple because it has the figure of Ādinātha in the main cell, appears to be a cross-shaped *trikūṭācala* with straight sides having three *garbhagṛha*s with open *sukhanāsī*s and a common *navaraṅga* with a porch of two *ankana*s, all these faces towards the north. The *śikhara*s are of various shapes, the one on the east being round, on the north is square and on the west it is octagonal. There is a pair of twin temples, about 10 ft in height, and facing each other in front of the porch of the Trikūṭācala is almost similar in character to the central shrine of Ādinātha in the Trikūṭācala. There appears to have been a compound wall enclosing these five shrines, which are collectively known as Pañcakūṭa Basadi.

At a distance of about 20 ft. to the north of the compound wall of this temple is another large temple dedicated to Śāntinātha whose image is 12 ft. high. The basement is high and has a finely carved frieze of ridden horses, elephants, wild lions and *yati*s. This frieze is of great interest, its workmanship being superior to that occurring in any other Hoyasala temple. The building has no towers.[62]

Haḷebeḷgoḷa

The village Haḷebeḷgoḷa is at a distance of about four miles to the north of Śravaṇbeḷgoḷa. The *jina* temple at this place consists of a *garbhagṛha*, an open *sukhanāsī*, a *navaraṅga* and a porch. The plinth is supported at the corners and other places by the figures of elephants. The outer walls are decorated with pilasters and shallow niches. The central ceiling of the *navaraṅga* is beautifully carved with a standing figure of Dharaṇendra holding bow and conch under a five-hooded canopy in the centre and the *aṣṭadikpālaka*s around. There are *cāuri*-bearers and a headless *jina* figure in the *navaraṅga*. The temple is in a ruined condition.

---

62. *Ibid.*, p. 47.

An inscription on the temple Cennarayapatna of AD 1094, states that a Hoyasala prince Ereyaṅga, the father of Viṣṇuvardhana, granted to the Jain *guru* Gopanandī the villages of Rachanahulla and the Beḷgoḷa for the repairs of the twelve *basadi* at Beḷgoḷa and others places.[63]

Nothing would flourish without the royal patronage. Fortunately, Jainism received patronage from royal persons, royal ladies, rich merchants, traders, moneylenders and lay *śrāvaka-śrāvikās* since its inception. Śravaṇbeḷgoḷa is adorned with many Jain temples and monuments which were built and maintained by many royal families and others. The following is the brief survey of royal patronage to Śravaṇbeḷgoḷa during the third century BC to the ninth century AD.

SPREAD OF JAINISM IN KARNATAKA

(From Fourth Century BC to Ninth Century AD)

Karnataka became the second home of Jainism right from the third century BC. A number of Jain shrines came into existence and developed rapidly across Karnataka. The political condition of Karnataka was congenial to the spread of Jainism as several dynasties extended patronization to Jainism in this state.

The following is a brief account of the spread of Jainism in Karnataka from the third century BC to the ninth century AD and how Sātavāhanas, Kadambas, Cāḷukyas, Rāṣṭrakūṭas and Gaṅgas extended royal support to Jainism in Karnataka.

After the rule of the Mauryas in the first century AD, Karnataka did not remain under political control of one dynasty. On the contrary, there were kings of several dynasties who ruled for varying duration over different areas of Karnataka and patronized Jainism.

63. *Ibid.*, pp. 47-48.

Jainism under Sātavāhana (first to third century AD)

In the Deccan, the Mauryan empire was followed by the rule of the Sātavāhanas, which lasted for four and a half centuries from about 230 BC. The Sātavāhana empire extended to the whole of the Deccan including Karnataka and spread far into the northern India, perhaps, even as far as Magadha.[64]

Karnataka and Maharashtra were a part of the Sātavāhana empire. Pratiṣṭhān or modern Paiṭhan (in the Aurangabad district of Maharashtra) was the capital of Sātavāhanas. Sātavāhana rulers were the followers of Vedic religion but they also patronized Jainism. Some rulers of this dynasty were inclined towards Jainism. The Sātavāhana were ardent patrons of Brāhmaṇism. But they respected Jainism too.[65]

Śimūka was the founder of Sātavāhana dynasty who ruled for 23 years from 235 BC to 212 BC. According to the Jain accounts, Śimūka grew so wicked towards the end of his reign that he was dethroned and killed. He was successed by his brother Kānhā (207 BC – 189 BC).[66]

The seventeenth ruler of this dynasty was Hala, who ruled for AD 20-24 and was famous as a compiler of *Sattasai* (*Saptaśatī*), a collection of 700 erotic *gāthā*s in the *āryā* metre in Marāthi Prākr̥t. It is said that King Hala was under the influence of the Jain thoughts when he composed his *Gāthā Saptaśatī*, a Prākr̥t work.[67] During the Sātavāhana period, Prākr̥t literature was encouraged.

After Sukastin, the saint Kālakācārya (first century BC) is said to have gone to the king of Pentha in the Deccan to invite

---

64. K.A. Nilakanthasastri, *A History of South India*, India, 1966, pp. 83-84.
65. B.N. Luniya, *Life and Culture in Ancient India*, Agra, 1978, p. 292.
66. K.A. Nilakanthasastri, *op. cit.*, pp. 46-47.
67. Rajamala Jain and Laxmichandra Jain, *op. cit.*, p. 16.

him to attend his discourses at Pajjusana. May be, he was Hala of the Sātavāhana dynasty (who is believed to have been a Jain) ruling from Paiṭhan (Pratiṣṭhānapura). The early existence of Śvetāmbara Jains in the north Deccan is also indicated by references to Padaliptācārya's visit to Manyakheta (Malkhed, in the Nizam's dominions). The *Samyaktuasaptati* of Haribhadrasūri related that the people of Manyakheta would not allow Padaliptācārya (first century BC) to leave them and go elsewhere. It also says that in all the neighbourhood there existed Jain *saṁgha*s noted for their piety.[68]

The Sātavāhana rulers followed the Vedic religion and performed Vedic sacrifices. But the rulers of this dynasty practised complete religious toleration. Apart from them, there were writers of Jain works and reputed teachers of the Digambara sect of Jainism in the Deccan and south India in the early centuries of the Christian era. The Digambara (Jain teacher Kundakundācārya) was the teacher of Sātavāhana princes. Kundakundācārya and Sāmantabhadra were in the Kannaḍa region. As told earlier, Jainism had entered into this land with the Mauryan emperor, Candragupta, and his spiritual guide Bhadrabāhu in about 300 BC. The place of their penance, viz., the mount of Śravaṇbeḷgoḷa is the oldest and the holiest centre of Jainism in the south. The disciples of Bhadrabāhu propagated the Jain faith carrying conviction to the people by their precept and practice. Initially in Gaṅgavāḍī and then in different parts of Karnataka Jainism grew in popularity, though in the far-off centres of Śravaṇbeḷgoḷa, Karkala, Koppam and Manyakheta. Its principles of *ahiṁsā* and spiritual self-reliance must have had their impact on the rulers and their people following the Vedic religion. Thus

68. S.R. Sharma, *Jainism and Karnataka*, Dharwar, 1940, p. 7.

the Sātavāhana set a very good example of religious tolerance.[69]

Jainism under Kadambas (Third to Sixth Century AD)

Śimogā district and Karnataka was controlled by Kadambas of Banavāsī after the fall of Sātavāhanas. Kadambas were the rulers of Karnataka during the third to fifth centuries AD and their capital was first at Karnataka (modern Karad) and later Vajihayanti and then Banavāsī. Kadambas were the followers of Brāhmaṇism but they also extended patronage to Jainism. Some rulers professed Jainism. It is said that the second king of dynasty Śivakoṭi took *dikṣā* from the famous Jain *ācārya* Sāmantabhadra.[70]

Another king, Kakutsthavarmā, who belonged to the fourth century AD, granted a village to the Jain temples and paid reverence to Jinendra and Ṛṣabhadeva. S.R. Sharma gives the following account of this grant. The next contemporary epigraphical foothold that we possess in following the history of Jainism in Karnataka, is a grant made by the Kadamba Kakusthavarmā, when he was *yuvarāja*, to the General Śrutakīrti. The gift consisted of a field called Bodhavara-Kṣetra which was in the village of Khetagrāma which belongs to the holy *arhats*; and the record concludes with "reverence to Ṛṣabha."[71] The circumstances which led the king to gift was that Śrutakīrti, a Jain, had once saved his life. Possibly, therefore, out of sheer gratitude, he patronized Jainism only for the satisfaction of the donee. Kakusthavarmā also made similar grants to brāhmaṇas, but he never

---

69. K.R. Basavaraja, *History and Culture of Karnataka*, Dharwar, 1984, p. 502.
70. Rajamala Jain and Laxmichandra Jain, *op. cit.*, p. 16.
71. J.F. Fleet, "Sanskrit and old Canarese Inscription," *Ind. Ant.*, vol. VI, p. 24.

expressed before them his "reverence to Ṛṣabha." Had he himself been an "Avowed Jain" he would surely have done.[72]

In this connection, the following observations of Prof. Moraeas on the religion of the Kadambas may be borne in mind, "these kings nevertheless were of a very tolerant disposition, and allowed other religions to flourish in their kingdom side by side Śaivism." The numerous grants which they made to the Jains are clear evidence of their toleration. Such grants led J.F. Fleet, K.B. Pathak and others to suppose that the Kadambas were of Jain persuasion. The error, however, was corrected by Fleet in the second edition of his book entitled *Dynasties of the Kanarese Districts*, which he published after the discovery of the inscription of Śāntivarmā at Talaguṇḍa. He has established here that the religion of the Kadambas was Brāhmaṇism and not Jainism.[73]

Nevertheless, under the liberal patronage of the Kadambas, Jainism prospered in Karnataka is evident from the various grants referred to below. It is evident that despite their personal beliefs, some of the Kadamba rulers came to be very closely associated with the Jains. For instance, Mṛgeśavarmā, (AD 450-78) a grandson of Kakusthavarmā, gave fields, to the divine supreme *arhat*s, at Vajjayanti for the purpose of the glory of sweeping (the temple) and anointing (the idol with *ghī*) and performing worship, etc., entirely free from taxation.[74]

Another grant by the same monarch bears "the seal of Jinendra" and is important as showing Mṛgeśavarmā's impartiality towards both the sects of Jains, viz., the Śvetāmbaras and the Digambaras.[75] Mṛgeśavarmā gave grants to the Jain

72. S.R. Sharma, *op. cit.*, p. 9.
73. George M. Moras, *The Kadamba Kula: A History of Ancient and Mediaeval Karnataka*, Bombay, 1931, p. 250.
74. J.F. Fleet, *op. cit.*, pp. 36-37.
75. *Ibid.*, p. 38.

religious centres. The grants of Ravivarmā and Bhānuvarmā (AD 478-520), both sons of Mṛgeśavarmā, manifest this growing influence of Jainism yet more clearly.[76]

Ravisena at Palasika or Halsi in the Belgaum district, is both interesting and important from a historical point of view. Besides recounting the grant of Kakusthavarmā to Ravikīrti and Śrutakīrti, it also states that king Śāntivarmā son of Kakustha, and his son "the pious" Mṛgeśa gave the grant to the mother of Damakīrti, for the sake of piety and at the direction of his father.[77]

Another grant of Ravivarmā "to the god Jinendra" describes him as "the mighty king," the sun of the sky of the mighty family of Kadambas.[78] Hence their personal allegiance to the Jain faith must have had considerable influence in spreading the religion among the masses as well.[79]

Similarly, his brother, Bhānuvarmā's devotion to Jainism is also attested by a grant. By him, a desirous of prosperity, this land was given to the Jains in order that the ceremony of ablutions might always be performed without fail on the days of the full moon.[80] Harivarmā (AD 520-40) also made another grant to the Jains "at the request of Bhānuśakti of the family Sendraks."[81] He gave the village of Marade "for the holy people and for the proformance of rites of the temple, as a property belonging to the sect of *śramaṇa*s called the *aharisti* and the authority of which remained with the *ācārya* Dharmanandi,"[82] despite of the fact that the Kadamba rulers

76. *Ibid.*
77. S.R. Sharma, *op. cit.*, p. 11.
78. J.F. Fleet, *op. cit.*, p. 27.
79. *Ibid.*, p. 30.
80. *Ibid.*, p. 29.
81. *Ibid.*, p. 31.
82. S.R. Sharma, *op. cit.*, p. 14.

were followers of Hinduism. Since they patronized Jainism also, the religion flourished during Kadamba's reign.

Jainism under Cāḷukyas of Bādāmī (AD 500-754)

The Cāḷukyas of Bādāmī were the rulers of Karnataka as well as Maharashtra during the sixth to eighth centuries AD. Jainism flourished during this period too. The rulers liberally patronized it. Ravikīrti, a Jain author of the famous Aihoḷe inscription, had received the highest favour from Pulakeśin II (AD 610-42). He built a temple of Jinendra, now known as Meguti temple. Vinayāditya, Vijayāditya and Vikramāditya gave rich gifts to the Jain teachers and for building *basadi*s or temple. A cave temple in Bādāmī was dedicated to Jain.[83]

Bhandarkar has noted that Jainism achieved prominence under the early Cāḷukyas of Bādāmī.[84] We get many glimpses of the Jain religion in the inscription of the Cāḷukyas which reveals their patronage for that faith.[85]

A Jain inscription of Śravaṇbeḷgoḷa speaks of the Jain teacher Guṇacandra as a worshipper at the feet of Mallikamoda Santisa at Balipura.[86] Mallikamoda being a title of Jayasiṁha I of the Cāḷukya dynasty, it is reasonably supposed that the Beḷagoḷa inscription represents him. If this supposition is true then we have here our first reference to the patronage of Jainism under the early Cāḷukyas. This is greatly supported by the fact that the same inscription also speaks of another Jain celebrity, Vasucandra as having attained fame as "Balsara Swati" at the Cāḷukya capital. Likewise, another epigraphs states that Vādirāja, also a Jain

83. K.R. Basavaraja, *History and Culture of Karnataka*, p. 503.
84. R.G. Bhandarkar, *Early History of the Deccan*, Poona, 1927, p. 59.
85. S.R. Sharma, *op. cit.*, p. 21.
86. B.L. Rice, *EP*, p. 69.

teacher, was honoured by Jayasiṁha I at whose capital he too won his celebrity.[87]

Rāṇārāya, son of Jayasiṁha I, and his son Pulakeśin I, both appear to have kept up this tradition of patronage of the Jains. The latter endowed a Jain temple at Alaktanāgarāja and the inscription recording this fact states "Satyasraya in his piety bestowed a field (and) a chapter worthy of that shrine of Jina." His successor was Kīrtivarmā I, and according to an earliest Kannaḍa inscription at Dhārwār, he too made grants to the Jains. But of all the Cāḷukya inscriptions of Pulakeśin II, the Ahioḷe is the most famous. In it, Ravikīrti, the Jain poet who composed the inscription says "This stone temple of Jinendra which is the abode of glory was caused to be constructed by the learned Ravikīrti."[88]

There is also a Jain cave towards the eastern end of the south face of the Meguti temple. Jayasiṁha II is thus stated to have as his spiritual preceptor a Jain teacher named Nirvādya Paṇḍita.[89] An inscription of Vijayāditya tells us that this king made a grant to Udayadeva Paṇḍita, or Niravādya Paṇḍita, who was the house pupil of Śrī Pūjyapāda and belonged to the Devagan division of the Mūlasaṁgha. Vijayāditya's son Vikramāditya II also got repaired a Jain temple and gave a grant to the Jain *ācārya* Vijayadeva Paṇḍita.[90]

Thus Cāḷukyas of Bādāmī extended patronage to Jainism. Ravikīrti was a Jain poet in the court of Pulakeśin II and his Ahioḷe *praśasti* dated AD 634 is remarkable. From the study of Cāḷukyas inscriptions, we come to the conclusion that Jainism was in prosperous condition during this period.

---

87. B.L. Rice, *op. cit.*, p. 41.
88. S.R. Sharma, *op. cit*, p. 22.
89. R.G. Bhandarkar, *op. cit.*, p. 59.
90. *Ibid.*, p. 59.

Jainism under the Rāṣṭrakūṭas (AD 754-974)

The Rāṣṭrakūṭas were a great power in south India for more than two centuries, and like the Gaṅgas of Talakaḍ, they were zealous patrons of Jainism. Jain literature, in particular, had its golden age under their patronage. The Gaṅgas had set-up this tradition before the Rāṣṭrakūṭas rose to power, and Cāḷukyas, which was an another important dynasty, almost sandwiched between the Gaṅgas and the Rāṣṭrakūṭas, were also inclined to patronize Jainism. Although they were votaries of the Vedic religion, they were greatly interested in Jainism and supported it with a big heart. Their period is considered as the golden age of Jain literature.

The Cāḷukya ruler Kīrtivarman II was defeated by Dantidurga in AD 752-53. The latter was the founder of Rāṣṭrakūṭa dynasty. The age of Rāṣṭrakūṭas (AD 754-974) was a period of great activity among the Jains of the Deccan and the Kannaḍa country.[91]

Akalaṅka was the most celebrated name and a great intellectual in Jain history. He was an important figure in the south Indian Jain *saṁgha*. This great logician Akalaṅka, who was the founder of the Jain school of logic, lived around AD 642 and was connected with the country of Śubhatuṅga of Manyakheta and of Himaśītala of Kāñcīpuram. His teacher was Ravigupta, (Ravikīrti of Ahioḷe inscription dated AD 634) and Akalaṅka is said to have studied Buddhism in the College of Kānherī. He distinguished himself in his disputations with Buddhists and won laurels. His career is associated with the courts of the Rāṣṭrakūṭa king Kṛṣṇa I, who is identified with Sahastuṅga and is held as Akalaṅka's patron. He is said to have defeated Buddhists at Kāñcīpuram and driven them to Ceylon.[92]

---

91. A.S. Altekar, *The Rāṣṭrakūṭas and their Times*, Poona, 1934, pp. 21-25.
92. S.K. Rao Ramachandra, *Jainism in South India*, pp. 27-28.

Dhanṭivarman was succeeded by Kṛṣṇa I, also called Akālavarṣa Śubhatuṅga, who ruled from AD 757-73 and was also the king of Maharashtra and Karnataka. The famous Ellorā Jain temples and caves were erected during his reign. He conquered all the Cāḷukyan territory. He was the patron of *ācārya* Parvadhimalla.[93]

Prof. S.R. Sharma writes about the patronization of Kṛṣṇa I to Jainism in the following way, "According to the *Kathākośa* of the Digambaras, Akalaṅka was the son of Śubhatuṅga whose capital was Manyakheta."

But this is a mere belief and the identity of the persons is by no means easy to establish. However, in the light of our knowledge of the galaxy of great writers who lived about this time, the belief is not without its value. The *Akalaṅka-Carita* or the traditional biographs of Akalaṅka states that he was the son of Puruṣottama, a minister of Śubhatuṅga. An inscription at Śravaṇbeḷgoḷa also alludes to Akalaṅka's challenge to the *paṇḍitas* at the court of Śubhatuṅga. He is supposed to have belonged to the *Devasaṁgha* of Manyakheta. From all these it becomes clear that Akalaṅka must have had some intimate connection with the Rāṣṭrakūṭa king, so persistently named; and it is possible that he lived at the court of Kṛṣṇa I in the eighth century AD as suggested by Hiralala.[94]

Kṛṣṇa I was succeeded by Dhruvadharavarṣa who ruled during AD 779-93. His queen was the daughter of Cāḷukya ruler Veṅgī who was the follower of Jainism. Dhruva was the patron of *ācārya* Jinasena who composed *Harivaṁśa Purāṇa* in AD 783.[95]

---

93. Rajamala Jain and Laxmichandra Jain, *op. cit.*, p. 20.
94. S.R. Sharma, *op. cit.*, pp. 30-31.
95. Rajamala Jain and Laxmichandra Jain, *op. cit.*, pp. 20-21.

King Dhruva was succeeded by Govinda III who ruled during AD 793-814. During his time, the Rāṣṭrakūṭa empire had expanded in all directions. Govinda III was not a follower of Jainism but he extended patronization to the Jain scholars. He donated land to the Jain temple at Manyakheta in AD 802. Again he donated one village Jalamaṅgal to the Jain Muni Arkakīrti.[96]

Samrāṭ Amoghavarṣa (AD 815-77)

Jainism reached its pinnacle during the reign of Amoghavarṣa, who ruled Deccan including Karnataka during AD 815-77. Therefore, Dr. A.S. Altekar, an authority on Rāṣṭrakūṭa history, rightly pointed that among the Rāṣṭrakūṭa emperors, Amoghavarṣa I was more a Jain than a Hindu. In his *Pārśvābhudaya*, Jinasena calls himself as the chief preceptor, *parama guru*, of the king who used to regard himself as purified by the mere rememberance of that holy saint. *Sārasaṁgraha*, a Jain mathematical work, also mentions that Amoghavarṣa I was a follower of the Syādvāda. Amoghavarṣa's offering of one of his fingers to the Goddess Mahālakṣmī, in order to extricate his kingdom from an epidemic, indicates that he worshipped some Hindu deities too along with Mahāvīra. He seems to have taken an active interest in Jainism.

This emperor had appointed Guṇabhadra, the author of the last five chapters of *Ādi Purāṇa*, as the preceptor of his son Kṛṣṇa II. The latter is known to have given a donation to a Jain temple at Mulguṇḍa. It can be said on this basis that although he was not a full-fledged Jain but was at least a patron of Jainism.[97] Many of the feudatories and officers of the Rāṣṭrakūṭas were also Jains. Most of the Ratta rulers of Saundati were followers of the Jainism. Banavāsī, Governor

---

96. *Ibid.*, p. 21.

97. A.S. Altekar, *op. cit.*, pp. 311-12.

of Amoghavarṣa I, was a Jain who had got the imperial sanction for the alienation of a village to a Jain establishment at his capital.[98]

Thus Amoghavarṣa I was one of the greatest royal patron of Jainism in the Rāṣṭrakūṭas dynasty. Amoghavarṣa himself was a poet king. In the opening verses of the *Gaṇita Sārasaṁgraha* by Mahāvīrācārya, it is stated that, it was written under Amoghavarṣa I (AD 815). It is supposed that the author might have been one of the court poets. The *Jayadhavalā-Ṭīkā*, one of the rarest Jain works, was composed by Vīrasenācārya almost during the same time. Its concluding portion is attributed to Jinasena who also commenced the *Ādi Purāṇa* under Amoghavarṣa I. The author calls himself the *paramaguru* or chief preceptor of Amoghavarṣa.[99]

Amoghavarṣa prostrated himself before Jinasena and purified thereby himself. In his *Pārśvābhudaya*, Jinasena blesses his royal pupil and wishes that he might reign long. But more interesting than anything else is the composition of the *Ratnamallikā* or more fully *Praśnottararatha-mallikā* attributed to Amoghavarṣa's own authorship.[100]

Thus Jainism was a state religion during the reign of Amoghavarṣa (I). Emperor Amoghavarṣa was the author of *Kavirājamārga* and Jinasena and Guṇabhadra were the two great Jain scholars who flourished during this period.

Jinasena Svāmī (AD 770-850) not only completed his master's commentary *Jayadhavalā* but also wrote the well-known poetical biography of Tīrthaṅkara Pārśvanātha, namely *Pārśvābhudaya* and the *Mahāpurāṇa*. He was a refined scholar who belonged to the Senagaṇa. He was a teacher of Amoghavarṣa I (AD 815-77), the Rāṣṭrakūṭa king, during whose

98. *Ibid.*, pp. 312-13.
99. S.R. Sharma, *op. cit.*, p. 31.
100. *Ibid.*

reign he completed the *Jayadhavalā* commentary of Vīrasena. His fame rests on the *Pārśvābhudaya* which was written at the request of a fellow student Vijaysena as a challenge to Kālidāsa's *Meghasaṅdeśa.* He commenced writing *Ādi Purāṇa* soon after in about AD 800 as a *mahākāvya* in 47 sections, but he could complete only 40 sections and three verses in the 43rd section (a total of 10,380 verses), as he passed away there- after. This encyclopaedic work was completed by his student Guṇabhadra who wrote another 1620 verses in AD 898.[101]

Emperor Amoghavarṣa's great commander-in-chief, Bankya, was a staunch follower of Jainism. He established a village named Bankapur in Karnataka, which later emerged as the Jain centre.[102] Amoghavarṣa I assigned a huge territory of Banavāsī 30,000 to Bankya who built a city named Bankapur and made the capital of this territory.[103] He built some Jain temples and donated land too. Bankya's son Lokāditya is described by his preceptor Guṇacandra as the propagator of religion founded by *jina.*[104] Bankapura was the headquarter of Lokāditya, a Jain feudatory of Kṛṣṇa II. It is said about Lokāditya that he ruled the province of Vanavāsa (Banavase, Dhārwār district) and encouraged the spread of Jainism.[105] Amoghavarṣa I was succeeded by Kṛṣṇa II who ruled from AD 878 to AD 914. Ācārya Guṇabhadra, a composer of the *Uttara Purāṇa,* was his teacher. He patronized Jain religion and also built some Jain temples as well as granted some lands to the Jain temples.[106]

---

101. S.K. Ramachandra Rao, *op. cit.,* p. 32.
102. Rajamala Jain and Laxmichandra Jain, *op. cit.,* p. 21.
103. Jyothi P. Jain, *Pramukha Aitihāsika Jain Puruṣa Aur Mahilāyen* (Hindi), New Delhi, 1975, p. 105.
104. *Ibid.*
105. S.R. Sharma, *op. cit.,* p. 33.
106. Rajamala Jain and Laxmichandra Jain, *op. cit.,* p. 21.

Kṛṣṇa II was succeeded by Indra III who ruled during AD 914-22. He was also a patron of Jainism. Indra IV was the last ruler of the Rāṣṭrakūṭas dynasty and he was overthrown by Tailappya II in AD 973 the founder of Cāḷukya dynasty of Kalyāṇī. The mighty Rāṣṭrakūṭas Empire thus came to an end.[107]

The Gaṅgas of Talakaḍ and Their Contribution to Jainism

The Gaṅgas rose to power along with the Kadambas and ruled over the southern parts of Karnataka. They did not rule as independent rulers for long, but they acted as powerful feudatories under the Karnataka Empires. They also enriched Karnataka culture.

According to a legendary account, the two Ikṣavāku princes, namely Didiga and Madava, came southwards after the dismemberment of the Ikṣavāku kingdom and reached a place called Gaṅga Perūr where they met Siṁhanandī, a Jain teacher, who helped them in founding an empire.[108]

In the beginning, the Gaṅgas had their capital at Kuluvala (present Kolar). Later, it was shifted to Talakaḍ or Talavanapura. Formerly, their royal residence was located in Mankuṇḍa but later in the seventh century, it was shifted to Manyapura, situated in the north of Nelamaṅgala. The founder of this dynasty was Didiga or Koṅganivarmā. He fought with the Banas and led a successful expedition to Koṅkaṇ coast. He was able to establish the Gaṅga power on firm foundation through these victories. The Gaṅgas grew in strength in course of years and attracted attention of the Kadambas.[109] Perhaps a daughter of Kakusthavarmā had been

---

107. A.S. Altekar, *op. cit.*, p. 313.
108. H.V. Sreenivasa Murthy, *A History of Karnataka* (*From the earliest times to the present day*), New Delhi, 1966, pp. 63-64.
109. *Ibid.*, p. 64.

married to Talakaḍ Mādhava II and their son was Avinīta. Avinīta's son Durvinīta (AD 605-50) was the most remarkable of the early Gaṅga rulers, equally proficient both as a warrior and a man of letters.

Durvinīta performed many sacrifices and, therefore, it may be held that the early Gaṅgas were not the followers of Jain religion. But it is equally true that he patronized the great Jain Pūjayapāda on whose grammar, *Jinendravyākaraṇa*, he wrote a commentary, *Śabdāvatāra*.

After Durvinīta, Muskara, Bhuvikarma and Śivamāra I reigned in succession. Then came Śrīpuruṣa (AD 729-88), one of the most distinguished rulers of the dynasty.

Śrīpuruṣa was not an undefeated warrior. He was defeated by Rājasiṁha Pāṇḍya and had agreed to give his daughter in marriage to the latter's son. He was also defeated by Rāṣṭrakūṭa Kṛṣṇa I after which Gaṅgāvāḍī was converted into a vassal power of the imperial Rāṣṭrakūṭas.

Śivamāra II, son of Śrīpuruṣa, had to bear the full brunt of the Rāṣṭrakūṭa invasions led by Dhruva and Govinda III. Śivamāra was a great scholar of logic, philosophy, drama, grammar, etc. He wrote *Gajaśataka* in Kannaḍa dealing with the methods of elephant management. He is credited with the authorship of another work titled *Setubhanāda*.[110]

After Śivamāra II, Rachmalla I made a successful attempt to re-establish the Gaṅga's independence. This was made possible through the conciliatory policy framed by Amoghavarṣa. Amoghavarṣa also gave his daughter Candrabhalajji in marriage to Yuvarāja Bhutaga I. Bhutaga's son was Nītimārga II. His successor Rachamalla II was ousted by Kṛṣṇa III and Bhutaga II was placed on the throne. Bhutaga rendered invaluable assistance to Kṛṣṇa III in the battle of Takkolam. He was followed by Mārasiṁha III.

---

110. *Ibid.*, p. 65.

Jainism under Gaṅgas (Southern Dynasty)

Toleration was the accepted principle of the state in matters of religion. Gaṅga rulers like Mādhava II made grants to Buddhism and Jainism. But Buddhism declined gradually in Gaṅgavāḍī owing to the preponderance of Jainism. While Siṁhanandī is said to have helped Mādhava Koṅgaṇivarmā in establishing his power, Vakragrīva and Vajranandī were able to maintain the supremacy of Jainism over all the religions.[111] The Jain teacher Siṁhanandī, who is generally credited with the creation of the Gaṅga kingdom, appears only in the later records of the Gaṅgas. We have thus some doubt regarding his support in the establishment of Jain tradition in the Gaṅga kingdom; and even if we believe so then we can only presume the possibility of the relation between Siṁhanandī and the progenitor of the Gaṅga race on the ground of the events that followed one after another during the period from the fourth to the tenth centuries.[112]

From the fourth century onwards, we have ample evidence to show the close relation between the Jain teachers and the Gaṅga kings in south Karnataka. The first important record dated AD 370 refers to the Ācārya Vīradeva who was the preceptor of the Gaṅga king Mādhava II. He is said to have granted some plots of land and the village for the benefits of the Jain sanctuary. In another record of AD 425, Avinīta donated the Vennelkarni village on the advice of his preceptor Vijayakīrti.[113]

The Gaṅgas, from the time of Śrīvikrama, were staunch followers of Jainism. Rulers like Nītimārga Bhutuga and Mārasiṁha were proficient in Jain philosophy. Kings and

---

111. *Ibid.*, p. 66.

112. Prasad B.R. Singh, *Jainism in Early Mediaeval Karnataka*, Delhi, 1975, p. 6.

113. *Ibid.*

ministers made liberal grants for temples and temple buildings.[114]

The following interesting account shed light on the *sallekhana* rite observed by the various Jain *sādhus* and *śrāvakas* at Śravaṇbeḷgoḷa which occupied religious importance since early days. The fame of Śravaṇbeḷgoḷa spread not only in the south but also in north India due to the visits of the many religious persons from north India to Śravaṇbeḷgoḷa who observed *sallekhana*. Thus the importance of Śravaṇbeḷgoḷa had been increasing and number of Jain *śrāvakas* and *śrāvikās* extended help in erecting monastery in this place. Some inscriptions, from AD 500 onwards found at Śravaṇbeḷgoḷa, furnish the following information about the religious importance and *sallekhana*.

The first inscription which is dated AD 600 opens with a reverential salutation to Bhagavān Mahāvīra and refers to his unique creeds of high merit, enlightening all creatures and providing them with guidance most beneficial in their mundane living. It refers to the arrival of Bhadrabāhu Swāmī who hailed from the holy line of Gautama Gāndhāra and who, from his knowledge of the past, present and future, predicted at Ujjain that there was to occur a severe famine for twelve years. He set out from the north towards the south with his *saṁgha*. Ācārya Prabhacandra, who was a member of the *saṁgha*, perceived that he had little span of life left to him and hence adopted the vow of *samādhi*, the goal of every righteous person. He bade farewell to all the members of the *saṁgha* and in the company of a single disciple, lay on the cold rock of the small hillock (Cikka-beṭṭa) and became engrossed in meditation without taking any food or water till the soul went out from the body to its heavenly abode. It is further stated that about 700 saints accomplished the vow

114. H.V. Sreenivasa Murthy, *op cit.*, pp. 66-67.

thereafter as a tribute to the victorious doctrines of the *jina*. This inscription is on a rock to the south of the Pārśvanātha temple on the Candragiri or Cikka-beṭṭa.[115]

The second inscription of AD 650 describes the beauty of Cikka-beṭṭa as being surrounded by the green paddy fields and water lilies growing therein. One Baladeva Muni, the disciple of Kanakasena and well-versed in the knowledge of religion taught by the Bhagavān, was full of mercy for all living creatures. He departed to the world of the *siddhas* by adopting the vow. The next five inscriptions of AD 700 refer to the observances of the vow respectively by the *guru* of the holy place, by the *guru* of Ullikkal, a nun by name Dhannekuttirevi, by Guru Guṇasena and by Panapabhatar.[116]

Ācārya Ariṣṭanemi came to the south along with his disciples. He was worshipped by queen Kāmpila and king Dindik with the holy lamp, incense and sandal. The group following him consisted of members of the four castes. The *Ācārya* ascended the hill, gave up all food, engaged himself in lofty meditation, attained perfection, and was honoured by the *siddhas* and the *vidyādharas* of AD 650. Just above this inscription another inscription of AD 700 refers to the *sallekhana* practised by Municaritaraśrī Śrī, who by his glorious conduct destroyed all his sins and false notions of other religions (*maithyatva*). He conquered all his senses and acquired that knowledge which showed him the path of salvation. He observed the vow on the hill Kalbappa and attained the heavenly abode after being praised by gods and sages. There is a brief inscription of AD 800 which merely states that Ariṣṭanemideva attained liberation on the Kalbappa. The next

---

115. T.G. Kalghatgi (ed.), Articles (T.K. Tukol), *Gommatesvara Commemoration Volume* (Inscription on *sallekhana* at Śravaṇbeḷgoḷa), p. 51.

116. B.L. Rice, *Epigraphia Carnatica*, vol. II, S.B. (Translations inscriptions on Candragiri or *Chikk-beṭṭa*), p. 2.

inscription refers to Bhagavān Mahāvīra but the name of the person who adopted *saṁnyāsa* has been erased.[117]

There are numerous inscriptions which are assigned AD 700. Akṣayakīrti, one who had come from Mathurā, was bitten by a snake on the hill and yet he observed the vow amidst great suffering and attained the happiness of the world of gods. There is reference to an eminent *guru* who practised meditation for many years and attained perfection after accomplishing the vow.

The next inscription refers to one Guṇadeva Sūri who was proficient in many sciences and had practised the twelve kinds of penances on the holy hill. He attained the abode of gods after successfully observing the vow. Baladeva, an another *guru* and a disciple of Dharmasena *guru* of Valmadi as well as of Ugrasena Guru, observed *saṁnyāsa* and attained the heavenly abode. Mahasena Muni of supreme glory also observed the vow and attained the heavenly abode. There is a reference to one *muni* whose name has unfortunately been erased. He has been described as being adorned with virtues (*guṇabhūṣaṇa*) and descended from the *guru*s of Sandvi Gaṇa.[118]

There is an important inscription (no. 31) which expressly mentions that Jainism prospered when the Muni Bhadrabāhu along with Candragupta came to this region and awakened the people to the glory of Jainism. Though it did not prosper for sometime but Muni Śāntisena restored its popularity to its pedestal of renown. He climbed the hill at Śravaṇbeḷgoḷa, gave up food, and drink and attained immortality. It may be noted here that the place is described in this inscription as merely *beḷgoḷa* and not as Śravaṇbeḷgoḷa (AD 650).[119]

---

117. B.L. Riche, p. 4.
118. *Ibid.*, p. 7.
119. *Ibid.*

Singanandī Guru, who was the disciple of the *guru* of the hills, observed the vow and expired (inscription no. 32). There is an inscription (numbered 32 of AD 700) where the name of the Muni is not clear; it states that he observed the vow of *saṁnyāsa* for 21 days and ended his life. The next inscription refers to Nāgasena Muni, the disciple of Ṛṣabhasena, who ended his life by the observance of vow *saṁnyāsa*. He was renowned for his virtues by which he conquerred all his passions and was respected by the kings. He too went to the heavenly abode.[120]

Koṅgunivarmā, who was the king of Gaṅga line, had gained numerous victories in different parts of the country. He built many temples at various places and holy pillars (*mānasthambhas*). He performed many acts of piety and thereafter relinquished his kingdom. He observed the vow for three days by worshipping at the holy feet of Ajitasena Bhaṭṭāraka at Bankapur and accomplished *samādhi*.[121]

Vṛṣabhanandī, who was famous for his fasts, was a very learned ascetic. He was distinguished for his austerities and meditation. With his clairvoyance he saw his approaching death and as such adopted *saṁnyāsana* formally on the summit of Katavapra. He burnt his *karmas* by meditation and attained the celestial happiness (inscription no. 75 of AD 650). There are brief references to ascetics Soucadarya (inscription no. 79 of AD 750) and Mahādeva who performed the great penance and entered the heaven (inscription no. 80 of AD 700).[122]

Candradevarāya was an ascetic free from all weaknesses. He had distinguished himself for his modesty and purity of character. He had attained high reputation for his austerities.

---

120. *Ibid.*, p. 8.

121. T.G. Kalghatgi (ed.), Articles (T.K. Tukol), *op. cit.*, p. 53 (inscriptions on *sallekhana* at Śravaṇbeḷgoḷa).

122. B.L. Rice, *op. cit.*, p. 41.

He ascended the hill Kalbappu, abandoned the body and his soul, ascended to the heaven in a happy condition and was praised by gods (inscription no. 84 of AD 700). Nandisena was an *ācārya* amongst ascetics. He was of strong will and had become convinced that beauty, wealth and pleasure were as transient as a rainbow, disappearing in a moment like that of dew. This, according to him, was the supreme truth. He adopted *saṁnyāsana* and went to the world of god (inscription no. 88 of AD 700). Indranandī *ācārya* was very noble and self-controlled. He conquered all his passions and achieved victory over the delusions of life. He achieved *samādhi* on the Katavapra hill and attained immortal splendour in the kingdom of Indra (inscription no. 95 of AD 700). [123]

Guṇakīrti was perhaps an ascetic of lofty devotion. He abandoned his body on the peak of the beautiful golden mountain (inscription no. 105 of AD 700). Vr̥ṣabhanandī was the disciple of Ācārya Muni belonging to the Navilur *saṁgha*. He realized that worldly existence was of transient nature and followed the path of Jainism incessantly with devotion. Devasena and Nandī Muni was a great ascetic. He was adorned with numerous virtues (AD 700).[124]

The Gaṅga king Śivamāra II built the Śivamāra Basadi at Śravaṇbeḷgoḷa in AD 810.[125] He had also contributed to the spread of Jain *dharma*. He had erected temples and *basadis* at Kumadavāḍā and Śravaṇbeḷgoḷa (AD 780-812).[126]

There are some other inscriptions relating to the observances of this vow but the names of *munis*, nuns or the householders have been erased. Some of the inscriptions are in verse and are highly poetical, while others are obscure.

---

123. *Ibid.*, p. 43.
124. T.G. Kalghatgi (ed.) Articles (Tukol. T.K.), *op. cit.*, p. 54.
125. B.L. Rice, *EC*, vol. II, *SB*, 415, p. 81.
126. M.V. Krishnarao, *The Gangas of Talakad*, Madras, 1936, p. 65.

The long inscriptions usually bear the name of person who engraved them and/or at whose instance it was engraved so far as the inscriptions relating to *sallekhana* are concerned. Most of the inscriptions relating to the observance of this vow seem to have been carved out somewhere between AD 500 and AD 700.

It is noteworthy that everybody seems to have chosen the Chikka-beṭṭa or Candragiri as that had been hallowed by the *sallekhana* of many saints who accompanied *śrutakevalin* Bhadrabāhu; there are only three or four instance of *sallekhana* by persons who seem to have chosen the village nearby; it might probably be Jinanāthapura. From this fact, it can be safely inferred that Jainism had a great hold in the area; that there were numerous pious householders of great merit, and eminent ascetics who kept the torch of the *tīrthaṅkaras*' religion ever blazed. It is these saints that seem to have been responsible for the construction of numerous beautiful temples of great architectural beauty.

On the basis of the famous Bhadrabāhu-Candragupta Jain tradition as mentioned in an inscription of the seventh century, the origin of this rite may be traced as back to the fourth century BC. It narrates, as told earlier, that Bhadrabāhu, who predicted a twelve year famine in the north, went to Śravaṇbeḷgoḷa in Mysore, accompanied by his chief disciple Candragupta Maurya. On reaching Śravaṇbeḷgoḷa, he ordered the Jain community to proceed on their journey, while he himself stayed back at Candragiri hill. He died there by submitting himself to the Jain rite of fasting. After the death of Bhadrabāhu, Candragupta lived there as an ascetic, worshipping the footprints of his *guru* (teacher) until his death through the Jain rite of *sallekhana*. But there is no doubt that the practice of *sallekhana* prevailed among the Karnataka Jains from the seventh century.

The ritual became very popular in Karnataka by the eighth century. While we have evidence of only five cases of death through fasting in the seventh century, but about 54 cases have been found recorded in the eighth century. Of the 54 cases mentioned above, 43 refer to men, mostly monks, and ten commemorate the death of nuns. The nuns also accepted this mode of death as bravely as the monks. They did not lag behind the monks in religious ansterities and exhibited the same tenacity in observing *sallekhana.*[127]

Most epigraphs refer to Candragiri hill in Śravaṇbeḷgoḷa in the Hassan district as the most sacred place of performing this rite. It appears that the Jains tried to choose a place which was supposed to be peaceful and free from living beings. This is why they preferred to die on the summit of the mountain. The epigraphs of Śravaṇbeḷgoḷa show that people from distant places came to spend their last days here, during the seventh-ninth centuries. But in the later times, we notice some change in the selection of the place for performing this rite. These Jains appear to have observed this vow in the Jain temples.

Thus from the third century BC to the ninth century AD, Jainism received patronization from various dynasties like Sātavāhana, Kadamba, Cāḷukyas, Rāṣṭrakūṭas and Gaṅgas of Talakaḍ. Number of land grants and other donations as well were received by various Jain temples and monasteries in south India. Jainism prospered in south India including Karnataka.

But the installation of Bāhubali collosal image in AD 981 at Śravaṇbeḷgoḷa by Gaṅga's Commander-in-Chief, Cāmuṇḍa-rāya, is an outstanding event in the history of Jainism in south Karnataka.

---

127. A.L. Bhushan, *Jainism in Early Mediaeval Karnataka* (*AD 500-1200*), pp. 64-65.

Therefore, rapid development of Śravaṇbeḷgoḷa has been narrated in detail in the third chapter.

3

Rapid Development of Śravaṇbeḷgoḷa as a Jain Centre After AD 981 (Second Phase)

IN the last chapter, we have discussed development of Śravaṇbeḷgoḷa from the fourth century BC, i.e., from the advent of Bhadrabāhu and Candragupta Maurya to the ninth century AD. Candragiri was adorned with many Jains temples during this period and we also found some old inscriptions from the Candragiri hill.

The installation of colossal idol of Bāhubali on the Indragiri hill by Cāmuṇḍarāya, the General of Racamalla II in AD 981, is an outstanding event in the history of Jainism in south India in general and Karnataka history in particular. Bāhubali's icon at Śravaṇbeḷgoḷa has become one of the wonderful attraction for all Jain community all over India.

A number of Jains and also others have flocked to Śravaṇbeḷgoḷa since AD 981 onward to pay pious homage to the colossal image of Bāhubali every year and this has led to the rapid development of Śravaṇbeḷgoḷa and adjoining areas. Even royal families, feudatories, nobles, royal ladies, rich persons extended their patronage to Śravaṇbeḷgoḷa. We have a number of evidences of the land grants given to Śravaṇbeḷgoḷa during the ancient and medieval times and also the construction of new temples by various persons.

An attempt has been made in this chapter to study the massive growth of Śravaṇbeḷgoḷa since AD 981 and how this place held a special interest and attraction in the south Karnataka.

History of Bāhubali

It would be interesting to have a look into the life history of Bāhubali who was the son of Ādinātha, the first Jain *tīrthaṅkara*. The following few pages are devoted to narrate the brief account of Bāhubali who occupied importance in Jain canons next to *tīrthaṅkaras*.

Śravaṇbeḷgoḷa is known all over the world for its colossal image of Bāhubali or Gommaṭeśvara which is regarded as one of the wonders of the world. This marvellous image was caused to be erected on the Vindhyagiri hill in the year AD 981 by Cāmuṇḍarāya.

But the legendary accounts say that this magnificent image of Bāhubali was already there on the hill in a concealed manner and that Cāmuṇḍarāya discovered the image and consecrated it in a proper way. Hence to find out the real facts, it is necessary to know the original story of Bāhubali's life, the traditional account of Bāhubali's image and the historical evidence about the actual installation of the image of Śravaṇbeḷgoḷa in the last quarter of the tenth century AD.

Bāhubali, the first Jain saint to attain liberation, in this *avasarpiṇīkalā*, i.e., the descending half arc of time, was the son of lord Ṛṣabha, the first Jain *tīrthaṅkara*, who flourished at the dawn of civilization and taught mankind the first lessons of a cultured life. Lord Ṛṣabhadeva, the son of Nābhirāja and Marudevī, was a patriarch king of Ayodhyā. Lord Ṛṣabhanātha had many sons, among whom Bharata and Bāhubali were very prominent. Bharata was the crown prince and he succeeded his father to the throne of Ayodhyā. By his powers Bharata became the first universal monarch and due to his profound impact on the country, India came to be known as Bhāratavarṣa, i.e., the land of Bharata.[1]

---

1. V.A. Sangave, *The Sacred Sravanbeḷgoḷa (A Socio-Religious Study)*, Delhi, 1981, p. 66.

Bāhubali was given the kingdom of "Asmaka" in south India which he ruled from its capital seated at Podanapura. In this way after dividing his kingdom among his sons, Lord Ṛṣabhadeva retired to the Himālayas and adopted the Jain ascetic way of life to teach mankind the path of salvation.[2]

The Legendary Account of Bāhubali

Bāhubali is known by three names, Vahurali, Bhujabali, and Gommaṭeśvara. As mentioned above, he was the son of Ādijina Ṛṣabhanātha, the first *tīrthaṅkara* of the Jains. Ṛṣabhadeva, according to the tradition, was a king and had two wives, Nanda (some say Sumaṅgala) and Sunandā. Nanda or Sumaṅgala gave birth to a twins, Bharata and Brāhmī, a boy and a girl. Bharata was crowned by Ṛṣabhadeva when he decided to seek absolute knowledge. Bāhubali and his sister Sundarī were born of Sunandā, and the former ascended the throne of Takṣaśilā (modern Taxila), when his father distributed his kingdom among his sons. Bharata possessed a wonderful *cakra* (discus), which no warrior could withstand in a fight. With the help of this *cakra*, Bharata conquered the earth and returned to his capital. But the discus could not enter the capital (or, according to another account, the armoury). Bharata then took this as a sign that there was still another territory on earth which had not been conquerred by him, and, after reflection came to the conclusion that there was only the kingdom of Takṣaśilā, ruled by his brother Bāhubali, which had not been subdued by him.[3]

Bharata then declared war on his brother Bāhubali at Podanapura. In the terrible event of fight between the two brothers when both the armies were about to attack one another, the ministers of both the kings stepped forward,

2. V.A. Sangave, *The Sacred Sravanbeḷgoḷa (A Socio-Religious Study)*, Delhi, 1981, pp. 66-67.
3. S.C. Ghoshal, *The Sacred books of the Jains*, vol. I, Arrah-India, 1917, pp. 28-29.

prayed to their lord not to fight and said, "O Lords, both of you are divine personalities and your bodies are invulnerable, why should these innocent soldiers be massacred and driven to the saws of death? You may kindly decide your superiority by a dual-combat." Ultimately the spirit of *ahiṁsā*, i.e., non-violence, triumphed over *hiṁsā*, i.e., violence, and both the contending brothers, who were also naturally averse to any form of injury to any life, agreed to decide their question by the three methods of righteous fight, viz.

(1) *Dṛṣṭi-yuddha* — looking at each other without winking,

(2) *Jala-yuddha* — throwing water on each other's face, and

(3) *Malla-yuddha* — wrestling.

In all the three combats Bāhubali came out victorious and his army shouted with applause. Thereupon Bharata lost his temper and resorted to his all powerful *cakra*, with which he strove to kill his brother. But even this *cakra*, could not harm Bāhubali. Lastly Bāhubali pitied his brother's aggressive nature and the selfish ways of the world.[4] In other words, Bāhubali was victorious. Despite of his victory Bāhubali had suddenly lost in meditation, thinking of the vanity of this world. Bharata made obeisance to Bāhubali and returned to his palace, but Bāhubali went to the summit of Kailāsa mountain, remained standing there (or, according to another account, stood on the very field of battle) in a statuesque posture for one year and "the creepers, wreathing round the boughs of the trees on the bunk clung to his neck and crowned his head as a canopy and the blades of *kuśa*-grass grew between his feet, and he became in appearance like an ant hill." Subsequently, Bāhubali obtained absolute knowledge and became one of the *kevalis*.

An another inscription, however, mentions that Puru was

4. V.A. Sangave, *op. cit.*, p. 66.

the father of Bāhubali and Bharata. Then the inscription goes to say that:

> Bharata, the son of Purudeva, surrounded by all the kings conquered by him, erected in glee, an image, representing the victorious Bāhubali Kevali, which was 525 bows in height, near Podanapura. After a long time, innumerable Kukutasarpa (dragons having the body of a fowl and the head and neck of a snake) terrifying the world, grew up in the place surrounding (the image of) that Jina, for which the image became known as Kukkutesvara.[5]

According to the another traditional account, Gommaṭa is mentioned in an inscription of poet Boppana of AD 1180 and is repeated with some additional and varied in the details in several literary works such as the *Bhujabali-Śataka, Bhujabali-Carite,* etc.

The particulars mentioned about Gommaṭa in the inscription are that he was the son of Purudeva, the first *tīrthaṅkara,* and the younger brother of Bharata and that his name was Bāhubali. In a struggle for the empire between the brothers, Bāhubali won, but generously handed over the kingdom of the earth to the defeated elder brother and retired from the world in order to do penance. He thus became a *kevali,* attaining such eminence by his victory over *karma*. Furthermore, Bharata erected an image in his form at Podanapura. In course of time the region around the image became infested with innumerable Kukkaṭa Sarpas or Cockatrices. The initiated image afterwards became visible to all.

But Cāmuṇḍarāya having heard a description of it, set out with the desire of seeing it. Finding that the journey was beyond his power, he resolved to erect such an image himself at Śravaṇbeḷgoḷa. An arrow shot by him from Candragiri struck a boulder on Indragiri which appeared to him in the form of Gommaṭa. With the great effort Cāmuṇḍarāya succeeded in

5. S.C. Ghoshal, *op. cit.*, 29.

getting this statue made under the supervision of the monk Ariṣṭanemi. The literary works mentioned above support this tradition but differ only in minor details.[6]

The Legendary Accounts of the Establishment of the Image by Cāmuṇḍarāya

The knowledge of this colossal image of Bāhubali erected by Emperor Bharata at Podanapura created an intense desire in the mind of devoted Cāmuṇḍarāya. As a result, Cāmuṇḍarāya set out in search of it. But on his way, at Śravaṇbeḷgoḷa, he was informed in a dream that the journey was beyond his power owing to the distance and inaccessibility of the region and that the same image of Bāhubali would manifest itself on the larger hill at Śravaṇbeḷgoḷa by performing a particular feat. Accordingly, Cāmuṇḍarāya did the feat, the colossal image of Bāhubali became visible on the summit of the Vindhyagiri hill at Śravaṇbeḷgoḷa.

The account given of Gommaṭeśvara is repeated with some additions and variations in the details in several literary works, composed in Sanskrit and Kannaḍa language such as the *Bhujabali-Śataka* written by Doddaiya of Piriyapaṭṭana in AD 1550; the *Bhujabali-Carite* of AD 1614, by Panchabana of Śravaṇbeḷgoḷa; the *Gommaṭeśvara-Carite* of about AD 1780, by Anantakavi; the *Rājāvalikathe*, of AD 1838, by Devacandra; and the *Sthala Purāṇa* of Śravaṇbeḷgoḷa.[7]

THE STORY IN BHUJABALI-ŚATAKA

A well-known Kannaḍa poet Panchabana, in his *Bhujabali-Śataka* mentions of the tradition related to the image in detail. It states that in the city Madhuro (now as Madurā) in the Draviḍa country there was a king, named Rājamalla, who encouraged the spread

6. R. Narasiṁhachar, *Epigraphia Carnatica*, vol. I, *Sravanbeḷgoḷa*, Bangalore, 1923, p. 12.

7. *Ibid.*, p. 13.

of Jain tenets and was the worshipper of Siṁhanandī, belonging to the Deśīya Gaṇa. His minister was Cāmuṇḍarāya. One day when the king sat with his minister in the royal court, a travelling merchant came there and told them that in the north there is a town called "Podanapura," where there is an image of Bāhubali, also called Gommaṭa, established by Bharata. Hearing this, the devout Cāmuṇḍarāya resolved to visit the shrine of the image, and at home he narrated about the meeting with the travelling merchant and also about Gommaṭa to his mother, Kālikā Devī whereupon she also wished to go with him to that sacred spot. Cāmuṇḍarāya then went to his spiritual preceptor, Ajitasena, who revered Siṁhanandī and made a vow before the latter that he will not drink milk till he sees the image of Bāhubali.

Accompanied by Nemicandra, his mother and numerous soldiers and attendants, Cāmuṇḍarāya started on his pilgrimage and reached the Vindhyagiri at Śravaṇbeḷgoḷa. In the night, the Jain Goddess Kuṣmāṇḍinī (the *yakṣī* of 22nd *tīrthaṅkara*) appeared in the dream of Cāmuṇḍarāya, Nemicandra and Kālikā, and told them that it was very difficult to go to Podanapura but on that hill there is an image of Bāhubali, formerly established by Rāvaṇa, which will be visible, if the hill be cleft by a golden arrow. According to the dream, Cāmuṇḍarāya stood on the hill next morning with his face towards the south and let loose a golden arrow from his bow. Immediately a cleft in the mountain was formed which led the image of Bāhubali become visible. Cāmuṇḍarāya then established and consecrated the image and granted lands for the worship of this image. When king Rājamalla heard of this affair, he conferred the title of "Rāya" on Cāmuṇḍarāya and granted further lands for the regular worship of the image.[8]

THE STORY IN GOMMAṬEŚVARA-CHARITE

Further, the *Gommaṭeśvara-Carite* of Anantakavi tells us that when

---

8. S.C. Ghoshal, *op. cit.*, Introduction, p. 29.

Cāmuṇḍarāya shooted arrows, the image of Gommaṭa revealed itself to him. He got it raised and improved by sculptors and then had it consecrated.[9]

THE STORY IN STHALA PURĀṆA

Besides, the *Sthala Purāṇa* also holds that the image of Bāhubali was already in existence at Śravaṇbeḷgoḷa. It states that Cāmuṇḍarāya, king of Dakṣiṇa Madhurā and the descendant of Jain *kṣetrī* Pāṇḍu, set out with his family, escorted by an army of infantry, cavalry, elephants and charriots with a view of visiting to god Gommaṭeśvara (500 bilu high) at Podanapura and 1254 other gods in the smaller temples scattered throughout the surrounding country. Enroute, he came to "Śravaṇbeḷgoḷa Kṣetra." Having heard a good deal about the god Gommaṭeśvara (18 bilu high), he repaired the ruined temples and performed among other ceremonies that of sprinkling the god. He appointed *siddhācārya* as *guru* of *maṭha*, to conduct the daily, monthly, annual and other processions. He established in the *maṭha*, a *chattra* where food, medicine, and education were provided for the pilgrims. Villages giving an annual revenue of 1,96,000 *pagoḍās*, were made over to the temple for this purpose.[10]

THE STORY IN RĀJĀVALIKATHE

On the same lines is the Kannaḍa work, *Rājāvalikathe*, written by Devacandra in AD 1838. It states that, Cāmuṇḍarāya was a feudatory of king Rājamalla. His mother learnt from the *Ādi Purāṇa*, when this work was being read to her, that there was an image of Bāhubali at Podanapura. Thereupon, she set out with her son to see this image. But on her way on the hill where Bāhubali Svāmī died, she dreamt one night that Padmāvatī appeared to her and said that, there is an image of Bāhubali on that hill covered by stones, which was formerly

9. V.A. Sangave, *op. cit.*, p. 71.
10. R. Narasiṁhachar, *E.C.*, vol. II, S. 13, p. 15.

worshipped by Rāma and Rāvaṇa and also by the latter's wife Mandodarī. An arrow was shot the next morning and the image of Bāhubali became visible.[11]

Cāmuṇḍarāya and Gaṅga Dynasty

The benevolent kings of various dynasties who ruled over different areas of Karnataka from the ancient times had generously extended their royal patronage for the proper upkeep and adequate maintenance of the holy place of Śravaṇbeḷgoḷa. Their Chief Ministers and Military Generals also, in the like manner, took personal and special interest in giving not only the sufficient protection to Śravaṇbeḷgoḷa in the days of turmoil and disturbances but also in continuously enhancing the sanctity and importance of Śravaṇbeḷgoḷa by incessantly making varied and rich contributions of an enduring nature.

Among such noteworthy, the Chief Ministers and Military Generals of Karnataka, Śivamāra, Mārasiṁha II and Cāmuṇḍarāya of the Gaṅga dynasty, Gaṅgarāja and Hullagarāja of the Hoyasala empire stand out very prominently in the history of Śravaṇbeḷgoḷa and in the promotion of Jain religion.[12]

Śivamāra of Gaṅga Dynasty

Among the ancient royal dynasties of India, the Gaṅgas of the west were devoted followers of Jainism. There is a tradition that a Jain *ācārya*, named Siṁhanandī, belonging to the Nandīgaṇa, helped Śivamāra, the first king of the Gaṅga dynasty, to rise to the throne. In one inscription we find the fact that Śivamāra Koṅgunivarmā was the disciple of Siṁhanandī, and from another inscription that the race of the Gaṅgas prospered through the sage Siṁhanandī. It is therefore no wonder that we shall find in Jain works verses to the effect that, the Gaṅga kings worship the feet of

11. V.A. Sangave, *op. cit.* pp. 71-72.
12. *Ibid.*, p. 50.

Siṁhanandī, or that a dynasty which owed its origin to the help of Jain *ācārya* should be staunch to the Jain religion. There are records which establish beyond doubt that the kings of the Gaṅga dynasty were the promoters and protectors of Jainism. Numerous inscriptions, dating from the fourth to the twelfth century AD, testify to the building of Jain temples, consecration of Jain images of worship, hollowing out caves for Jain ascetics and grants to Jain *ācārya* by the rulers of the Gaṅga dynasty.[13]

Mārasiṁha II of Gaṅga Dynasty (AD 961-74)

In this dynasty, there was a king, named Mārasiṁha II, mentioned in the inscriptions as "Dharma-Mahārājādhirāja Satyavāka Koṅgunivarmā Padmanandī Mārasiṁha." The reign of this king was conspicuous by great and decisive victories over the Ceras, the Coḷas, the Pāṇḍyas and the Pallavas of the Nolambadi country. The most notable success of Mārasiṁha II against his enemies was the Vajjaladeva, and his most terrible fights were fought at Gonur and Ucchaṅgi. Faithful to the doctrines of Jainism, this great king after a glorious reign, abdicated his throne and gave up his life by a three days fast, in the presence of his spiritual preceptor, the great Ajitasena, at Bankapur, in the Dhārwāḍ district. The epitaph of Mārasiṁha II is contained in the inscription engraved on the four sides of the base of the pillar known as Kuge Brahmadeva *khambha* near the entrance to the temples on Candragiri hill at Śravaṇbeḷgoḷa (Mysore). Though this inscription is without date, the year of the death of Mārasiṁha II is inferred from an another insciption which mentions it to be AD 975.[14]

Cāmuṇḍarāya

No single individual could be given credit for building Śravaṇbeḷgoḷa, for it is built over a millennium and half by a number of pious, saints, rulers, chieftains, merchants, artists,

13. S.C. Ghoshal, *op. cit.*, pp. 19-20.
14. R. Narasiṁhachar, *op. cit.*, p. 44.

scribes and pilgrims. The men who contributed materially to strengthen and enhance its spiritual, artistic and historical value are, however, recognized as early as the twelfth century. Among them

1. Cāmuṇḍarāya (AD 974-84)
2. Gaṅgarāja (AD 1108-42)
3. Hullarāja (AD 1142-73)

are considered to be the greatest.[15]

Among these three benefactors of Jain religion, however, the contributions of Cāmuṇḍarāya are by far the most outstanding, inspiring and lasting nature. By his rich personal accomplishments and varied achievements in different fields, Cāmuṇḍarāya has made a permanent mark and there is hardly any other personality of his stature and competence in the history of Karnataka.[16]

Cāmuṇḍarāya has emerged in the history of Karnataka as a faithful minister, a loyal General, a profound scholar and a great patron of Jainism.

B.A. Saletore refers to the pre-eminent position of Cāmuṇḍarāya in the following terms:

> The first great name in the constellation of brilliant Jain Generals, we meet with, is that of Cāmuṇḍarāya, popularly known as Rāya. A braver soldier, a more devout Jain, and a more honest man than Cāmuṇḍarāya, Karnataka had never seen.[17]

Cāmuṇḍarāya was born to Mahābalayya and Kalaladevī, and from his wife Ajitadevī he got a son named Jinadevana. Had the record of AD 1090 of Kuradahalli (Hassan Dt.) was issued by this person, we would have to assume that he had two other sons named Madirāja and Ellappayya. His teachers were saints

---

15. S. Setter, *Sravanbeḷgoḷa*, Dharwar, 1981, p. 70.
16. V.A. Sangave, *op. cit.*, p. 51.
17. B.A. Saletore, *Mediaeval Jainism (with special reference to the Vijayanagara empire)*, Bombay, 1938.

Ajitasena and Nemicandra. A lady named Puliappa, who died at Vijayamaṅgalam (Coimbatore Dt.), is believed to be his younger sister.[18] Cāmuṇḍarāya was a great scholar and a soldier. He composed the *Triśaṣṭiśalākā Mahāpurāṇam*, a work on the life of the 24 *tīrthaṅkaras* in AD 978. He was the first to introduce in Kannaḍa what had been earlier written in Sanskrit under the title of *Mahāpurāṇam*. It is one of the two earliest prose works in the language. He is also credited with the Kannaḍa translation of Nemicandra Siddhānta Cakravartī's *Gommaṭasāra*, a summary of *Dhavalā* and *Jayadhavalā* in Prākṛt. He patronized Ranna and Nāgavarmā, poets who earned a lasting place in the history of Kannaḍa literature.[19]

The place held by Cāmuṇḍarāya in Indian history is also unrivalled. The colossal and an ornate pillar on the large hill, a granite Draviḍian structure on the small hill, are among the celebrated works in the history of Indian art. Thus, in the fields of religion, literature and art Cāmuṇḍarāya acquired a niche. Because of these multiple achievements he is deservedly called Saṁyuktaratnākara, Caucabharaṇa Satya-Yudhiṣṭhira.

Had Cāmuṇḍarāya not consecrated the colossal image of Gommaṭa in Śravaṇbeḷgoḷa the place would not have been as attractive as it is today. As minister under the Gaṅgas of Talakaḍ, he served Mārasiṁha II and Rachamalla IV (AD 974-99). He distinguished himself as a warrior, fighting against the Śilāhāras, Molambas, Cāḷukyas and other minor chieftains. Besides serving the Gaṅgas, Cāmuṇḍarāya also served the cause of Rāṣṭrakūṭas as well. The political interests of these two dynasties were closely interconnected in the tenth century.[20]

Cāmuṇḍarāya — A Great Jain Minister of Gaṅga Dynasty

Kṛṣṇa III (AD 939-66) was the last great Rāṣṭrakūṭa ruler. Between

18. S. Setter, *op. cit.*, p. 72.
19. R. Narasiṁhachar, *op. cit.*, p. 12.
20. S. Setter, *op. cit.*, p. 72.

the Rāṣṭrakūṭas and the Gaṅgas, there was at this time not only political alliance, but there were a number of matrimonial alliance also. Kṛṣṇa III's sister Revakī had married the Gaṅga king Butuga II (AD 925-60). Butuga II and Kṛṣṇa III had formed a powerful and invincible military alliance. They strengthened their friendship further by marriage alliance. Kṛṣṇa III's daughter married Butuga II's son Maruladeva. Butuga's daughter married a son of Kṛṣṇa III and to this pair was born the last Rāṣṭrakūṭa prince Indrarāja.[21]

Butuga's first son Maruladeva, for some reason, did not rule. The second son Mārasiṁha III succeeded his father. Mārasiṁha continued the policy of friendship with the Rāṣṭrakūṭas and fought with all their enemies both in the north and in the south of India. He was the last great Gaṅga ruler. It was under him that Cāmuṇḍarāya came to the limelight. Cāmuṇḍarāya came from a family of Brahmakṣatriyas who were loyal for generations to the Gaṅga ruling family. His grandfather was Govindamayya. Govindamayya and his younger brother Īśvarayya were, as it appears, like Bhīma and Arjuna of the *Mahābhārata*. They both served under Mārasiṁha. Cāmuṇḍarāya's father Mahābalayya was known as a virtuous and able man.[22]

Cāmuṇḍarāya proved his loyalty to his master Mārasiṁha by defeating his two rivals who aspired for the Gaṅga throne. The first was Caladanka Gaṅga and the second Muduracayya. The latter in addition to being a rival of his master had also offended Cāmuṇḍarāya by killing his younger brother Nāgavarmā. Thus with one stroke, he avenged his brother's death as well as saved his master.[23]

---

21. T.G. Kalghatgi (editor), Articles (G.S. Dikshit), *Gommatesvara Commemoration Volume* (Cāmuṇḍarāya — A Great Jain Minister of Karnataka), Śravaṇbeḷgoḷa, 1981, p. 46.
22. *Ibid.*, p. 46.
23. T.G. Kalghatgi (editor), Articles (G.S. Dikshit), *Gommatesvara Commemoration Volume* (Cāmuṇḍarāya — A Great Jain Minister of Karnataka), Śravaṇbeḷgoḷa, 1981, p. 47.

He fought along with his master Mārasiṁha against the Nolambas. The Nolambas who were ruling in Tumkur, Citradurga and Anantapura districts had opposed the Rāṣṭrakūṭas and thus incurred the wrath of the Gaṅgas. Mārasiṁha made almost a clean sweep of the Nolambas. They were throroughly defeated and in achieving this result Cāmuṇḍarāya had a lion's share. He won a victory over them at Gonur and earned the title of *Vīramārttaṇḍa*; he also defeated Rājāditya, who had the title of *Ranaraṅga-singha* or *Rāṇā-Rājasiṁha*, and took his hill-fort to Ucchaṅginī and bore the title of the defeated king. He defeated one Vajvala, younger brother of Patalamalla. Vajvala is identified by Hultzch with a local chief ruling in the Cittor region.[24]

RACHAMALLA II

After the death of Mārasiṁha II of the Gaṅga dynasty, Pañcaladeva, fully known as Dharmamahārājādhirāja Satyavākya Koṅgunivarmā Pañcaladeva, ascended the throne and he was succeeded by king Rachamalla II, fully known as Dharmamahārājādhirāja Satyavākya Koṅgunivarmā Parmanandi Rachamalla. Cāmuṇḍarāya was also the minister of Rachamalla II. In one inscription, he has been mentioned as "Rāya" (i.e., Cāmuṇḍarāya), the excellent minister of the King Rachamalla II, and in another "Cāmuṇḍarāya" second in glory to King Rachamalla. In a manuscript, Cāmuṇḍarāya has been described as having the titles of Rāṇāraṅgamalla, Akṣayaparākrama, Guṇaratnabhūṣaṇa, Samyaktvaratnanilaya the Mahāmātya Cāmuṇḍarāya (highest minister) of Rachamalla of the Gaṅga dynasty and graced by the great sage Siṁhanandī.[25]

INSTALLATION OF BĀHUBALI IMAGE

The traditional accounts about the Bāhubali image maintain that

24. V.A. Sangave, *op. cit.*, pp. 52-53.
25. S.C. Ghoshal, *op. cit.*, p. XXIV.

the image was already there on the Vindhyagiri hill at Śravaṇbeḷgoḷa from the ancient times, though, in a concealed form; and that Cāmuṇḍarāya came to know about it through the divine suggestion after which he merely discovered the image and started its worship. But this account is neither tenable nor accepted by the modern historians.

On the summit of the hill stands the image of Gommaṭeśvara in an open court surrounded by a battlemented verandah enshrining the image of Jains saints. This enclosure is again surrounded at some distance by a heavy wall, a good part of which is picturesquely formed by boulders in their natural position.

Date of Gommaṭeśvara

Inscriptions definitely state that the statue of Gommaṭa was caused to be erected by Cāmuṇḍarāya, the minister of the Gaṅga king Rājamalla Satyavākya, whose reign began in AD 974.[26]

Since, according to tradition, the consecration took place during the reign of Rachamalla, the statue must have been erected between these two dates. But a Kannaḍa work, popularly known as *Cāmuṇḍarāya Purāṇa* composed in AD 978 by Cāmuṇḍarāya does not mention the erection of the statue in the long account it gives of the author's achievements. It is, therefore, reasonable to conclude that the image was set-up after AD 978.[27]

In the absence of more precise information, the date of completion of the colossus may be taken as AD 983. The traditional date of the consecration of Gommaṭa by Cāmuṇḍarāya, given in several literary works however is Sunday, the fifth lunar day of the bright fortnight of Caitra of

---

26. K.A. Nilakanthasastri, *Sravanbeḷgoḷa*, Mysore, 1981, p. 14.
27. R. Narasiṁhachar, *E.C.*, vol. II, S.B., p. 15.

the cyclic year Vibhāva, corresponding to the year 600 of the *kali* or *kalki* era, which might correspond to AD 1028.[28]

DESCRIPTION OF GOMMAṬEŚVARA

The colossal image of Gommaṭeśvara standing erect on the summit of the large hill is nude and faces north. The shoulders of the image are very broad and the arms hang straight down the sides with the thumbs turned outwards. The waist is small. From the knee downwards, the legs are rather short and thick. The figure has no support above the thighs. Up to that point it is represented as surrounded by ant hills from which emerge the serpents, and a climbing plant (*mādhavī*) twines itself round both the legs and arms terminating at the upper part of the arm in a cluster of berries or flowers.

The pedestal is designed to represent an open lotus. The image is carved in fine grained light grey granite. It looks as bright and clean as if it had just come from the chisel of the artist. It is probable that this image was cut out of a granite mass of huge size which stood on the spot as it would have been otherwise an impossible task to transport it there. The statue of Gommaṭa is more impressive both on account of its position and size than the statues of *Rameses* in Egypt and is bigger than any other monolithic statue in the world. Two more colossal images of Gommaṭa are known to exist, one at Karkala and the other at Venur, both in the South Canara district.[29] These two images are identical with the Śravaṇbeḷgoḷa statue in the way in which they are represented, but differ considerably in the delineation of the features. The image of Karkala erected by Vīrapāṇḍya in AD 1432, is 41'5" high, while that of Venur, erected by Timmarāja of the family of Cāmuṇḍa at the instance of Cārukīrti Paṇḍita of Beḷgoḷa in AD 1604, is 35' high.[30]

---

28. R. Narasiṁhachar, *E.C.*, vol. II, S.B., p. 16.
29. K.A. Nilakanthasastri, *op. cit.*, p. 15.
30. *Ibid.*, p. 16.

Gommaṭa Name of the Image

The real name of the ascetic son of Ṛṣabhadeva is Bāhubali and the image set by Bharata at Podanapura is known as the image of Lord Bāhubali. The image, about which there is a popular belief that Cāmuṇḍarāya had discovered at Śravaṇbeḷgoḷa, is generally and popularly known as the image of Lord Gommaṭeśa also called Gommaṭeśvara, Gommaṭadeva, Gommaṭaprabhu, Gommaṭajina and at times, just Gommaṭa.

There has been a lot of controversy over the origin of the term *gommaṭa*, its meaning and appellation. A majority of scholars support the view that the term *gommaṭa* meaning good, handsome, benefactor, etc., is a local (*deśī*) word found with a slightly varied form in the south Indian languages like Kannaḍa, Telugu, Koṅkaṇī and Marāṭhī.

Anyway the word *gommaṭa* is derived from the Sanskrit word "*manmatha*" and refers to "Kāmadeva." Since Bāhubali is the first "Kāmadeva" of this age according to the Jain scriptures; and also "Manmatha," he popularly became known as Gommaṭa.[31]

Measurement of Gommaṭeśvara

There had been a great curiosity to know the exact dimensions of the colossal image of Gommaṭeśvara. Different estimates of the height of the image of Gommaṭa were given — 70'3" by Buchanan and 60'3" by Sir Arthur Wellesley. But Mr. Browing, the Chief Commissioner of Mysore, holds it as 57 ft. by actual measurement and in his book *Eastern Experiences* he said that "The colossal statue was measured by my order on 1 January, 1865 and the height then assigned was 57 ft."[32]

1. **Height**

   Height of foot : 2'8"

31. B.K. Khadabadi, *Gommatesa-thudi, Hymn of Gommatesa*, New Delhi, 1990, pp. 7-8.
32. R. Narasiṁhachar, *op. cit.*, pp. 15-16.

	Foot tip to knee	:	15'2"
	Foot tip to waist line	:	31'4"
	Foot tip to navel	:	34'1"
	Foot tip to neck line	:	45'10"
	Foot tip to neck	:	47'8"
	Knee to waist line	:	16'2"
	Waist line to navel	:	2'9"
	Navel to neck line	:	10'11"
	Neck line to neck	:	2'8"
	Neck to the tip	:	11'10"
	Head		
	Length of arms	:	30 ft.
	Length of penis	:	4 ft.
	Length of ears	:	5'10"
	Length of nose	:	3'9"
	Length of Hands		
(a)	Wrist to the tip of the middle finger	:	8 ft.
(b)	Wrist to the index finger	:	7 ft.
(c)	Wrist of thumb	:	5 ft.
	Total height	:	58'8"
2.	**Width**		
	Face (ear to ear)	:	8'10"
	Waist line	:	9'1"
	Shoulder tip to shoulder tip	:	23'9"
	Chest (arm-pit to arm-pit)	:	12'8"
	Neck (across)	:	6'4"[33]

33. S. Setter, *op. cit.*, p. 52.

The Inscriptions Below the Image of Gommaṭeśvara at Śravaṇbeḷgoḷa

There are inscriptions of the slabs near the right and left foot of the image of Gommaṭeśvara at Śravaṇbeḷgoḷa. The inscription on the right hand slab is as follows:

śrī-cāmuṇḍarājam medisidam;
śrī-cāmuṇḍarājan (se) yv(v)ittan;
śrī-gaṅgarāja suttalayara madisida;

That is to say —

Śrī Cāmuṇḍarāya caused to be made.
Śrī Cāmuṇḍarāya caused to be made.
Śrī Gaṅgarāja caused the *caityālaya* (enclosed) to be made.

The alphabet and language of the first and third lines are Canarese. The second line is a Tamil translation of line I and consists of two words of which the first is written in the *grantha* and the second in the Vattelutta alphabet.

The first two lines record that Cāmuṇḍarāya caused to be made the image at the foot of which the inscription is engraved, and the third line lays that Gaṅgarāja caused to be made the buildings which surround the image.[34]

The Marāṭhī Inscription on the Slab

Marāṭhī Inscription on the slab on the left hand is as under :

śrī cāmuṇḍarājem karaviyalem
śrī gaṅgarāje suttale karaviyale;

That is to say —

Śrī Cāmuṇḍarāya caused to be made.
Śrī Gaṅgarāja caused the *caityālaya* (enclosure) to be made.

The alphabet is Nāgarī, and the language is Marāṭhī. . . . The

---

34. E. Hultzsch, "Inscriptions on the Three Jain Colossi of Southern India" (*Ep. Indica*), vol. VII, pp. 108-09.

35. *Ibid.*, pp. 108-09.

Marāṭhī language was perhaps adopted for the benefit of the Jain pilgrims from the Marāṭhā country.[35]

In this inscription mentioned above, beginning with those on the left from the identical type used in both the lines, the inscription is supposed to be engraved during the reign of Gaṅgarāja when he erected the building round the image of Gommaṭeśvara established by Cāmuṇḍarāya. It is all the more probable, as the inscription on the left is nothing but a repetition of that on the right in a different language.[36]

The Art of Gommaṭa

The labour bestowed on this image is really astonishing and the image is on the whole a very successful masterpiece of sculpture. The best part of the image is its face, its wonderful contemplative expression touched with a faint smile with which Gommaṭa gazes out on the struggling world. The spirit of Jain renunciation, with its stiff and erect posture suggests perfect self-control. The benign smile on the face shows the inward bliss and sympathy for the suffering world. In spite of its slight anatomical defects, the image looks majestic and impressive. Fergusson exclaimed, "Nothing grander or more imposing exists anywhere out of Egypt and even there no known statue surpassed it in height."[37]

The majesty and the beauty of this great image has led many Kannaḍa poets, old and new, to sing their praises of it in beautiful poetry. From the terrace around the Gommaṭa image, a wonderful sight meets the eye on all sides extending over a radius of about 40 miles. Many well-known places can be identified through field glasses on a clear day. This sacred place assumes an indescribable charm at dawn, sunset, and by moonlight and in the darkness of a starlit night.[38]

---

36. *Ibid.*
37. K.A. Nilakanthasastri, *op. cit.*, p. 18.
38. *Ibid.*

Royal Patronage to Śravaṇbeḷgoḷa

The golden period of Jainism was attained during the later half of Gaṅga rule in Karnataka. Some of the later Gaṅgas themselves were Jains and almost all the Gaṅga kings were patrons of Jainism. In course of time, Jainism became popular as a result of the proselytizing zeal of the Jain *ācārya*s who moved from place to place spreading their religion and this was an important reason for Jainism taking deep roots in the south. The spread of Jainism was greatly promoted by a number of Jain teachers such as Sāmanthabhadra, Akalaṅka, Pūjyapāda, Jinasena, Śrīvijaya and Ajitasena. They held an important place in the Jain *saṁgha* of south India.

It is mentioned in the Śravaṇbeḷgoḷa inscription that Akalaṅka was such with folded hands. Vidyānandī, Akalaṅka's successor is styled as the master of the Jain doctrine Syādvāda Vidyāpati.[39]

Further, Jainism received consistent patronage from the rulers of the south. Some of the kings of the Gaṅgas, the Rāṣṭrakūṭa, the Kalacūri, and the Hoyasala dynasties professed Jainism. There must have been a considerable number of Jains in Karnataka at the time when Gaṅgas established their power.

It is a matter of great interest to enquire whether the early Gaṅga monarchs professed Jainism or not, but many of the scholars have accepted the view expressed in the later inscriptions of the Gaṅgas that Jainism was the state religion from the time of Koṅgunivarmā I. The early Gaṅgas were Jains and as tolerant monarchs they bestowed liberal grants to the Jain *guru*s and temples. On the other hand, ever since the advent of Jainism in south India, it was slowly gaining ground and attracting the attention of all classes of people. The credit for this must go to the Jain *guru*s who performed a difficult task. They were responsible for securing royal patronage and almost all the

39. B. Ali Sheik, *History of the Western Gaṅgas* (*Comprehensive History of Karnataka*, vol. I), Mysore, 1976, p. 321.

Gaṅga monarchs encouraged Jainism and made liberal grants. The Jain *guru* won the support of the provincial governors, the feudal lords and military commanders.

The construction of various *basadis* and the installation of image indicate that Jainism was taking deep roots in Gaṅgavāḍī. Particularly in the later phase from the ninth century onwards, it made rapid strides and became the state religion.[40]

The masses were attracted by the offer of basic needs such as food, clothing and shelter. The great Jain teachers appealed to the wealthy sections of the society to bestow grants liberally and out of these generous grants that came from the king and rich people, the Jain teachers managed to remove the economic distress of those who accepted Jainism.

We have numerous inscriptions to show that the Gaṅga monarchs made very liberal grants for such purpose. Koṅganivarmā I is supposed to have established a *caityālaya* at Mandali near Śimogā.[41] According to the Mahāmaṅgala copper-plates, Tadangala Mādhava made a grant to the Arhat temple of wet land under the big tank, and the Kumārapura village. According to the Mercara copper-plates, Avinīta is supposed to have made a gift to Caṇḍanandī Bhaṭṭara and presented the village of Badhanaguppe to the Śrīvijaya Jina temple of Talavananagara together with the twelve Khandukas of land.[42] It is quite clear from these and numerous other inscriptions that there was a considerable Jain population in Karnataka at the time the Gaṅgas established their power. There were quite a few important centres of Jainism in south such as Śravaṇbeḷgoḷa, Humcha, Karkala and Moodabidri.

The Gaṅga rulers continued the tradition of patronizing Jainism. Durvinīta is said to have built a *basadi* at Kogali in Bellāry

40. *Ibid.*, p. 323.

41. B.L. Rice, *Mysore Gazetteer*, p. 311.

42. B.L. Rice, "*Coorg Inscriptions*," *E.C.*, I, p. 51.

district.[43] He regarded the famous Jain divine Pūjyapāda as his teacher. His son Mushkara constructed the Mokkara Basadi which was a Jain temple in Bellāry district.[44]

Śivamāra I continued the tradition of promoting Jains in Gaṅgavāḍī and gifting lands to them. When we come to the rule of Śivamāra II, the son of Śrīpuruṣa, we find the position of Jainism to have further strengthened. We regard that Śivamāra was not only a patron of Jainism but also professed Jainism as his personal faith. He built a *basadi* on the smaller hill of Śravaṇbeḷgoḷa. The Gaṅga monarchs, from Śivamāra II onwards, changed their faith and accepted Jainism as their personal creed. From the time of Śivamāra II to the end of the dynasty, the Gaṅga monarchs were all staunch followers of Jainism. One of them was under the impact of the Rāṣṭrakūṭa policy of the Gaṅgas. Śivamāra II himself was under the custody of the Rāṣṭrakūṭas for sometime. This was a very opportune moment for him to be acquainted and impressed by the Jain creed.[45] He must have been in contact with numerous Jain saints, scholars, poets and philosophers who must have brought about a change in him. Inscriptions mention the names of Siṁhanandī, Vakragrīva, Vīradeva, Jinasena, Toraṇācārya, Prabhānandī and several other teachers who were greatly instrumental in popularizing Jainism.

The rulers, who followed Śivamāra II, were Rājamalla I, Nītimārga III, Rājamalla IV and Rakkasa Gaṅga. All these rulers had not only adopted Jainism but were also well versed in the Jain philosophy and above all were men of great piety.[46]

The Gaṅga king Śivamāra II built the Śivamāra Basadi at Śravaṇbeḷgoḷa in AD 810. About the same time, the younger

43. P.B. Desai, *Epigraphia Jainica,* Chap. II (Jainism in South India), Solapur, 1957, p. 46.
44. B. Ali Sheik, *op. cit.,* p. 323 and *Indian Antiquary,* vol. VII, p. 107.
45. R. Narasiṁhachar, *E.C.,* vol. II, S.B., p. 43.
46. Ali Sheik, *op. cit.,* p. 325.

brother of Śivamāra II, also gave specified land to the Koil Basadi. The same *basadi* received land from the inhabitants of three villages.[47] They built *basadis*, monasteries and *mānasthambas*. Rājamalla II, the successor of Śivamāra II, took keen interest both in the construction of Jains basadis and also cave temples for the Jains.[48]

Mārasiṁha III was equally a great supporter of Jainism. The Kugebrahmadeva inscription near Śravaṇbeḷgoḷa give us a detailed account of Mārasiṁha as the follower of a particular Jain doctrine, known as the Syādavāda doctrine. Mārasiṁha constructed Jain *mānasthambha* on the Candragiri hill. The record states that he observed the vow of *sallekhana* in the presence of his religious preceptor Ajitasena and died three days later.[49]

Rājamalla IV (AD 974-84) — Mārasiṁha's son and successor Rājamalla IV continued the royal patronage to Jainism. He was also a devout Jain — a mutilated stone inscription found in Aṅgādi in Mudigere *tāluka* relates that his religious preceptor was Vajrapāṇi, who belonged to Mūlasaṁgha.[50]

The period of Rājamalla IV is very noteworthy in the history of Jainism. Rājamalla called the *jina dharma* a moon of the ocean.[51] This was also the period of his great minister Cāmuṇḍarāya, who was responsible for the installation of the Gommaṭa statue at Śravaṇbeḷgoḷa. He was also the author of the work titled *Cāmuṇḍarāya Purāṇa*. He constructed the Cāmuṇḍarāya Basadi at Śravaṇbeḷgoḷa. His preceptor Nemicandra wrote a classic on the Jain doctrine called *Dravyasaṁgraha*. According to the *Cāmuṇḍarāya Purāṇa*, its author never uttered untruth even in Jest. He practised the principles of Jainism so scrupulously that

47. P. Rambhushan Singh and Mysore Archaeological Report, 1932, *Jainism early Medieval Karnataka, c.* AD *500-1200*, Delhi, 1975, p. 103.
48. B. Ali Sheik, *op. cit.*, p. 324.
49. *Ibid.*, pp. 324-25.
50. B.L. Rice, *E C.*, vol. VI, Mudigere 18, p. 61.
51. B.A. Saletore, *op. cit.*, p. 93.

he received the title of Satyayudhiṣṭhira. In short, he was the very embodiment of a very true follower of *jina*, and he well deserved the title conferred on him — Guṇratnabhūṣaṇa and Kavivijanaśekhara.[52]

Another preceptor of Cāmuṇḍarāya was the celebrated Ajitasena. Both Ajitasena and Nemicandra Siddhārtha were responsible for shaping the character of Cāmuṇḍarāya. An inscription of AD 1159 gives us a hint of Cāmuṇḍarāya as being a devout Jain. It says that this Rāya alone could truly be called a firm promoter of Jain *dharma*.[53] His endowments for the cause of Jainism have been numerous. Apart from the statue of Gommaṭeśvara, he installed a pillar on the Candragiri. We have already noted the reasons which prompted him to install the statue of Śravaṇbeḷgoḷa while studying the political history of Southern Karnataka.

Cāmuṇḍarāya's younger sister, Pallavva, died by observing the *jina* rite of *sallekhana*. She died in the Candranātha Basadi at Vijaymangalam in Coimbatore district.[54] Gaṅgarāja is described as a hundred times more fortunate than the former Rāya of the Gaṅgas, that is what Cāmuṇḍarāya referred to the visitor Śubhakarayya, who, it says, was the accountant of Rachamalla-deva, probably king Rachamalla IV. The last record to be noticed under this head is which refers to the erection of a Jain temple at Beḷgoḷa by Jinadeva, son of Cāmuṇḍarāya and a lay disciple of Ajitasena. Ajitasena was also the *guru* of Cāmuṇḍarāya who built a temple at Śravaṇbeḷgoḷa.[55]

It was on the Candragiri hill at Śravaṇbeḷgoḷa that Cāmuṇḍarāya erected in AD 982 a magnificent temple containing the image of 22nd Jain *tīrthaṅkara*, Neminātha. Subsequently, the upper storey of the building was added an image of the

52. B.L. Rice, *E.C.*, vol. II, S.B.P. 148.
53. B. Ali Sheik, *op. cit.*, p. 325.
54. *Ibid.*, p. 325.
55. R. Narasiṁhachar, V.A. Sangave, *E.C.*, vol. II, *S.B.* p. 46, *op. cit.* p. 58.

23rd Jain *tīrthaṅkara*, Pāraśvanātha by Jinadeva, son of Cāmuṇḍarāya in the year AD 995. Both the storeys give a fine idea of the beautiful architecture of that age.

Cāmuṇḍarāya died after a very hectic and eventful career by about AD 990, during the reign of the Gaṅga monarch Rakkasa Gaṅga, the successor of Rājamalla IV. It was unfortunate that Cāmuṇḍarāya had to leave this world only after 9 years of his making outstanding contribution to the world culture, that is, the installation of the colossal image of Gommaṭeśvara in the year AD 981. But it is pertinent to note that Cāmuṇḍarāya's dedicated service to the cause of Jain religion did not go in vain. Cāmuṇḍarāya's monumental works provided continuous inspiration for centuries. As a result, we find that the renowned Military Generals and Chief Ministers like Gaṅgarāja and Hullarāja of the Hoyasala Empire continued with zeal work of Cāmuṇḍarāya during the twelfth century.[56]

GAṄGARĀJA

Gaṅgarāja, also known as Gaṅga, Gaṅgana and Gaṅgayupa, was the Military General and Chief Minister of the Hoyasala monarch Viṣṇuvardhana (AD 1090-1152). Gaṅgarāya or Gaṅgarāja was probably a scion of the Gaṅgas of Talakaḍ. His place in Jain history is second only to that of Cāmuṇḍarāya.[57]

From the time of his great grandfather Nāgavarmā, who belonged to the *Kauṇḍinya gotra* of the brāhmaṇa *varṇa*, the observance of Jain religion was an established family tradition. Gaṅgaraja's father, Echa, who worked as the General and Minister of Hoyasala king Nṛpukāma, was a devout Jain and a disciple of saint Kanakanandī of Mallur in Coorg area. Similarly, Pochaladevī, the mother of Gaṅgarāja was a staunch follower of Jainism. She made several religious endowments at Śravaṇbeḷgoḷa and other places and ultimately left this world in AD 1121 by the Jain rite of *sallekhana*. On the same lines, General

56. V.A. Sangave, *op. cit.*, p. 59.
57. S. Setter, *op. cit.*, p. 72.

Gaṅgarāja and his talented wife Lakṣmīdevī continued their patronage to Jainism under the guidance of their saint preceptor Śubhacandra Siddhanāthadeva.[58] He had two brothers among whom one was Bommanayya. As a warrior, he was responsible for liberating the Hoyasala from the Cāḷukya overlordship and for wresting Talakaḍ from the Coḷas. His heroic career earned several titles for him among which *drohagharatta* (a grindstone to traitors) is one.[59]

In addition to his military successes and benevolent administration, Gaṅgarāja has to his credit a number of religious activities which greatly increased the importance of Śravaṇbeḷgoḷa as a sacred place. In this respect, Gaṅgarāja is very favourably compared with Cāmuṇḍarāya in an inscription at Śravaṇbeḷgoḷa.[60]

Viṣṇuvardhana was so pleased with the military achievements of his General that he granted all that Gaṅgarāya needed to maintain the *basadi*s at Śravaṇbeḷgoḷa. It is during this time that Beḷgoḷa grew into a town and the temples of this centre attained an institutional status.

Besides laying the foundations of the present town of Śravaṇbeḷgoḷa and of Jinanāthapura, Gaṅgarāya and members of his family were responsible for the Kattle Basadi Śāsana Basadi, Eradukatte Basadi and Śāntinātha Basadi on the small hill; the Gommaṭa enclosure on the large hill, the Aregal Basadi at Jinanāthapura and several others at Dorasamudra, Kambadahalli, etc. They were also responsible for securing the rich endowments and village grants from the ruling kings.[61]

Gaṅgarāja made the following major contributions in the religious field of Śravaṇbeḷgoḷa.

---

58. V.A. Sangave, *op. cit.*, p. 60.
59. S. Setter, *op. cit.*, p. 27.
60. R. Narasiṁhachar, *E.C.*, vol. II, 513, p. 49.
61. S. Setter, *op. cit.*, p. 72.

CONSTRUCTION OF ENCLOSURE AROUND GOMMAṬA IMAGE

Gaṅgarāja built a heavy wall at some distance around the colossal image of Gommaṭeśvara. This high solid wall built in AD 1117 has made the area around the image on the Vindhyagiri hill into a compact enclosure. By this wall the overall impressiveness of the image from a long distance is reduced to some extent. But it appears that the marvellous image of Gommaṭeśvara needed such protection from the attacks of sectarian fanatics.[62]

GRANT OF VILLAGE GOVINDAVĀḌĪ

It is stated in the inscription numbered 240, 251 and 397 that Gaṅgarāja, after his victory over the Coḷa feudatories at Talakad, obtained, as a boon from the king Viṣṇuvardhana, the village of Govindavāḍī and granted it for the worship of Gommaṭeśvara.[63]

ERECTION OF ŚĀSANA-BASADI

It is recorded in the inscription no. 74 that Gaṅgarāja erected the *jina* temple, Indirākulagṛha, now known as the Śāsana Basadi. The temple was built in AD 1117, in the middle of the temple sector, on the Candragiri hill.[64]

ERECTION OF THE KATTALE-BASADI

It is recorded in the inscription no. 70 that Gaṅgarāja erected this temple for his mother Pochaladevī. This temple is dedicated to Ādinātha, the first *tīrthaṅkara*, but it is popularly known as the Kattle Basadi, i.e., the temple of darkness, due to lack of sufficient light in the temple. The temple was built in AD 1118 in the middle of the temple sector on the Candragiri hill.[65]

FOUNDATION OF VILLAGE JINANĀTHAPURA

Gaṅgarāja founded a new village at a distance of about 1 mile

---

62. V.A. Sangave, *op. cit.*, p. 62.
63. B.L. Rice, *E.C.*, vol. II, S.B. 103-06.
64. R. Narasimhachar, *op. cit.*, p. 40.
65. *Ibid.*, p. 37.

to the north of Śravaṇbeḷgoḷa and named it as "Jinanāthapura" in the year AD 1117. The village became famous for its beautiful Śāntinātha Basadi erected round about AD 1200 by Rachimayya who was the minister to Hoyasala king Ballāla II (AD 1173-1220).

GRANT OF VILLAGE PARAMA

Gaṅgarāja asked for and obtained from the king the village of Parama and granted it to the *jina* temples erected by his mother Pochaladevī and his wife Lakṣmīdevī. The aforesaid information is given in the inscription no. 73 and 125 at Śravaṇbeḷgoḷa.[66]

HELP IN ERECTING ERADUKATTE-BASADI

Inscription no. 130 states that Lakṣmīdevī, the wife of Gaṅgarāja and a lay disciple of Śubhacandra, caused the *jina* temple, now known as the Eradukatte Basadi, to be built in AD 1118. The temple is said to belong to the *pustaka-gaccha* of the *deśīyagaṇa* of the *mūla-saṁgha*. The inscription further describes Lakṣmīdevī as Chelana, in the worship of *jina*, and as the lady of policy in business and the lady of victory in battle to Gaṅgarāja. This temple is dedicated to Ādinātha, the first *tīrthaṅkara*, but is popularly known as Eradukatte Basadi on account of the two stairs in the east and west of the approach to it. The temple is situated on the eastern side of the temple sector on the Candragiri hill.[67]

HELP IN ERECTING ŚĀNTINĀTHA TEMPLE

Gaṅgarāja encouraged his son General Boppanna to build a temple at Kambadahalli, a village situated at 11 miles away from Śravaṇbeḷgoḷa. Accordingly, Boppanna built the temple and dedicated it to Śāntinātha, the 16th *tīrthaṅkara*. The temple is popularly known as the Śāntīśvara Basadi and it is thought that

---

66. V.A. Sangave, *op. cit.*, p. 63.
67. R. Narasiṁhachar, *op. cit.*, pp. 57-58.

its construction work must have been completed after the death of Gaṅgarāja.[68]

HELP IN THE ERECTION OF A TEMPLE AT SANEHALLI

Due to the encouragement of Gaṅgarāja, Jakkimavve, the wife of his elder brother, built a temple three miles away from Śravaṇbeḷgoḷa. The temple is known as Hale Basadi, i.e., old temple.[69]

Had not Gaṅgarāya and the members of his family erected this temple the great saints and pious Jains would not have received the *nisidhi* memorials, and Śravaṇbeḷgoḷa would not have been enriched with as many ponds and tanks as are seen at present. Gaṅgarāja renovated all the temples built by his predecessors, and also ensured endowments for the maintenance of each of these. Because of this, he was considered even greater and blessed than Cāmuṇḍarāya.

When Gaṅgarāja died in AD 1133, he was honoured by his son with two temples; one at Halebiḍ and another at Kambadahalli. Both temples were called Drohagharatta Basadis after the title of Gaṅgarāja.[70]

HULLARĀJA

Hullarāja, a minister under the Hoyasalas, is acclaimed in a record as the greatest of the Jains after Cāmuṇḍarāya and Gaṅgarāja. This is substantiated by his contribution to Śravaṇbeḷgoḷa.

Gaṅgarāja's tradition of extending support to Jain religion was ably continued by the Military General and Chief Minister Hullarāja of Hoyasala King Narasiṁha I (AD 1152-73). Minister Hullarāja, also known as Hulla, Hullappa or Hullamayya had unique distinction to serve in this high office to three Hoyasala

68. V.A. Sangave, *op. cit.*, p. 63.
69. *Ibid.*, p. 64.
70. S. Setter, *op. cit.*, p. 72.

kings in succession. Hullarāja started his service as a minister under king Viṣṇuvardhana AD 1090-1152 and became Chief Minister under king Narasiṁha I (AD 1152-73) and continued to work under King Ballāla II (AD 1173-1220) as *bhanḍārī* (treasurer) and *mahāpradhānī* (minister).[71]

Hullarāja belonged to a devout Jain family. He was a lay disciple of saint Nayakīrti Siddhāntadeva and devotee of Mahāmaṇḍalācārya Devakīrti. Like Cāmuṇḍarāya and Gaṅgarāya, Hullarāja also worked strenuously as a promoter of Jain faith. Hullarāja's major contributions to the Jain religion is given in the inscriptions at Dhārwāḍ, Rāicūr and Śravaṇbeḷgoḷa.[72]

Besides making a lavish gift at Kopana (Koppal in the Rāicūr District), Hullarāja renovated and beautified two *basadi*s, one at Bankapura (Dhārwāḍ district) and another at Kellangere. He was the earliest to build a *basadi* (AD 1159) in the town of Śravaṇbeḷgoḷa and it is, even to this day, the largest of the structures in the city. Dedicated to the 24 *tīrthaṅkara*s, the patron called it Caturviṁśati-Tīrthaṅkara Basadi, but the ruling king who visited it was so much pleased by its workmanship that he called it Bhavyacūdāmaṇi. Hullarāja was also responsible for establishing the first settlement of Jains in the town. Two strongly built Jain dwellings which he put up near the Bhanḍāra Basadi probably, became the basis of the later monastic institution.

He erected a memorial in the honour of his Guru called Devakīrit-Paṇḍitadeva on a small hill, (now in the *Mahānavamī Maṇḍapa*) and an alms-house at Jinanāthapura. King Narasiṁha I and Ballāla II granted him three villages (named Savaneri, Kaggere and Bekka) for the maintenance of the *basadi* at Beḷgoḷa in appreciation of his services to the kingdom. He is one of those responsible for the establishment of a large tank called

71. *Ibid.*

72. V.A. Sangave, *op. cit.*, p. 64.

"Siṁha Samudra" then and Bekka-tank now. It was probably because of him that Hoyasala king Narasiṁha I personally visited Śravaṇbeḷgoḷa in about AD 1159.[73]

Thus, this trinity of ministers namely Cāmuṇḍarāya, Gaṅgarāja and Hullarāja enriched the old traditions of Śravaṇbeḷgoḷa by their valuable and lasting contributions.

THE RĀṢṬRAKŪṬAS

The Rāṣṭrakūṭas, like the Gaṅgas of Talakaḍ, were a great power in south India for more than two centuries. They were zealous patrons of Jainism. Jain literature, in particular, had its golden age under their patronage. The Gaṅgas had set-up this tradition before the Rāṣṭrakūṭas rose to the power, and the Cāḷukyas, who were another important dynasty sandwiched almost between the Gaṅgas and the Rāṣṭrakūṭas, were also inclined to patronize Jainism. Although they were votaries of the Vedic religion, they were no less adherent to Jainism and supported it with a big heart.

The period from AD 754 to AD 974 is considered as the age of Rāṣṭrakūṭas in the Deccan. The rulers had embraced the Jain religion as their personal faith and had bestowed liberal patronage.[74]

The most famous Rāṣṭrakūṭa king was the Amoghavarṣa Nṛpatuṅga (AD 814-78). Although involved in wars almost incessantly, he was by inclination a pacifist. Moreover, he was more scholarly than militant and an author by choice and a warrior by necessity. His *Kavirājamārga*, one of the oldest Kannaḍa work available today, is a work on poetics and is a masterpiece on the subject. He also wrote a book entitled *Praśnotara Ratnāvalī* dealing with Jain ethics in Sanskrit.[75] He was

---

73. S. Setter, *op. cit.*, p. 72.

74. K. Jain Utter (ed.) Articles (Prof. Kumari Vasanta), *Jinamanjari* (Rāṣṭrakūṭas and the dawn of Jain Culture in Southern India AD 783 — AD 988) (vol. I, October, 1990), p. 40.

75. V.A. Sangave, *op. cit.*, p. 40.

one of the most prominent Jain rulers. The credit of establishing the new capital Manyakheta, a centre of rich antiquary, is attributed to him. The most prominent Jain *ācārya*s namely Prabhacandra and Jinasena were his preceptors, while Vīrasena, Mahāvīra, Guṇabhadra, Sākaṭāyana were those intellectuals who also contributed to the glory of their eminent ruler. Amoghavarṣa was known for his scholarship and political idealism.[76]

Kṛṣṇa II (AD 878-914), son and successor of Amoghavarṣa, was highly inspired to follow his father's policy. Renowned *ācārya* Guṇabhadra was his preceptor. Lokāditya, son of General Banksena and a Jain by faith, was his courageous Governor and supporter in the southern region.

Kṛṣṇa III (AD 939-67) witnessed further expansion of the political authority of the Rāṣṭrakūṭas. Bharata and his son Nanne were his great Jain Ministers and Generals : Jainism also witnessed a great period of ascendancy during this period.[77]

King Indra IV (AD 973-87), the last monarch of Rāṣṭrakūṭa dynasty, was also a patron of Jainism and a great warrior as seen from the various titles conferred on him. When the Rāṣṭrakūṭa power was waning owing to a quick succession of weak rulers, the Gaṅga King Narasiṁha had to interfere in getting the crown to Indra IV, his nephew and the last ruler of the Rāṣṭrakūṭa. Indra IV died at Śravaṇbeḷgoḷa in AD 987 observing *sallekhana*. He is bestowed with lavish praise for he never uttered falsehood, and is highly honoured as a believer in the doctrines of *jina* Mahāvīra.[78]

The *praśasti* of the *Uttara Purāṇa* refers to the prominent *ācārya*s, Vīrasena, Jinasena, Sadakarma, Daśaratha, Guṇabhadra and Lokasena of Senagaṇa. *Ācārya* Ajitasena inspired his disciple Cāmuṇḍarāya, the great minister of successive Gaṅga rulers

76. Vasanta Kumari, *op. cit.*, p. 41.
77. *Ibid.*
78. *Ibid.*

Mārasiṁha II, Rachamalla VI and Rachamalla V — the feudatory of the Rāṣṭrakūṭas, to cause the erection of the monolithic statue of Gommaṭa at Śravaṇbeḷgoḷa in AD 981.

These Jain *ācāryas* evidently moulded the character and career of the many kings and generals. Akalaṅkadeva, the celebrated logician, disputant and rhetorician in the court of Śubhatuṅga, who is identified as Kṛṣṇa I (AD 788) is said to have hailed from Śravaṇbeḷgoḷa. Rice opines that Akalaṅka belonged to the line of *ācāryas* of Mallyur Maṭha which was a subaltern to Śravaṇbeḷgoḷa Maṭha.[79]

THE HOYASALAS

The Hoyasalas, whose kingdom included modern Mysore, were staunch Jains and their rule which spread over a period of more than three centuries (AD 1006-1345) forms the brightest chapter in the history of Medieval Karnataka. The rulers of the Hoyasala dynasty steadfastly followed Jainism and actually patronized it because the very foundation of the Hoyasala rule was laid by the efforts of a Jain ascetic teacher. It is recorded in the inscriptions at Śravaṇbeḷgoḷa that the progenitor of the Hoyasala dynasty was Sala, an eponymous hero, who was a devout Jain.

On a certain occasion, we are told, he went to worship at the temple of his family deity at Sosavura. After worship, he came to his ascetic teacher called Sudatta Vardhamāna to receive religious instruction. While he was receiving instructions, a fierce tiger came out of the forest and flared at them with rage.[80]

At this the sage said to Sala with reference to the fierce tiger "Poyasala" (i.e., strike it, Sala); and from this event Sala adopted the sage's words as his name, i.e., Poyasala or Hoyasala, as also the tiger crest. In this way the utterance of the *guru* "Hoya(poya)Sala," itself became the name of the

79. *Ibid.*, p. 45.

80. B.L. Rice, Mysore and Coorg, p. 95.

dynasty which succeeded in expelling the Coḷas from Mysore region and in establishing its rule in the eleventh century.

Thus, just as the great Jain saint Ācārya Siṁhanandī helped in establishing the Gaṅga kingdom in the fourth century AD and gave advice to Koṅgunivarmā I, the first Gaṅga king, similarly, the renowned and politically conscious Jain saint Ācārya Sudatta guided the foundation of the Hoyasala kingdom in the eleventh century AD and took a prominent part in the administration of the Hoyasalas.[81]

It is clear from the inscriptions that the first three Hoyasala rulers viz., Sala, the founder; his son Vinayāditya I (AD 1016-22) and the latter's successor Nr̥pakāma (AD 1022-47) were under the spiritual guidance of Ācārya Sudatta. The fourth Hoyasala ruler Vinayāditya II (1047-98) was a staunch devotee of the Jain sage Śāntideva who has been respectfully mentioned in the inscription numbered 67, dated AD 1129, at Śravaṇbeḷgoḷa in the following terms: "who is able to describe 'such and such' is the ability of the ascetic Shantideva and the Hoyasala King, Vinayaditta, being blessed, brought the Goddess of wealth to the territory under his rule?"[82]

What king Vinayāditya II did as a Jain, obviously on the advice of his preceptor Śāntideva, is described in a stone record found in the Gandhavaraṇa Basadi (viz., Inscription no. 143, AD 1131) at Śravaṇbeḷgoḷa in the following words "King Vinayaditta gladly made any number of tanks and temples, any number of Jina shrine, any number of *nadu*s (or districts), villages and subjects."[83] The erection of Jain temples by Vinayāditya, the great builder, is thus described : "The pits dug for bricks became tanks, the mountains quarried for stones became level with the ground, the roads by which the mortar carts passed became raviness."

81. B.A. Saletore, *op. cit.*, pp. 62-63.

82. R. Narasiṁhachar, *op. cit.*, p. 30.

83. B.L. Rice, *E.C.*, vol. II, *S.B.*, pp. 70-71.

Such enormous was the scale at which Hoyasala built the Jain temples. There are many inscriptions found at other places that reveal the utmost care with which King Vinayāditya II looked after the Jain interests.[84]

Ereyaṅga (AD 1098-1102), the son and successor of Vinayāditta II, was a devoted disciple of Jain saint Gopanandi whose qualifications and achievements are graphically described in a stone inscription at Hale-Beḷagoḷa dated AD 1094. King Ereyaṅga, while ruling the Gaṅgamaṇḍala, granted villages Rachanahalli and the Śravaṇbeḷgoḷa 12 to this great Jain logician Tribhuvanamalla Ereyaṅga for the repairs of the *basadis*, i.e, temples in the holy place round the Kalbappu hill and Katavapra or Candragiri hill at Śravaṇbeḷgoḷa.[85]

It is also mentioned in an inscription that saint Gopanandī with the patronage of king Ereyaṅga "caused the Jain religion, which had for a long time been at a standstill, to attain the prosperity and fame of the Gaṅga kings."[86]

King Ballāla I (AD 1102-08), the eldest son of king Ereyaṅga, was a disciple of the Jain *guru*, Paṇḍitadeva Cārukīrti, whose accomplishments are mentioned in a stone inscriptions dated AD 1398 and AD 1432. These inscriptions are the Siddheśvara Basadi records of Śravaṇbeḷgoḷa and they depict *guru* Cārukīrti's proficiency in medicine as well. It is stated therein that "when king Ballāla was verily in a moribund condition through severe illness, he quickly restored him to health." Even the air that had touched his body cured disease; was it such (then) that his medicine cured King Ballāla of his disease?[87]

Bittideva-Viṣṇuvardhana (AD 1108-42)

Bittideva (AD 1108-42), who, later, adopted the name

---

84. B.A. Saletore, *op. cit.*, p. 74.
85. B.L. Rice, *op. cit.*, No. 148, pp. 189-90.
86. B.A. Saletore, *op. cit.*, p. 77.
87. B.L. Rice, *E.C.*, vol. II, *S.B.*, No. 254, p. 113.

Viṣṇuvardhana, was one of the most brilliant monarchs of the Karnataka. He was a great king and his achievements both in war and in peace were very remarkable. Many of the notable victories which marked his rule were won by his great Jain generals. King Viṣṇuvardhana's reign was also important from the point of his continued support to Jainism in spite of his alleged conversion from Jainism to Vaiṣṇavism in AD 1116[88] under the influence of the great Ācārya Rāmānuja, who had taken refuge in the Hoyasala country to escape persecution at the hands of a Coḷa king. While this legend is popular and persistent, it appears unfounded as none of the numerous inscriptions of this king contains any reference to this event and neither mentions the influence of Ācārya Rāmānuja on the king.[89]

Even after about AD 1125, when Ācārya Rāmānuja is supposed to have left Mysore region, King Viṣṇuvardhana made grants to Jain teachers like Śrīpāla Traividyavratī and saw merit in the consecration of the image of Pārśvanātha. Another stone inscription at Belūr dated AD 1129 commemorates a gift to the *basadi* named "Malli Jinālaya" by the same King Viṣṇuvardhana.[90] Further, it is recorded that when the famous Pārśvanātha Jain temple was built in the Hoyasala capital city by one of his many great Jain generals, King Viṣṇuvardhana christened his son Prince Vijaya Narasiṁhadeva after the god Vijaya Pārśvadeva and granted the village Javagal for a Jain temple in the capital Dorasamudra near Haḷebiḍ.[91]

All these records clearly reveal that Viṣṇuvardhana, whatever his patronage to Vaiṣṇavism might have been, continued till the end of his rule to be a pious *bhavya* (Jain householder).

---

88. B.L. Rice, *Mysore and Coorg*, p. 99.
89. B.A. Saletore, *op. cit.*, p. 78.
90. R. Narasiṁhachar, *E.C.*, vol. II, *S.B.*, No. 131-124, p. 83.
91. *Mysore Archaeological Report*, 1119, p. 43.

SANTALADEVĪ

Queen Santaladevī, the eldest and the principal wife of King Viṣṇuvardhana, was undoubtedly a Jain enthusiast and played a prominent role in the history of Jainism in Karnataka. The inscription numbered 132 of Śravaṇbeḷgoḷa records the erection of the famous temple Savatigandharvana Basadi on the Candragiri hill by Queen Santaladevī[92] in AD 1123.

The same inscription eulogizes queen Santaladevī: "The eldest daughter of Narasiṁha and Machikabbe. She was to king Viṣṇu the Goddess of victory in battle, the Goddess of wealth always resting on his breast and the Goddess of fame spreading the greatness of his volour to the remotest points."[93]

Among the epithets applied to her are a Bṛhaspati in discriminations; a *vācaspati* in ready wit; the cause of the elevation of the four *samaya*s or creeds; an expert in singing instrumental music and dancing and a rutting elephant to ill-mannered co-wives (*udvṛtta-savatigandhavarane*).[94]

The last epithet is interesting as the temple founded by her on the Candragiri hill was named after it, i.e., Savati-Gandhavarana Basadi. She endowed the temple with a village and certain lands, which she presented to her Jain teacher, the saint Prabhacandra, after washing his feet. She died in AD 1131 at Śivagaṅga. Her mother Machikabbe, resolving not to survive after the death of her daughter, went to Śravaṇbeḷgoḷa and observed fasting for one month. She thus died by the Jain rite of *sallekhana*, in the presence of her teachers, namely the saints Prabhacandra, Vardhamāna and Ravicandra.[95] Several verses glorify her sacrifice and severe penance in the inscription no. 143.

---

92. N. Lakshminarayan Rao, Eminent Women of Karnataka, *Q.J.M.S.*, vol. 45, no. 1, Bangalore 1954, p. 12.
93. R. Narasiṁhachar, *E.C.*, vol. II, *S.B.*, p. 56.
94. *Ibid.*
95. *Ibid.*

There are six inscriptions of this reign. Of these, the one on the car-like structure in front of Terina Basadi on the smaller hill at Sravanbeḷgoḷa is perhaps the earliest, dating to AD 1117. The car-like structure perhaps represents what the Jains call a *mandara*. The inscription, which is in verse throughout says, that there were two royal merchants (Raja Sreshtigal) named Poyasalaseṭṭi and Nemiseṭṭi, who were the abodes of *jina-dharma* at the court of king Poyasala; that their mothers Machikabbe and Śāntikabbe, who were devoted Jains, caused a Jain temple and a *mandara* to be built; took *dīkṣā* from Bhānukīrtimuni and became famous in the *mūla saṁgha* and *deśīya-gaṇa*; and that the two merchants casued special worship to be offered to *jina* in honour of the occasion and arranged for the feeding of the Jain *gurus*. The temple built by the ladies is no doubt the Terina Basadi and the *mandāra*, the car-like ornamental stone structure on which the inscription is engraved.

Another inscription of Viṣṇuvardhana is engraved on a rock to the south-west of Jinanāthapura near Śravaṇbeḷgoḷa. This inscription, though mostly worn out, informs that the king's senior *daṇḍanāyaka*, Svāmīdrhagharatta, Gaṅgapayya, made Jinanāthapura at Beḷogoḷatīrtha. A grant also appears to have been given by him on the king's advice. It is curious that the inscription ends thus: The arrow shot by Drohagharatta. Perhaps, the mark of an arrow served as his signature, though no such mark is now visible. The information that Gaṅgarāja brought Jinanāthapura into existence is new.[96]

The remaining two inscriptions are of some importance as they give an account of Gaṅgarāja's exploits. One of them is on a stone to the west of Brahmadeva *maṇḍapa* on the large hill at Śravaṇbeḷgoḷa and the other on a stone at Saehalli near the same village. Both of them are similar to inscription no. 90 at Śravaṇbeḷgoḷa in their description of Gaṅgarāja's greatness and his victory over the Coḷa feudatories. But the inscription at

96. K.S. Chandrasekhar Aiyar, *Archaeological Report*, Nov. 1909, pp. 18-19.

Saehalli, dated AD 1119, gives an additional information that apart from Govindavādī, which was granted by Viṣṇuvardhana to Gaṅgarāja for worship, the villages Aruhanhalli, Bekka and Chalya were also named. The fact that its name mentioned in an old inscriptions of Śravaṇbeḷgoḷa numbered 24 establishes its great antiquity. The grant was made after washing the feet of Śubhacandra Siddhāntadeva, the *guru* of Gaṅgarāja, in the presence of Pattanasvāmī Mallisetti, Gaṇḍanarāyaseṭṭi and others. The engraver was Gaṅgacāri, an ornament of titled sculptors.[97]

An important information given in the inscription no. 66 of Śravaṇbeḷgoḷa may be mentioned here. It was supposed on the strength of this inscription that Gaṅgarāja's son were named Echana and Boppa. This supposition was inferred from an incorrect reading of the second half of the second verse. The correct reading, however is Boppanaparanamanka-Caityālayam. It was the name given to the temple by Echana.

Boppana-Caityālaya mentions of only one son of Gaṅgarāja whose name was Boppa. But he is mentioned as Agratanaya, the eldest son of Gaṅgarāja in some inscriptions (e.g., Śravaṇbeḷgoḷa 144 and Cannarāya Patna 248). Echana, related the present inscription, is the other son who built Boppana-Caityālaya in memory of his elder brother Boppana.[98]

Two inscriptions on the pedestals of Bāhubali and Bharateśvara near the entrance, known as Akhaṇḍa, on the large hill at Śravaṇbeḷgoḷa record that the images were set-up by Bharateśvaradaṇḍanāyaka, a lay disciple of Gandavimukta Saiddhāntadeva of the *mūla-saṁgha, deśīya-gaṇa* and *pustaka-gaccha*. This fact is also mentioned in Śravaṇbeḷgoḷa inscription no. 115. Gandavimukta was the *guru* of Śubhacandra who died in AD 1123 (Śravaṇbeḷgoḷa inscription 43), the date of these records however is AD 1115. Another inscription around the

---

97. *Ibid.*
98. *Ibid.*

central ceiling panel in the *maṇḍapa* in front of Gommaṭa, tells us that the Arasaditya (or king Āditya) and Achambike had three sons, namely, Pamparāja, Harideva and the chief of ministers Baladevana, who were ornaments of the Karnatakakula, uncles of Machirāja and devoted worshippers of *jina*. Baladevadaṇḍanāyaka is praised at length in Śravaṇbeḷgoḷa inscription 53, but he is quite different from Baladeva of the present inscription as his parents were Nāgavarmā and Chandikabbe. The date of this record may be about AD 1120.[99]

Two inscriptions near Jokkikatte, Śravaṇbeḷgoḷa, say that Jakkamavve — wife of the elder brother *daṇḍanāyaka* Gaṅgarāja — was the mother of *daṇḍanāyaka* Boppadeva. She is also stated to have built the tank which is known after her name even now. The date of Jakkivavve's records may be ascertained to about AD 1120.

One of the inscription dated about 1160 is engraved near the left foot of Gommaṭa. It is similar to Śravaṇbeḷgoḷa inscription 80 in its contents and tells us that the great minister, senior *bhaṇḍārī*, Hullamayya received the village Savaneru from Bittideva's son Pratāpa-Narasiṁhadeva and granted it for Gommaṭa.[100]

KING NARASIṀHA I (AD 1142-73)

King Narasiṁha I, the third son and successor of Viṣṇuvardhana, carried on the tradition of Hoyasala kings. King Narasiṁha gave the name Bhavya-Cūdāmaṇi Basadi to the famous Chaturviṁśati-tīrthaṅkara Basadi built by his General Hullarāja in the village of Śravaṇbeḷgoḷa in AD 1159 and granted the village Savaneru for its upkeep. The temple is popularly known as Bhaṇḍārī Basadi, since Hullarāja was also *bhaṇḍārī* or treasurer of king Narasiṁha I.[101]

99. K.S. Chandrasekhar Aiyar, p. 19.
100. *Ibid.*, 20.
101. S.R. Sharma, *op. cit.*, p. 42.

KING BALLĀLA II OR VĪRA BALLĀLA I (AD 1173-1220)

King Ballāla II organized the kingdom upon a footing of peace and prosperity and like his predecessors showed marked favour to the spread of Jainism. His titles and achievements are given in inscription nos. 327 and 335 at Śravaṇbeḷgoḷa. Inscription no. 327 records the erection of the Pārśvanātha Basadi (now known as Akkana Basadi) at Śravaṇbeḷgoḷa, by Achiyakka, the wife of the king's minister Candramauli, in AD 1181. Achiyakka who got the temple built, was a Jain and a lay disciple of Bālacandramuni, the chief disciple of Nayakīrti-Siddhānta-Cakravartī.[102]

It is evident from inscription no. 240, dated AD 1175, that the king gave his confirmation to the grant of three villages awarded by his father king Narasiṁha I for temples of Gommaṭṭa, Pārśvanātha and the twenty-four *tīrtaṅkara*s. The greater part of the inscription is taken up with an account of the exploits of Gaṅgarāja. The record seems to conclude with the statement that Adhyātmī-Bālacandra, disciple of Nayakīrti, made a Jain temple, a great *śāsana* or inscription, a group of epitaph and a series of tanks and ponds in memory of his *guru*.[103]

King Ballāla II thus gave the village Bammeyanahalli for the temple of Pārśvanātha, set-up by Acalādevī and granted the village Bekka for the worship and the upkeep of the Caturviṁśati-Tīrthaṅkara Basadi at Śravaṇbeḷgoḷa. Further, in AD 1176 a Jain temple was built by a Jain merchant who called it Vīra-ballāla Jinālaya in honour of the king, and king Vīra Ballāla I granted it a village.[104] The kingdom was organized "upon a footing of peace and prosperity and the king assumed for the first time the titles of independent royalty."[105]

About twenty years later, in AD 1195, Nāgadeva, the minister

---

102. R. Narasiṁhachar, *op. cit.*, p. 60.

103. *Ibid.*

104. B.A. Saletore, *op. cit.*, p. 150.

105. S.R. Sharma, *op. cit.*, p. 42.

and *pattanaswāmī* of Ballāla II a discible of Nayakīrti, built the Nagara Jinālaya. The king Ballāla II made a grant to this temple built at his own capital Dvārasamudra for feeding the Jain ascetics and bringing on the eight-fold worship of the temple.[106] Nāgadeva built in AD 1195 a dancing hall and a stone pavement in front of the god Pārśva at Śravaṇbeḷgoḷa.[107] Nāgadeva, having made a tank under the name of Nāgasamudra and a garden, granted it alongwith certain worship of Gommaṭeśvara. The period of these records may be about AD 1200.[108]

An inscription on the pedestal of the image in the Śāntiśvara temple at Jinanāthapura near Śravaṇbeḷgoḷa say that he set-up the god and handed over the charge of the temple of Sāgaranandi. Another inscription at the same village, dated AD 1213, is engraved on a Jain tomb.[109]

KING NARASIṀHA II (AD 1120-35)

In the thirteenth century AD too, the ardour of the citizens for the cause of the *anekāntamata* never flagged. Paduma-Seṭṭi was a typical *bhavya*, endowed with all good qualities and devoted to the stories relating to the *sad-dharma* (i.e., Jainism) delighting in the four kinds of gifts.[110] King Narasiṁha II followed the policy of his father king Ballāla II. The inscription no. 186 at Śravaṇbeḷgoḷa ascribes paramount titles to him and records that in AD 1231 the king confirmed the grant made by one Śrī Gommaṭa Seṭṭi as a perpetual endowment for the worship of Gommaṭeśvara and the 24 *tīrthaṅkaras*.[111]

NARASIṀHA III (AD 1254-92)

Similarly king Narasiṁha III, the grandson of king Narasiṁha II and the son of Someśvara, also confirmed the grants of land

106. *Mysore Arachaeological Report*, 1923, pp. 36-40.
107. B.A. Saletore, *op. cit.*, p. 150.
108. R. Narasiṁhachar, *op. cit.*, p. 61.
109. K.S. Chandrasekhar Aiyar, *op. cit.*, p. 21.
110. B.A. Saletore, *op. cit.*, p. 182.
111. *Ibid.*, p. 182.

made by Śambhudeva and others with a view to provide milk-offerings for Gommaṭeśvara and the 24 *tīrthaṅkaras* temple situated in the enclosure on the Vindhyagiri hill.[112]

Purchasing land and freeing it from all obligations and bestowing it as charitable endowment for the Jain institutions was a noteworthy feature of the times.[113]

Likewise, in AD 1280 during the reign of the same monarch, all the farmers of Arakottara were exempted from all the obligations of money payments pertaining to the *basadi* of that locality and were granted the water-rate, alms, house tax, poll-tax, the *nicandi* and other dues as well for the same basadi.[114]

The same procedure was adopted in AD 1282 when all the Jewel merchants (*māṇikya nagaraṅgal*) of Śravaṇbeḷgoḷa desired to make some endowments. Together with the royal *guru* Nemicandra Paṇḍita's disciple Bālacandradeva, these merchants, who belonged to the Balātkāra *gaṇa* and who were the disciples of the Mahāmaṇḍalācārya Māghanandi purchased wet land from Bālacandradeva and gave it along with other lands for the worship of the god Ādi of the Nagara Jinālaya.[115]

This king Narasiṁha III and his brother Rāmanātha of AD 1254-95, who ruled over a section of the Hoyasala Empire, were devout Jains. We have evidence about king Narasiṁha III's piety as a Jain in the Pārśvanātha Basadi stone record found at Bastihalli near Halebid, the Hoyasala capital. The spiritual adviser of this king was famous Jain saint Māghanandi Siddhānta of the Balātkāra *gaṇa*, i.e., section. This is gathered from the Benneguda inscription at Halebiḍ dated AD 1265 and the Nagara Jinālaya inscription at Śravaṇbeḷgoḷa dated AD 1282. In this inscription at Śravaṇbeḷgoḷa, the saint is styled as *mahāmaṇḍalācārya* i.e., best of the *ācāryas*, royal *guru* to the

112. B.L. Rice, *E.C.*, vol. II, S.B. No. 246, p. 104.

113. B.A. Saletore, *op. cit.*, p. 182.

114. R. Narasiṁhachar, *E.C.*, vol. II, S.B., Ch. 84, p. 10.

115. *Ibid.*, *E.C.*, II, No. 334, pp. 141-42.

Hoyasala king and the emperor of philosophers.[116]

King Narasiṁha III granted village Kallangere together with fourteen hamlets attached to it to the saint Māghanandi for maintaining the Jain temple called "Trikūṭaratnatraya-Śāntinātha-Jinālaya." This temple was called "Trikūṭaratnatraya-Narasiṁha Jinālaya;" obviously as a mark of esteem and loyalty to the king. An inscription on the pedestal of the *gaṇadhara* image in the enclosure around Gommaṭa on the larger hill at Śravaṇbeḷgoḷa, recording a grant for Gommaṭa in AD 1279 by a subordinate of the Maha-pasayila Tirumappa and a fragmentary Tamil inscription at the Kadalur pond, recording a grant for the god Surabhūpati of the place, may also belong to his reign.[117]

BALLĀLA III (AD 1292-1343)

During the reigns of the last two Hoyasala monarchs, viz., Ballāla III (AD 1292-1343) and Ballāla IV (AD 1343-45) Jainism did not get as much royal patronage as it had received during the reigns of all other Hoyasala kings from AD 1006. Yet there is ample proof to show that Jainism still dominated in Karnataka in the reigns of these two rulers.[118] The various Hoyasala kings thus not only built many Jain temples but gave a large number of grants to them.

THE VIJAYANAGARA RULERS

Although the rulers of the Vijayanagara Empire were devotees of Viṣṇu and Śiva, they not only tolerated Jainism but encouraged it as well. The finest example of this noble tradition of tolerance is found in the inscription no. 344 at Śravaṇbeḷgoḷa which refers to a reconciliation brought by the Vijayanagara King Bukka-Rāya I (AD 1355 to 1377) between the *bhavya*s (Jains)

---

116. V.A. Sangave, *op. cit.*, p. 45.
117. K.S. Chandrashekhar Aiyar, *Arachaeological Report*, 1989-90, p. 28.
118. V.A. Sangave, *op. cit.*, p. 45.

and the *bhaktas* (Vaiṣṇavas) in AD 1368.[119]

It opens with a verse in praise of the Śrīvaiṣṇava apostle Rāmānujācārya and proceeds to say that when the Jains made petition to the king about the injustice meted out to them by the Vaiṣṇavas, the king pacified the Jains by taking their hands and placed these in the hand of the Śrīvaiṣṇavas of the 18 *nāḍus* (i.e., districts) including the *ācāryas* of Śrīraṅgam, Tirupati, Kāñcī and Melkoṭe and other Vaiṣṇava sects, and declared, at the same time, that there was no difference between the Vaiṣṇava and the Jain *darśanas*, i.e., creeds, decreed thus.[120]

The Jain creed is, as before, entitled to the privileges of five great musical instruments and the *kalaśa* or vase. If loss or advancement should be caused to the Jain creed through the Vaiṣṇavas, the latter will kindly deem it as a loss or advancement caused to their own creed. The Śrīvaiṣṇavas will, to this effect, kindly set-up a *śāsana* or inscription in all the basadis or temples of the kingdom. For as long as the sun and moon endure the Vaiṣṇavas, creed will continue to protect the Jain creed. The Vaiṣṇavas and the Jains are one body and should not be viewed as different.

Tatayya of Tirupati will, out of the money levied from every Jain house throughout the kingdom, appoint twenty servants as bodyguards for the god at Beḷagoḷa and repair ruined Jain temples. He who transgresses this decree shall be a traitor to the king, a traitor to the *saṅgha* and the *samudāya*.[121]

The details given of the administration of this unique edict seem to show that the king Bukka Rāya I was even partial to the *bhavyas*, as the Jains were called, and threw the burden of their protection upon his coreligionists, the *bhaktas* as the Vaiṣṇavas

---

119. B.L. Rice, *E.C.*, vol. VIII, T1, 197, pp. 206-07.

120. B.A. Saletore, *op. cit.*, pp. 288-89.

121. *Ibid.*, p. 289.

were called.[122]

Their attitude in regard to Jainism was by no means different. It is evident that King Bukka Rāya I exercized a great influence on his successors. Hence we find that kings, queens and members of the royal family gave unstinted patronage to the cause of the *anekāntamata* in the Empire. It is interesting to note in this connection that the impulse to support the cause of the *jina dharma* came from the queens of Vijayanagara, one of whom was a Jain herself. For, according to inscription no. 337 of about AD 1410 at Śravaṇbeḷgoḷa, Bhīmādevī, the queen of Devarāya I (AD 1406-22) of Vijaynagara, was a disciple of the Jain teacher Abhinava-Cārukīrti-Paṇḍitācārya and she set-up an image of Śāntinātha *tīrthaṅkara* in the Mangayi-*basadi* at the village Śravaṇbeḷgoḷa.[123] It may be noted that this temple had been built in about AD 1325 by Mangayi of Beḷagoḷa, "a crest jewel of royal dancing girls" and a lay disciple of Abhinava-Cārukīrti Paṇḍita of the same place.[124]

Queen Bhīmādevī may have been responsible for the generous attitude of king Devarāya I (AD 1406-22) towards the Jain *gurus*. What seems certain is that the Vijayanagara ruler showed his great concern about the famous centre of the Jains — Śravaṇbeḷgoḷa. Hence around AD 1420 he ordered the gift of the village Belame in Mepinad for a *vṛtti* for the worship of Gommaṭasvāmī of Beḷagoḷa. The great minister Baica Dannayaka carried it out of at royal behest.[125] Obviously, following the tradition of his noble father, Prince Harihara, as we shall narrate in latter's context, gave magnificent gifts to the *basadi* at Kanakagiri.

Further, inscription no. 253 of AD 1422 at Śravaṇbeḷgoḷa refers to Iruguppa, the general of Vijayanagara king Harihara II (AD

122. S.R. Sharma, *op. cit.*, p. 44.

123. B.L. Rice, *E.C.*, vol. II, Introd., pp. 29, 337 and p. 144.

124. *Ibid.*, p. 145.

125. *Ibid.*, *E.C.*, vol V, MJ 58, p. 273.

1377 to 1404) and records the grant made by him of Beḷgoḷa, together with a grove and a tank built by him, for Gommaṭeśvara. An inscription in that city tells us that Bukkavve, the queen of Vīra Harihara Rāya (i.e., Harihara Rāya II) gave a gift to the *basadi* built by General Irugappa in the cyclic year Īśvara AD 1397.[126]

A large portion of this inscription mentions the pedigree and praises of Iruguppa. He was a Sanskrit scholar and wrote the metrical lexicon *Nānārtharatnamālā*. Two of the other inscriptions found in Karnataka and bearing the dates AD 1382 and AD 1387 contain praises of Paṇḍitācārya and a third inscription, dated AD 1385 states that Iruguppa who adhered to the doctrine of the Jain teacher Siṁhanandi built the stone temple of Kumthu-Jinanātha at Vijayanagara.[127]

We may mention two more names of high officials of this age in order to complete the account of men of action of early Vijayanagara history; one is that of Masanahalli Kampana Gauḍa, the great lord of Bayinad. He was the disciple of Paṇḍitadeva. He granted the village of Totahalli situated in his own Bayinad in AD 1424 for the worship of Gommaṭa-nāthasvāmī of Beḷgoḷa.[128]

It is interesting to note that *mahāmastakābhiṣeka* of Bāhubali image was performed every 12 years right from AD 981. The following is the brief account of *mahāmaskābhiṣeka*. It is noteworthy that the 1000th one i.e., *sahastrābhiṣeka* took place on 21 February, 1981. The then Prime Minister Mrs. Indira Gandhi was present for this ceremony.

MAHĀMASTAKĀBHIṢEKA OF BĀHUBALI

HISTORICAL TRADITION

The great general Cāmuṇḍarāya not only installed the colossal image of Gommaṭeśvara on the top of the Vindhyagiri hill at

---

126. B.A. Saletore, *op. cit.*, p. 302.
127. R. Narasiṁhachar, *E.C.*, vol. II, *S.B.*, p. 64.
128. B.L. Rice, *E.C.*, vol. IV, Hg. 1, p. 65.

Śravaṇbeḷgoḷa but also performed the *Pratiṣṭhapanā Mahotsava,* i.e., the great ceremony of consecration of the image, on Sunday, 13 March, AD 981 in accordance with the detailed rituals prescribed in Jain scriptures for the purpose and on a very grand scale befitting both, the huge size of the image and the extremely high status of the *yajamāna,* i.e., the host. As a part of the sacred ritual, the ceremony of *pañcāmr̥tābhiṣeka,* i.e., bathing of the image with five liquids, viz., milk, curds, ghee or clarified butter, saffron and water, which is also known as *mastakabhiṣeka,* i.e., the head anointing ceremony, was performed with grandeur, dignity and solemnity in keeping with the extraordinary nature of the occasion. Later on, this festival of performing *mastakābhiṣeka* was continued and it came to be termed as *mahāmastakābhiṣeka,* since it used to be performed only at certain conjunctions of the heavenly bodies at intervals of several years and at a great cost.[129]

Written records are available to establish the *mahāmastakābhiṣeka* ceremonies having taken place in the following years. Inscription no. 231 of about AD 1500, seems to fix the amounts to be paid to the officiating priests, the stone-masons, carpenters and other workmen, and for the supply of milk and curds. The earliest reference to *mastakābhiṣeka* is found in inscription no. 254 (105) of AD 1398, which states that Paṇḍitarāya had it performed seven times. The poet Pañcabana refers to an anointment caused to be performed by one Śāntavarṇi in AD 1612. Anantakavi mentions another one conducted at the expense of Viśālākṣa-Paṇḍita, the Jain minister of the Mysore king Cikkadevarāja Oḍeyar, in AD 1677 and Śāntarāja Paṇḍita, attributes a third one having been performed by the Mysore king Kr̥ṣṇarāja Oḍeyar III in about AD 1825. Several further references are available to indicate a similar ceremony having been performed viz., in AD 1827 as per inscription no. 223 (98) in AD 1871 according to the *Indian Antiquary* (II, p. 129)

129. K.A. Nilakanthasastri, *op. cit.*, p. 18.

in AD 1887 in the harvest field (for may, AD 1887). The anointment performed in AD 1887 was at the expense of the Kolhāpur Svāmī, who is said to have spent Rs. 30,000 for the purpose.[130]

In the twentieth century the *mahāmastakābhiṣeka* ceremonies were held on the following days :

1. 30 March, 1910
2. 15 March, 1925
3. 26 February, 1940
4. 5 March, 1953, and
5. 30 March, 1967
6. 22 February, 1981 — 1000th Anniversary
7. 19 December, 1993.

The glorified *mahāmastakābhiṣeka* ceremony was held on 22 February, AD 1981. It would be worthwhile to note the important features of these six ceremonies. An extraordinary significance of historical nature has been attached to this ceremony as it marks the 1000th anniversary of the consecration of the image of Bāhubali, which was performed on Sunday, 13 March, AD 1981. This historic festival of worldwide importance was arranged on a huge scale and for the first time the then Prime Minister of India, Smt. Indira Gandhi, along with other Central Ministers and Chief Ministers of the States, attended the celebrations on 21 February, 1981 and showered flowers from the helicopter on Bhagvān Bāhubali.[131] The statue completed a thousand years of its phenomenal existence in February 1981 and this occasion was celebrated by the State Government and devotees on a grand scale during which millions of devotees and tourists gathered in this town to witness the event.

The last grand ceremony of the *mahābhiṣeka* of lord Bāhubali

---

130. R. Narasiṁhachar, *E.C.*, vol. II, S.B., pp. 18-19.

131. T.G. Kalghatgi (editor) Articles (R.S. Surendra), *Gommatesvara Commemoration Volume* (World's greatest sculptural colossus completes a thousand years), p. 95.

image at Śravaṇbeḷgoḷa took place on 19 December, 1993 on a grand scale by the hands of Sahu Ashok Kumar Jain.[132]

In nutshell, the period from AD 981 to 1565 was the golden era in the history of Śravaṇbeḷgoḷa because royal families, their rulers, royal ladies supported the cause of Jainism and spent money lavishly for the development of Śravaṇbeḷgoḷa, built many temples, erected *mānastambh*s and granted perpetual lands for the maintenance of these temples. During this period, the rulers of Gaṅga, Hoyasala, Vijayanagara dynasty continued their royal support to Śravaṇbeḷgoḷa and the fame of Gommaṭeśvara reached to each corner of India. Cāmuṇḍarāya made outstanding contribution to the world culture by installing Bāhubali's image at Śravaṇbeḷgoḷa manifestation of human culture for thw whole world.

132. V.A. Sangave, *op. cit.*, p. 99.

4

Humcha
The Capital of Santara Dynasty and a Seat of Goddess Padmāvatī

NEXT to Śravaṇbeḷgoḷa, is Humcha, a sacred place and abode of Goddess Padmāvatī, a *yakṣiṇī* of Pārśvanātha, who occupies an important place in the Jain history. From the third century BC to the ninth century AD, Śravaṇbeḷgoḷa played an important role in spreading the Jain culture in south Karnataka but from the ninth century onwards, Humcha became the pivotal centre of Jain culture because Santara rulers made Humcha their capital and these rulers and their queens were ardent devotees of Jainism, they built a great number of Jain temples at Humcha and surrounding it. They ruled this area from the eighth to the twelfth centuries AD and spread Jainism in south Karnataka. Many contemporary inscriptions speak of the glory of Humcha. They were subordinate to the Cāḷukya, the Hoyasala and the Vijayanagara rulers, and were finally subdued by the Keladi chiefs. The King Jinadatta, one of the rulers of the Santara dynasty, made Humcha his capital and built royal palaces, public offices, lakes, Jain temples and *maṭha*, etc.

While Śravaṇbeḷgoḷa is famous for the colossal image of Bāhubali, Humcha is famous for the goddess Padmāvatī. It is a holy place which is visited by lakhs of devotees throughout the year. According to a local legend, Jinadatta had come from north Mathurā and settled here, had iron converted into gold with touching it with the golden statue of goddess Padmāvatī. This resulted in his getting enormous wealth with which he constructed this town and a temple for *devī* Padmāvatī and ruled from here.

A great number of Jain devotees, even today, visit Humcha every year for seeking blessings from Goddess Padmāvatī. There are so many fine and beautiful architectural Jain temples at Humcha. The temple of Padmāvatī is the main attraction for the Jain followers. Besides, Humcha is also a seat of Śrī Devendrakīrti Bhaṭṭāraka Svāmījī. The historians and epigraphists also like this place because there are so many old historical monuments and inscriptions belonging to the eighth century AD onwards. An earnest attempt has, therefore, been made in this chapter to bring out the religious and historical significance of Humcha and its contribution in spreading Jainism in southern Karnataka. Humcha is a temple city in south India.

Description of Humcha

Humcha, at present, is situated in Śimogā district of Karnataka State. Humcha, a capital city of Santara, was first included in Nagar *tāluka* and at present it is located in Hosanagara *tāluka*. Humcha or Humbuja, a village about 22 miles to the north of Tīrthallī, situated at a distance of about 60 km. south-west of Śimogā city and 21 km. south-east of Hosanagar, and is a holy headquarter.

The Derivation of the Name Humcha

It is interesting to see the origin of name Humcha. It has been variously called Hombucha, Pomburchchha, Pattipomburchcha and Pombuchcha in old inscriptions. It was the capital of a principality founded by Jinadatta. The existing ruins of Humcha, situated at the foot of the Bileśvara hill, indicate the site of a large town. The name Hombucha means a golden bit. A local legend says that Jinadatta was asked by goddess Padmāvatī to touch her image with his horse's bit (i.e., the part of the bridle in horse's mouth) and on his doing so it was instantly changed into gold and brought him good fortune.[1]

Foundation of Santara Dynasty at Humcha

Humcha was once a historical capital, adorned with royal palaces, offices and temples having old inscriptions also. How Jinadatta conquered the area around Humcha is very interesting. B.A. Saletore, a historian, narrated the account regarding the foundation of Santara dynasty at Humcha in the following words:

> With Jinadatta Raya the Cantas or the Santaras, who were of the Ugra Vamsa, were the worshippers of the goddess Padmavati, boon lords of Northern Madhura, appear for the first time in the Nagar Taluka with Pattipombuccha as their capital. Now, we know that till the end of 8th century AD that city was under the Alupas. The fact that Jinadatta Raya made it as his capital, suggests that he wrested it from the Alupas somewhere in the 9th century AD. Not content with making Pattipombuccha their own, the Santaras made an attack on the capital of Alvakheda itself, Udayavara thereby showing the vigour which characterized the Santaras and the utter helplessness of the Alupas.[2]

The era from AD 800 to 920 was a period of confusion. Jinadatta founded a new dynasty at Humcha during this period. Jinadatta's fore-fathers were north Indians and how Jinadatta came to Śimogā district is narrated by B.L. Rice in the following words:

> The earliest mention of these kings is in the time of the Chalukya Vinayadita, the end of the seventh century. With the approval of the brother's son of the Chanter King Jaya Sangraha, who was lord of the city Madhura encircled by the Kalindi, and of the *Ugravamsa* but connected with the Yadu-Vamsa by marriage; a grant was then made by the wife of the Pandi Yuvaraja and it is said to be under the protection of "the

1. P. Gururaja Bhatt, *Antiquities of South Kanara*, p. 4.
2. B.A. Saletore, *Ancient Karnataka, History of Tuluva*, vol. 1, Poona, 1936, p. 224.

> three hundreds of the children of the house of the Chantas." That this was the original form of the name appears also from Sk 283 of about 830 AD, where too the King is said to be a Chanta.[3]

The following account is furnished by inscriptions:

> According to No. 35 and 48, the Santara Kingdom was founded by Jinadatta Raya, lord of the northern Madhura (Mathura), who was of the *Ugravamsa*. The Santaras are identified with Pattipomburchea, the modern Hombucha or Humcha in Nagar *taluka* as their capital, which previously may have been in the possession of the Aluvas. The remote Porgenitor of the line was Raha, from whom had descended Sahakara, who became a Cannibal. He was the father of Jinadatta, who escaped from him in disgust and came to the South, bringing an image of the Jain goddess Padmāvatī. She bestowed on him the power to transmute iron into gold, as exemplifed in his horse's bit being turned into golden bit on touching it with her image. Thus aided, he subdued the local chiefs around, and established his capital at Pomburcha (supposed to mean golden bit) and took the name Santara. His descendants the Santaras ruled over the Santalige Thousand which corresponds generally with the present Tirthahalli *taluka* and neighbouring parts. Jinadatta conquered the country Southwards as far as Kalasa (Mudgere *taluka*) and Northwards fortified Govardhangiri (Sagar *taluka*), which he named after the famous hill near Muttra in the north of Inida.[4]

The Origin and Early History of the Santaras of Santalige-1000

It is known from a number of inscriptions discovered in the western parts of the Śimogā and Cikmangalūr districts that this region was carved out into a subdivision bearing the name of Santalige-1000 and that from about the middle of the ninth century for over 400 years, this subdivision was subject to the rule of a family known as the Santarānvaya. Prior to the emergence of the Santaras as a ruling house, the region of

---

3. B.L. Rice, *Mysore and Coorg, From the Inscriptions*, London, 1909, p. 138.
4. B.L. Rice, *op. cit.*, pp. 138-39.

Santalige-1000 which fell within the bounds of the famous division of Banavāsī-12,000, was under the sway of the Alupas of Alvakheda-6,000 (i.e., the present-day district of South Kanara), its headquarters being located at the ancient city of Pombucchapura, which is the same as modern Humcha, Hosanagar *tāluka*, Śimogā district and which was also known by the names of Kanakapura and Patti.[5] We learn from the inscriptions discovered in South Kanara that some of the early Alupa rulers bore the epithet of Pattiodeya as a mark of their sovereignty over the Santalige region.[6]

A study of inscriptions shows that once a dynasty established itself as a stable power in the region and during its sway, legendary accounts were woven round the facts of its origin. The two records in question are:

1. Humcha (Nagar *tāluka*, Śimogā district) inscription of Nanni-Santara, belonging to AD 1077-78.[7]
2. Danasale (Tirthahalli *tāluka*, Śimogā district) inscription of Tribhuvanamalla Santara, belonging to AD 1103.[8]

Of these, Humcha inscription, which gives the legendary narrative in a greater detail, endows the progenitor of this family, Rāhā by name, with the epithets of *uttara-madhura-adhīśvara* (Lord of northern Madhura, i.e., modern Mathurā in Uttar Pradesh) and *ugra-vaṁśodbhavan* (i.e., born Ugra Vaṁśa). It then states that Rāhā played a victorious role in the *Mahābhārata* fought at Kurukṣetra and that in appreciation of his valour, Lord Nārāyaṇa (i.e., Viṣṇu-Kr̥ṣṇa) bestowed upon him the insignias of *ekaśaṅkha* and *vānara-dhvaja*. Throughout their known history, the Santaras professed the Jain faith and Rāhā

5. B.L. Rice, *Epigraphica Carnatica*, "Inscriptions in the Kadur District," vol. VI, Bangalore, 1901, SK., 103.
6. B.L. Rice, *Epigraphica Indica*, vol. IX, p. 19.
7. B.L. Rice, *Epigraphica Carnatica*, "Inscriptions in the Shimoga District," vol. VIII, Bangalore, 1904, No. 35.
8. *Ibid.*, T 1.192.

is described in the Danasale inscription as belonging to the Pārśvanātha Santara. The names of the immediate successors of Rāhā are not known and the Humcha inscription avers that many rulers had come and gone before the next Santara ruler, Sahakara by name, ascended the throne. Sahakara, according to the Humcha epigraph, was a cannibal by vow (*atam-naramamsa-vratan-age*) and had Siriyādevī as his queen. Both the Humcha and Danasale inscriptions mention Sahakara's son Jinadatta was the early members of this family, whose historicity is yet to be established by contemporaneous epigraphical evidence.[9]

Jinadatta — The Founder of Santara Dynasty at Humcha

Jinadatta was the most important ruler of the Santara Dynasty. Jinadatta was like a lion on the great mountain, the celebrated Ugrānvaya, and, all the kings in the world were just like deer before him. The particulars of this legendary achievement of Jinadatta are found given in the Humcha inscription as follows:

> While on his way to the South, Jinadatta encountered and killed the demon Simha-Lanchchhana. He then fought with and killed the demon Andhaka-Surai, he freed the fort of Kunda from the clutches of the demons Kara-Karadushana and goddess Padmāvatī, who pleased with this achievement of Jinadatta, came to stay on the Lokhe tree in the city of Kanakapura, also known as Pombuchchapura, took upon herself the secondary name of Lokhiyabbe and declared that city shall thenceforth be the headquarters (Rajya-Sthana) of Jinadatta's kingdom.

Only one fact emerges out of these unhistorical statements, namely that the Santaras were devout worshippers of the goddess Padmāvatī. This is substantiated by their distinctive epithet, *Padmāvatī-Labdha-Vara-Prāsāda*. The claim that Jinadatta, even if we were to assume that he was a historical figure, gained

9. T.T. Sharman (editor), Articles (Dr. K.V. Ramesh and Madhav N. Katt), *Quarterly Journal of the Mythic Society* (The origin and early history of the Santaras of Santalige-1000, XIVII) Bangalore, 1966-69, pp. 26-27.

control over the city of Pombuccapura is untenable, for as is shown by the inscription, the city was under the effective sway of the Alupas of South Kanara prior to the middle of the ninth century. On the same ground, the claim that Jinadatta was the first Santara ruler of Santalige-1000 also deserves to be dismissed.[10]

The Danasale inscription states that on gaining control over the city of Pombuccapura with the blessing of Padmāvatī, Jinadatta took upon himself the secondary name of Santara and that his family which was till then known as the Ugrānvaya came to be called Santarānvaya and also *balikkam-ugrānvayam santarānvayabhidhānamam padedudu.*

Jinadatta's Successor

We learn from the Humcha inscriptions that Jinadatta was followed by a number of rulers, who are not named, before Śrīkeśī and Jayakeśī ascended the Santara throne. From their being mentioned together, it may be concluded that they were brothers and in view of Jayakeśī having left behind an inscription of his reign, it may be considered as the earliest known record of that family. Engraved in inscriptions of the middle of the ninth century, it refers to the reign of Rāṣṭrakūṭa Nṛpatuṅga Amoghavarṣa (i.e., Amoghavarṣa I (AD 814-77) and states that Jageśī (i.e., Hayakeśī) of Caṇṭa-Rāja-kula, i.e., Santarānvaya was administering the entire Santalige region. This Jageśī may be safely be identified as Jayakeśī, the successor of Śrīkeśī. Like his father, Raṇakeśī, he has also not left behind any records of his reign. As a matter of fact, there is a break in the genealogical account given in the Humcha inscription which merely states that Raṇakeśī was followed by a number (Palabar) of rulers before the Santara throne was occupied by Vikrama Santara.[11]

10. *Ibid.*, pp. 27-28.
11. B.L. Rice, *EP. Carn.*, vol. VII, SK. 283.

Vikrama Santara

Vikrama was the most powerful of the early Santara rulers. The Humcha record states that, he had performed the *Hiraṇyagarbha* sacrifice and had given away much by way of gifts. He consolidated the claims of his family over Santalige-1000 by eliminating or driving out all rival chieftains and became the sole master of the kingdom[12] which was bounded on the south by the river Sulam, on the west by Tavanasi, and on the north by Bandage. By these courageous acts he earned the laudatory epithets of Kandukācārya and Danavinoda. He had as his queen Lakṣmīdevī, daughter of Kāmadeva, the ruler of Banavāsī.[13]

Two inscriptions, one from Humcha belonging to AD 898-99[14] and other from Salur, belonging to AD 902-03 are to be assigned to the reign of Vikrama Santara. Of these, the Humcha inscription which names him as *Tolapuruṣa Vikaramāditya Santara,* reveals that he had also performed the *Tulāpuruṣadāna* and refers him to belong to the reign of Kannara-Vallabha, i.e., Rāṣṭrakūṭa Kṛṣṇa II (AD 880-915). The Salur inscription which also belong to the reign of Kṛṣṇa II, mentions one Chanaliga as an officer serving under Vikramāditya-Santara. We have seen above that Jayakeśī was feudatory of Rāṣṭrakūṭa Amoghavarṣa I. It is, therefore, reasonable to suppose that the Santaras, ever since they made their appearance in the middle of the ninth century, owed their allegiance to this imperial dynasty.[15]

We may refer here to the three other inscriptions from Sorature, Honnali Tāluka, Śimogā district and belonging to AD 933-34. These refer to the reign of *Suvarṇavarṣa,* who is obviously the same as Rāṣṭrakūṭa Govinda IV (AD 930-35) and mention

---

12. B.L. Rice, *EP. Carn.*, vol. VIII, No. 35.
13. *Ibid.*, No. 35.
14. *Ibid.*, No. 60.
15. *Ibid.*, *EP. Carn.*, vol. VIII, SK. 284.

one Chaladānk-Rāma Santara as the governor of Banavāsī 12,000.[16]

With the information and knowledge gathered so far it is not possible to say, if this Santara is to be identified with Vikrama or with one of his immediate successors. However it can be assigned that by AD 933-34 the Santaras had gained much by their subservience to the Rāṣṭrakūṭas.[17]

Successors of Vikrama Santara

According to Humcha inscription of AD 1077-78, also discussed earlier, Vikrama Santara was succeeded by Chagi-Santara, his son by his queen Lakṣmīdevī. No inscriptions of his reign could be located. But the Humcha inscription states that, he had got a tank excavated (named Chagi-Samudra) after him and his queen, by whom he had a son named Vīra-Santara, was the daughter of Ranañjaya, the Alupa ruler of South Kanara.

The same record states that Chagi-Santara was succeeded by Vīra-Santara about whom the only other points mentioned in records are that he married Jakaladevī, daughter of a certain Śānti Varmā[18] and that he had two sons, Kannara-Santara and Kavadeva Kannara-Santara, who probably did not live long enough to ascend the throne, appears to have died without any issue and was succeeded by Kavadeva, whose queen, Chandaladevī, was the daughter of Vīra-Bayalnātha.[19]

Tyāgī-Santara, the son and successor of Kavadeva, married the daughter of Kadamba, and Harivarmā, Nagaladevī by name and had by her a son, Nanni-Santara. Arikesarī, the ruler of Pallasige, gave his daughter Sirīyadevī in marriage to Nanni-Santara. An inscription from Barur, Shikaripura Tāluka, Śimogā district may be assigned. This record belonging to AD 1027 refers

16. B.L. Rice, *EP. Carn.*, vol. VII, HI, pp. 21-23.
17. T.T. Sharman, *op. cit.*, p. 31.
18. *Ibid.*
19. B.L. Rice, *EP. Carn.*, vol. VI, Introd, p. 3.

to the reign of Annaladeva among whose numerous epithets Nanni-Santara also occurs.[20]

Political Status of the Santara

It is essential to see the political status of the Santaras. They started their career as the feudatories of the Rāṣṭrakūṭas. It is likely that they continued to acknowledge Rāṣṭrakūṭa suzerainty since AD 973, when the Rāṣṭrakūṭas made way for Cāḷukyas of Kalyāṇī. In the absence of epigraphical evidence, it is difficult to say whether the Santaras automatically transferred their allegiance to the Cāḷukyas or exploiting the changing conditions, declared independence. It is known, from inscriptions that, they served as the feudatories of the Cāḷukyas from at least the middle of the eleventh century.

It would have been difficult for a minor power to have existed outside the pale of imperial protection and it may not be far from the truth if we suggest that the Santaras became the subordinates to the Cāḷukyas immediately after the latter replaced the Rāṣṭrakūṭas as masters of the Karnataka empire.

The Santaras and Tuluva (Alupa)

B.A. Saletore gives the following account regarding the relations between Santara and Alupa's dynasty. Alupas were first the masters of Humcha territory. Later, Jinadattarāya wrested Humcha area from Alupas in the ninth century.

> With Jinadatta Raya, the Cantas or Santaras, who were of the *Ugravamsa,* and worshippers of the Goddess Padmavati, boon lords of northern Madhura, appear for the first time in the Nagar Taluka with Pattipombuccha as their capital. Now, we know that till the end of eighth century AD, that city was under the Alupas. The fact that Jinadattaraya made it, as his capital suggest that he wrested it from the Alupas somewhere in the ninth century AD. Not content with making Patti-Pombuccha their own, the Santaras made an attack on the capital of Alvakheda itself.

20. *Ibid.*, SK., 53.

> Vadyavara, thereby, showing the vigour which characterized the Santaras and the utter helplessness of the Alupas.[21]

This supposition of ours is proved by the non-appearance of the name Patti-Pombucca, henceforth in the Alupa records after the ninth century AD. It is not surprising that Patti-Pombucca was lost by the Alupas. The Tamil menace from the South, the Rāṣṭrakūṭa trouble in the north and the aggressive designs of Jinadattarāya from over the *ghāṭs* — all these explain the blank in the history of the Alupas after Cirtravāhana II for about 120 years.[22]

We are concerned here with the identification of Aluva Ranañjaya, Banki Alva, and the Aluva king whose daughter Acala (Bucala) Devī was given in marriage to Biruga Vīra-Santara. We have nine inscriptions of Trailokyamalla Vīra Santaradeva ranging from AD 1060 to AD 1070.[23] He may been identified with Biruga Vīra Santara. His first two sons were called Bhujabala and Nanni. Now a Bhujabala occurs in a record in AD 1066 and a Nanni in AD 1077.[24]

One of the queens of Biruga Vīra-Santara was Bijjala Devī, the daughter of Naolamba Narasinga Deva. The latter is mentioned as ruling over Kadambalige Thousand in AD 1050, and over the Kogari Five Hundred together with the Kadambalige Thousand in AD 1054. These records clearly prove that Narasinga Deva and Biruga Vīra Santara were contemporaries.

Biruga Vīra Santara's date may also be determined in the context of his third queen Vīra Mahādevī. She is called the younger sister of Cattala Devī, daughter of Rakkasa Gaṅga. Here daughter implies grand-daughter. The Gaṅga king Śrīpuruṣa slew Kaduvetti in battle in about AD 750 and Rakkasa Gaṅga's

---

21. B.L. Rice, *Mysore and Coorg*, p. 138.
22. B.L. Rice, *EP. Carn.*, vol. X, SP, 64, p. 281.
23. B.L. Rice, *EP. Carn.*, vol. VII, SK. p. 54.
24. *Ibid.*, SK. 63, p. 54.

grand-daughter Cattala Devī was married to Kaduvetti in about AD 1050 when she obtained the title of Kadava-Mahādevī. The Cattala Devī mentioned in the above grant could only have been the same Cattala Devī spoken of in the Santara genealogy. This again conclusively proves that the date AD 1060 assigned to Biruga Vīra Santara is correct.[25]

Temple Complex at Humcha and Royal Patronage

Even today, Humcha is, famous for the temples of Padamāvatī and Pārśvanātha. There are some Jain temples complexes which speak of the past glory of the site. These temples are not only old and historical but also have some 22 old inscriptions. These inscriptions belong to the period between the eighth to fifteenth centuries. Humcha being the capital of Santara dynasty, the Santara rulers and their queens probably built these Jain temples because they were followers of the Jain religion.

Even today, a number of Jain pilgrims visit this place every year. Some portions of the Padmāvatī temple have been renovated some years ago and remaining temples are old.

The following are some important old historical Jain temples at Humcha which have inscriptions and speak about the past glory of this place.

Pārśvanātha-Basadi

A large number of sculptures and architectures discarded from the ancient Jain foundations of differing dates gathered from within the town have been stored in the precincts of the temples of Pārśvanātha and Padmāvatī. Judging from their style they may reasonably be placed in the period of Jinadattarāya, for in context to the site they seem, not only relatively archaic but also very weather-worn, neither they are heavily adorned nor are the ornaments very detailed. They, moreover, possess traces of schematism characteristic of the

25. B.A. Saletore, *Ancient Karnataka, History of Tuluva,* vol. I, p. 230.

relatively earlier art of the Draviḍadeśa.[26]

The later Santara inscriptions credit Jinadattarāya with the foundation of *lokkiyabbe jina-gṛha* which was a temple attributed to Pārśvanātha with Padmāvatī as the tutelary deity. Lokiyabbe or Jakiyabbe Padmāvatī was also the patron goddess of the Santaras and the presiding deity of the city of Pombulcca, to whom Santara inscriptions refer to her time and again reverentially. A ceiling-piece containing the zoomorphic figure of the serpent king Dharaṇendra and a few sculptures assignable to the probable time of Jinadattarāya are the only relics of earlier art and architecture surviving in Humcha.[27]

Features of the Pārśvanātha Temple

This is an important temple. Pārśvanātha temple is on the right of Padmāvatī's temple. This Jain temple made of stone has a beautiful idol of Tīrthaṅkara Pārśvanātha inside it. The first temple of the early series is the southerly oriented *dvitala* of Pārśvanātha. The width of *vimāna* is only 7 ft 9 inches and the *maṇḍapa* 14 ft 8ū inches. It has most of the characteristics of the Bogara-basadi excepting the decorative enrichment. The wall plasters show some departure from the usual design, since it drops the upper *lasuna* member and retains only the bell-shaped member which is decorated with leaf motif, a feature adopted in later Karnataka temples. The *nāsikā*s of the *kūṭa*s and *śālā*s possess, in lieu of human heads, just lotus flowers in full bloom, which completely fill the *gaḍhā*.

The four pillars in the *mahāmaṇḍapa* are unadorned, but otherwise similar to their counterparts in the Bogara-basadi, including the *taraṅga-poṭika* (bracket capital). There is, moreover, a ceiling of *aṣṭa-dikpāla*s with a *yakṣa* figure in the central quadrant.

26. U.P. Shah, and M.A. Dhakey (editor), *Aspects of Jain Art and Architecture* (Santara Architecture), (Gujarat State, 1975), pp. 186-87.

27. M.A. Dhakey, "Santara Sculpture," *Journal of the Indian Society of Oriental Art*, New Series, vol. IV, Calcutta, 1971-72, p. 83.

Ceiling of this type became commoner about half a century later in the other styles in Karnataka, notably, those of Nolambavāḍī and Gaṅgavāḍī.[28]

There are two magnificent Pārśva images of the late ninth century carved to perfection, depicting the usual Jain mythological episode of the *Kamaṭhopasarga*, tormentation caused by Kamaṭha, kept inside the huge temple of Pārśva at Humcha of the eleventh century, in the spacious hall which has entrance from all the three sides. The icon of Jina Pārśva, the *mūlanāyaka*, seated in the *paryaṅkāsana*, is a feast to the eye.[29]

Padmāvatī as a Yakṣī of Pārśvanātha

Pārśvanātha was the 23rd Jain *tīrthaṅkara* and his worhsip was most popular in northern as well as south India prior to Mahāvīra. There were 24 Jain *tīrthaṅkara*s and every *tīrthaṅkara* had *yakṣa* and *yakṣī*. As earlier said, Humcha is the well-known abode of Padmāvatī who was *yakṣī* of Pārśvanātha. Therefore, it will not be out of place to give her detailed account here.

The worship of Padmāvatī was and has been very popular in Karnataka. Alongwith Ambikā, she seems to have asserted her importance soon after the first couple of centuries of the Christian era. We may venture to suggest here that the earliest temples of Padmāvatī may have been erected in Karnataka and her separate images carved and enshrined in them. In a recently found inscription of Kadamba Ravivarmā (AD 485-519) at Gudnapur near Banavāsī (Karwar District) reference is made to a grant registered for the temple Padmāvatī at Kallīgrāmam Padmavatyālyasya. Kadamba Ravivarmā is believed to have ruled during the last fifteen years of the fifth century.[30]

---

28. U.P. Shah and M.A. Dhakey, *op. cit.*, p. 189.
29. Nagarajaiah Hampa, *Jina Parsva temples in Karnataka*, Chap. IV, Second Phase, Hombuja, 1999, p. 13.
30. U.P. Shah, M.A. Dhakey, Editor, S. Setter, (The Classical Kannada Literature and the Digambara Jain Iconography), *Aspects of Jain Art and Architecture*, p. 40.

We may further presume that this temple may have existed at least in the beginning of the fifth century. However, the popularity enjoyed by the *yakṣī* and the number of temples built for her are borne out by the references made by Nemicandra.

The high images of Padmāvatī and also the miniature ones by the side of her lord are found in considerable number in Karnataka and in some Jain centres like Humcha. Her influence is far greater than that of her lord.[31]

Padmāvatī — A Jain Deity

Among the secondary deities of the Jain Pantheon chosen for individual adoration as an independent goddess, Padmāvatī, the *yakṣiṇī* of Pārśvanātha, stands foremost, being the most popular and widely invoked goddess in Karnataka. Though her cult might date from an earlier age[32], she frequently figures in the epigraphical sources all over Karnataka, roughly from the period of the tenth century AD. A large number of minor ruling families such as the Śilāhāras and the Rattas, and many a high official of the State of the Jain persuasion became votaries of this goddess and took pride in styling themselves as the favourite devotees of the deity, having adopted the title, *Padmāvatīdevī-labdhasvara-Prāsāda*, in their *praśasti*. This title is met with more frequently and prominently in the *praśasti* of these dignitaries, noted in the inscriptions of the eleventh to the thirteenth centuries AD in many parts of Karnataka. Thus this furnishes an idication in regard to the extent of popularity and the prevalence of the *yakṣī* in Karnataka.[33]

A well-known early instance of a family of subordinate chiefs, who adopted Padmāvatī as their tutelary goddess, are

---

31. *Ibid.*, p. 40.
32. B.L. Rice, *E. Carn.*, vol. VII, SH. 4.
33. P.B. Desai, *Jainism in South India and Some Jain Epigraphs*, Solapur, 1957, p. 171.

the Santaras, and how this took place is mysteriously narrated in the inscriptions furnishing their early history.

Jinadatta, a prince of ruling family of north India, we are told, came to the south with an image of Padmāvatī. The goddess blessed him with the power of transmuting iron into gold, and through her grace he founded the town of Pombuccapura, which became the capital of this kingdom. The goddess, it seems, chose her residence in a *Lakki* tree of the locality and therefore, came to be called Lakkiyabbe. These events may be referred to the ninth century AD, though the epigraphs describing them which are dated to the eleventh-twelfth century AD.[34]

Śrī Padmāvatī Temple at Humcha

Padmāvatī is the main deity of the Śrī-Kṣetra Humcha. It is believed that the idol of mother Padmāvatī was installed 1300 years before the King Jinadattarāya. An inscription of *S.* 991/ AD 1077 of Nanni Santara in the Pañcakūṭa Basadi at Humcha terms the dynasty as "Santara" and besides giving a legendary account of the earlier dynasties, recalls family history covering about two centuries and a half, beginning as it does with Jinadatta, claimed to be scion of Ugra *vaṁśa* who, through the grace of Yakkiabbe (*yakṣī* Padmāvatī) obtained the kingdom of Santalige-1000 and founded the town called Pombulccapura. The *yakṣī*, as the mythical account in the inscriptions goes on to say, came to live in the *Lakki* tree at Pombucca and secondarily named Lokkuyabbe (or Lokkiyabbe) on that account. The essence of the myth is that Jinadatta founded the temple of Padmāvatī in Pombucca.[35]

But the Kumsi inscription does mention Pombucca, the construction of Lokkiyabbe Jinageha (apparently by Jinadattarāya) and next to the grant of village Kumbsepura or

34. B.L. Rice, *E. Carn.*, vol. VII, No. 35, 48 and Mysore and Coorg from the inscriptions.

35. B.L. Rice, *E. Carn.*, vol. VIII, No. 35.

Kumbasika for the lustral ceremony of the Jina.[36] Now this Jinadattarāya can be none other than the one who is claimed to be the founder of the Santara dynasty and who, for that matter preceded Jayakeśī. The tradition linking Jinadattarāya, Lokkiya Basadi and Pombucca is so strong that it is mentioned in more than one Santara inscription, for example S. 984/AD 1062 of Vīra Santara's time on the pillar of the half of Pārśvanātha temple.

Santara tradition strongly suggests and moreover is, to hold that there existed a temple connected with the cult of Pārśva or Padmāvatī, assignable to about the earlier half of the ninth century, called the Lokkiya or the Nokkiya Basadi as referred to in the inscriptions.[37]

Features of the Padmāvatī Temple and Padmāvatī Deity

The Padmāvatī temple is situated in the compound of the Pārśvanātha temple. The annual *Navarātrī* festival here attracts a large number of people. Both the Padmāvatī temple and the Pārśvanātha temple appear to have been rebuilt of granite stone using a few materials of older Hoyasala and Cāḷukyan temples, particularly pillars and fine *toraṇa* doorway.[38]

There is an ancient *mānastambha* of 90 ft. height before the Padmāvatī temple. This *mānastambha* have the statues of the *yakṣa* and *tīrthaṅkara*. The door of the *garbhagṛha* is made of silver. The two beautiful images of goddess Padmāvatī are held on each side of the door of the *garbhagṛha*. There is another *sabhāmaṇḍapa* which is larger than first. There are two *dvārapālikas* which are of 6 ft. height held on the outer wall of the entrance door. These statues of *dvārapālikas* are made up of wood. There is also an ancient *dhvajastambha* made up of a stone in front of the Padmāvatī temple. There is a *Lakki* tree beyond the Padmāvatī temple. This blossoms throughout the year. There is also a statue of

36. *Ibid.*, No. 114.
37. M.A. Dhakey and B.L. Rice, *op. cit.*, p. 79, *E. Carn.*, vol. VIII, No. 47.
38. University of Mysore, *Annual Report of the Mysore Archaeological Department for the year* 1936, p. 40.

Jinadattarāya seated on the horse, and this statue is erected on the back at the right side of the Padmāvatī temple. Seven-hooded serpent images are also placed each side of the temple. The temple has been protected by a big wall surrounding it. The Padmāvatī Mandir is situated close to the Pārśvanātha Basadi. These two temples have enough space for *pradakṣiṇā*. There are also many monuments lying on the side of the protection wall. Late Jinacandra, the famous philanthropist of Kerala and a former Lok-Sabha member, did the renovation of the temple about 32-35 years back.[39]

The image of the goddess in the Padmāvatī temple is a seated figure with four hands; her hands in the back hold *aṅkuśa* and *pāśa*, while the front right hand is in the *abhaya-mudrā* and the front left hand holds a book.[40] The figure of the Jakiyabbe Padmāvatī is also noble, and her *hāra* having more number of pendants is as precious as those of the *yakṣa*'s. Her *karaṇḍa* crown with a diamond broach on the front and the festooning pearly strings coming down as they do from the broach's crest, and the golden ribbon at the base, go well with glory of the goddess. The lotus buds she holds are even more shapely than that of the *yakṣa*. The noose and the goad held in the upper arms are equally fine. The broad, ribbed anklets of silver look pretty just as is the jewel-studded *keyūra*. The face, somewhat squarish is sober and eloquent in a quieter way.[41]

Contribution of Vikrama Santara I (period AD 898-920)

Now much is known concerning the art and architecture of the immediate descendants of Jinadattarāya, though a few sculptures may fall into the dark phase. But the curtain is lifted in the late

---

39. Rajamala Jain and Laxmichandra Jain, *Bharat ke Digambara Jain Tirtha*, vol. V, Karnataka, Bombay, 1988, p. 127.

40. *Annual Report of the Mysore Archaeological Dept. Year 1929*, Part II (Survey of Monuments of Ancient sites), (Bombay, 1988) p. 6.

41. M.A. Dhakey, *Santara Sculpture*, Journal Series, vol. IV, (1971-72), p. 93.

ninth century, in the period of Vikrama Santara I whose period seems to span from AD 898 to early years of the next century, though he may have begun his career some years before the date and ended perhaps around AD 920.

Important Santara temples appear to have been built almost exclusively under the royal patronage. They can be categorized into two broad phases, the earlier ones and the later ones. The earlier buildings, excepting one, apparently date from Vikrama Santara's time.[42] Tolapuruṣa Vikramāditya-Santara (on the date specified) had a stone *basadi* made for Moni-Siddhānta Bhaṭṭāraka of the Koṇḍa-kundān-vaya and made grants for it.

Vikrama Santara's own inscription of *S*. 819/AD 897, refers to his founding a Jain *basadi* for the recluse Moni-Siddhānta-Bhaṭṭāraka of the Koṇḍakundānvaya.[43] Vikrama Santara himself founded a stone temple on the hill behind Humcha town in Shaka 819/AD 897, a notice to the effect being once recorded on a wall of this, which till its recent demolition was known as Guddada Basadi and was sacred to Bāhubali. Two other buildings in Humcha also seem to date to his time, the precise origins of which are namely the Sule-Basadi and Bogara-Basadi, which are otherwise in the same general style.[44]

There are two inscriptions relating to Vikrama Santara, one from Barur, whose date could be ascertained to be AD 890, as it refers to a *Santara* as a king, a feudatory of Pṛthvīvallabha Kannarddeva Rāṣṭrakūṭa Kṛṣṇa II (AD 880-915).[45] The other one has been found from Salur; it is of a *Santara* Candinga and is dated to AD 902-03, it refers to Vikramāditya *Santara* and his overlord Rāṣṭrakūṭa Kṛṣṇa II.[46] After the rule of Jinadattarāya

42. U.P. Shah, and M.A. Dhakey, *op. cit.*, p. 185.
43. B.L. Rice, *E. Carn.*, vol. VIII, No. 60.
44. *Ibid.*, 8, K.V. Ramesh, and M.N. Katti, *E. Carn.*, vol. VII, SK. 45b *The origin and early History of Santaras of Santalige-1000*, p. 35.
45. K.V. Ramesh, and M.N. Kitti, *op. cit.*, p. 30.
46. B.L. Rice, *E. Carn.*, vol. VIII, No. 35.

and many others there arose Śrīkeśī and Jayakeśī. To Śrīkeśī and his queen was born a son Raṇakeśī. Many others having ruled after him, there was *Hiraṇyagarbha* who made the *mahādāna*, slew or put to flight all the neighbouring kings, and with the Sula river on the south, Tavanāsī on the west, and Bandige on the north as its boundaries, formed the Santalige-1000 into a separate kingdom — being known as Kandukācārya, Dānavinoda, Vikrama Santara.

The Humcha inscription of Vikrama Santara's time calls him Tolapuruṣa referring to his ceremony. The inscription of AD 1077 from Humcha, cited earlier credits him with the performance of sacrifice and many donations which won him the feudatory epithets, Dānavinoda and Kandukācārya.[47]

Vikrama Santara seems to be a powerful king who consolidated Santara power and ushered in peaceful period which resulted as we are to notice here, in the flourishing of the Santara idiom of Karnataka art and architecture.

The style of the period of Vikrama Santara, however, differs from that of Jinadattarāya and although the course of its evolution cannot be firmly traced, it would appear that the pillar in its broad features, shows affiliation to both the early and late Rāṣṭrakūṭa types. Santara idiom would now appear to be a high quality provincial variation of the Rāṣṭrakūṭa style with some links, as an *adhiṣṭhāna* type, to the temples of lower Draviḍadeśa and later temples in Kerala. It also contains the seeds of the *koṣṭhapañjara* and other formal decorative devices which later on became viable in period of the Cāḷukyas of Kalyāṇī.[48]

GUDDADA-BASADI

As stated earlier, the sanctuary of Bahubali was built on the top of the hill, as earlier said, in AD 898 by Vikrama Santara for

47. U.P. Shah, and M.A. Dhakey, *op. cit.*, p. 185.
48. M.A. Dhakey, *op. cit.*, p. 190.

Mauni-Siddhānta Bhaṭṭāraka, pontiff of the Koṇḍakundānvaya of the southern Digambara Church.[49] The original temple had been very recently pulled down very recently to give place to a cement concrete structure. From the remains of the dismantled temple still spread over the site, it is clear that in style plan and dimensions was somewhat similar to the Bogara-Basadi.

The *adhiṣṭhāna* was of the *kapotabandha* class. The *miśraka* pillars that were once in the hall show a plane cubical base, the shaft immediately above is decorated with a pattern consisting of elongated overlapping petals with frilled edges. Next come two necking courses, a jewelled string and a cable moulding followed by a bell-shaped member, the lower part of which consists of a *grasakin kaṇikā* (lion with bell and chin) and the upper part either of a *maṇibandha* or a scroll band. Next follows the *malasthāna* and *lasuna* decorated all-around with a series of petalled ornaments. Altogether they seem to be rather rare type of decorated pillars, perhaps some of the most beautiful ones in whole Karnataka. Fragments of the *pañcaśākhā* doorframe indicate that it possessed *pātra*, *bāhya* and *ratnaśākhā*s, the other two being left plain.[50]

SULE-BASADI

In Kannaḍa, *sule* means prostitute. It is said that the temple might have been built by some prostitute. Therefore it is called as Sule-Basadi.

In all probability the oldest of the four early buildings at Humcha the Sule-Basadi. It is also the largest, being about 17 ft in width. The *adhiṣṭhāna* is of the general *kapotabandha* class. On the *karṇa* part of the wall is carved a *pañjara-koṣṭha* framed niche and *dormer* with a very shallow sit-niche, which is also found at the *bhadra*. While this feature is reminiscent of *panyan* building, the *makara toraṇa* crowning the niche, characteristically present

49. Jyoti P. Jain, *Pramukha Aitihasik Jain Purusha aur Mahilayen*, New Delhi, 1975, p. 171.

50. M.A. Dhakey, *op. cit.*, pp. 188-89.

in the buildings of lower Draviḍadeśa, does not apparently find a place in the Santara wall-scheme. The bosses of the *nāsikā dormers* of the *pañjara koṣṭha* as well as of the *kapota* of the *prastara* are unfinished. The temple has lost its *mahāmaṇḍapa*. The superstructure over the *vimāna* seems to have never been built, or if built at all, it might have been made of perishable materials such as timber, brick and plaster.[51] There are two inscriptions and one small temple without *śikhara* in front of the Sule-Basadi. There is an idol of seated (*padmāsana*) Mahāvīra. Bogara-Basadi and Sule- Basadi were built in the Vikrama period.

BOGARA-BASADI

The building immediately following the Sule-Basadi is the Bogara-Basadi. Of late, it has been saddled with unsightly additions but the older fabric is still intact. Judging from the elegant proportions as well as the high quality of workmanship, it must rank among the most beautiful temples of this period in whole Karnataka *deśa*.

The *vimāna* possesses an unusual variety of *adhiṣṭhāna*, probably of the *pratibandha* class and the wall is relieved by *brahmakānta* pilasters, very similar to those of the Sule-Basadi though a little less archaic. The *mukhapaṭṭī* of each *alpanāsī* shows a crisply cut, unusually rich and very elegant vine ornament, and the *gaḍhā* (cavity) harbours a seated *jin* figure.

The upper storey is formed by a *grahapiṇḍī* with a *bhadra* projection which is enriched with a *salakoṣṭha* while the *karṇa* bears a storied *kapotapañjara*. The latter feature is special to this style, and has a bearing to the development of wall surface of Karnataka temples built during the subsequent period of the Cāḷukyas of Kalyāṇī. The *śikhara* is now partially concealed by an ugly modern chamber with titled roof, its *mahanāsī*s containing seated *jin* figure. The curvature as well as the proportions of the *śikhara* also differs from contemporary

51. *Ibid.*, p. 187.

examples in lower Draviḍadeśa and is beautiful and blends with the lower structure.[52]

Vikrama Santara thus seems to have been a powerful prince who consolidated Santara power. He ushered in a peaceful period, and the Santara art and architecture fully flourished in his reign.

CAGI SANTARA (AD 920-45)

Vikrama Santara was succeeded by his son Cagi Santara by queen Lakṣmīdevī. According to 3 Soratur inscriptions dated AD 930-34 of Rāṣṭrakūta King Govinda IV clearly indicate that Cagi Santara was the contemporary king of Humcha. The Santara king, whose name is not given, was defeated in a battle with the Nolambas in about AD 920 and had slained and beheaded Gaṅga prince, the son of Pṛthvīpati AD 920.[53] After Vikrama Santara, his son Cagi ruled for some years. The events which followed next seem to have sent Santaras into temporary obscurity.[54]

Cagi is credited by Humcha inscription of AD 1077 to have built the reservoir Cagi Samudra.[55]

PALIYAKKAN-BASADI (AD 950)

The Pārśva-Basadi is possibly the Paliyakkan-Basadi founded by Paliyakkan according to an inscription of the mid-tenth century carved in its wall. Its style is a little more advanced than both the Bogara and the Guddada-Basadi, and it seems to be dated to first half of the tenth century, rather than the last quarter of the ninth one is likely to have been built in AD 950 Original Paliyakkan-Basadi.

---

52. *Ibid.*, pp. 187-88.
53. W. Meister Michand and M.A. Dhakey, *Encyclopaedia of Indian temple Architecture upper Dravidadesa* (Early Phase), p. 219.
54. *Ibid.*, p. 282.
55. B.L. Rice, *E. Carn.*, No. 35.

Renovation of Padmāvatī and Pārśvanātha Temples by Vīra Santara (AD 1062)

After Gagi Santara, the surviving dynasty passed for over a century but passed into political limbo. The name of the princes who followed in succession are known from the inscriptions dated after AD 1050, but they remain silent on their activities and status. The events that followed Cagi Santara's death in a battle in AD 940 had soon after, sent the Santaras into obscurity.[56]

The direct control of the Santara's land was then annexed, was under the Cāḷukya feudatories ruling from Banavāsī. There was, for example, one brāhmaṇa, a vassal of Cāḷukya Taila II (AD 973-97) governing Vanavāsī-12000 as well as governed Santalige-1000[57] as indicated by the inscription and thus the date of foundation of this temple is so ascertained. There is, however no evidence suggesting rebuilding. The shrine is too small and severe to be a royal foundation, if the builder is assumed to have had royal connections (date about AD 950).[58]

Be it well, when the fierce supporter of the faith (or, the great Ugra, firm in the faith), possessed of valour, champion over foreign kings (on the date specified), apparently PaliYakka was ruling. Tolapuruṣa, Santara's wife, on the death of her mother, had erected a stone *basadi* called Paliyaleka-Basadi, for which he made the various grants.[59] There is also a mention of disastrous invasion of Coḷa Rājarāja on Kuntaladeśa in the time of Cāḷukya Satyāśraya (AD 997-1008), and of Kundamarasa, a feudatory of Cāḷukya Vikramaditya V (AD 1008-14) who claims to be ruling over Santalige besides the Vanavāsī province.[60] The Santaras may still be there in Humcha or thereabouts, paying

56. M.A. Dhakey, *op. cit.*, p. 282.
57. R.C. Majumdar, *The Struggle for empire* (*History and Culture of Indian People*), vol. V, Bombay, 1957, p. 163.
58. M.A. Dhakey, *op. cit.*, p. 189.
59. B.L. Rice, *E. Carn.*, vol. VIII, No. 45, p. 146.
60. R.C. Majumdar, *op. cit.*, 165.

tribute to the Cāḷukya emperors' bigger vassals stationed at Vanavāsī. But family's real eclipse must have been brought about when Bijjarasa (with his brother Gonarāja), the feudatory of Jayasiṁha II (AD 1015-43) who seems to have been put directly in charge of Santalige, claimed to the "enjoying Santalige in AD 1042."[61] Subsequently, the occupation of the Santara kingdom by two Cāḷukyan princess Bijjaras and Gonarāja — brought about the eclipse of the dynasty from about the third quarter of the tenth century to around AD 1060.[62] Vīra Santara II lifted the dynasty up from gloom, dishonour and inaction, for he seemed to have freed Santalige from the usurpers and restored it to its former glory.[63]

It is not easy to say as to when Santara took full possession of his ancestral princedom. It may have been before AD 1060, because in this year, "the Santara's minister had become involved with the 'Hoyasala's hostile force' near the southern border of the Santara kingdom."[64] This is evident from the Santara records that appear in large numbers and also speak of the dynasty's achievements. The existing sculptures and architecture of that time in the capital town Humcha further attest to the dynasty's revived glory. For instance, Vīra Santara rebuilt the ancient family shrine of Jakiyabbe Padmāvatī in Humcha, to which his consort Cagaladevī added a *toraṇa* in AD 1062. More temples of this period have been found in Humcha.

The style of this period is quite different from the style of Vikrama Santara time. It shows a strong affiliation to the imperial style of the Cāḷukyas and Kalyāṇī, but the buildings are much simpler and austere in contradiction to the Cāḷukyan, which is disappointing.

---

61. M.A. Dhakey, *Santara Sculpture*, p. 190.
62. *Ibid.*
63. *Ibid.*
64. J. Derrt and M. Duncan, *The Hoyasalas*, Madras, 1957, p. 25.

ADDITIONS TO PĀRŚVANĀTHA AND PADMĀVATĪ TEMPLES DURING THE PERIOD OF VĪRA SANTARA (AD 1062)

Traditionally, *Lokkiyabbe-Jinageha* is the most ancient and sacred principal Jain temple in Humcha. The building seems to be a variation in Vīra Santara's time of the earlier edifice of Jinadattarāya (ninth century AD) and may be of a date little anterior to AD 1062.

The east facing temple is a plain oblong structure divided into three chambers, the *garbhagṛha*, the first closed hall, and the second closed hall. Inside the sanctuary are the beautiful sculptures of *jin* Pārśva, *yakṣī* Padmāvatī and *yakṣī* Sarvanabatti (converted into Dharendra). A cross inside this *garbhagṛha* has been supported by two simple but ancient looking pillars, perhaps the remainders of the ancient temples of Jinadatta's time.

Flanking the doorway, the first hall has a pair of standing figures of *jin* Pārśvanātha with a surrounding narrative of the *upsarga*. The second hall has *Śrīkara* pillars in the nave, elaborated, moulded, shaped and ornamented with *muktajala*, *maṇipaṭṭikā*, and *vasantapaṭṭi*. The second pretty hall, judging the style of pillars, may have been added in the early twelfth century AD.

A *mukha-maṇḍapa* in the Vijayanagara style was added to this latter hall in fifteenth century AD. A *toraṇa* had been set-up at some spot in front of this temple by Cagaladevī in AD 1062.[65]

The present remains of the sculpture of Vīra Santara, though sparse, certainly reflects the glorious history of Santara art. The eleventh century was a glorious time in Karnataka as revealed by the art particular of the time of the Cāḷukya emperor Āhavamalla Someśvara I (AD 1042-68). Vīra Santara was his contemporary (and also his subordinate) and the Santara art of

---

65. M.A. Dhakey, *op. cit.*, p. 283.

his time was a part of the greater movement that surged up and swelled in the Cāḷukyan empire.

The inscription of AD 1062 on the Pārśvanātha temple pillar credits him with the building of the temple of his family deity Lokkiyabbe which undoubtedly is the present sanctuary of Pārśvanātha. The cult image inside the sanctum is of *jin* Pārśvanātha. On *jin*'s left is the *yakṣa* Sarvahna which was converted at a later stage into Dharaṇendra by placing a slab with a shallowly carved *toraṇa* and the triple cobra-hood symbolic of the Nāgendra behind the head.

On the right is *yakṣī* Padmāvatī as the Humcha inscriptions affectionately address her. Since Jinadatta's original fan is no more to be found in Humcha today, it is very likely that Vīra Santara replaced it by a new building, the present temple of Pārśvanātha. Not only that, the images in the sanctuary also, by style, belong to this period, and by implication are a variation of the original.[66]

The inscription dated AD 1062 furnishines the following important information :

> The beloved of that Vira-Santara's mind and eyes was Chagala-devi. Numerous verses in her praise is — In front of the basadi of Nokkiyabbe, the family-goddess of her husband Vira Santara, she had a 'Makara torana' made. And at Baligave she had a temple made called Chagesvara, and making gifts of virgins to many brahmans, she performed the mahadana, and giving gold and baskets to the crowd of eulogists and thier dependents as much as they asked, and was thus distinguished for her liberality. And that Chagala-Devi's mother Arasikabbe also rose to fame. And the Sarvva-Pradhanam of Santara's house, Brahmadhiraja Kalidasa was distinguished.[67]

The above inscription indicate how royal ladies were influ-enced by the Jain religion and donated lands to temples.

---

66. B.L. Rice, *E. Carn.*, vol. VIII, No. 47 (dated AD 1062).
67. *Ibid.*, and Hayavadana C. Rao, *Mysore Gazetteer*, vol. V, p. 784.

TRITHADA-BASADI

In the same year (*S*. 984) or slightly earlier, the village headman, *burgher* and probably tradesman named Paṭṭana-Svāmī-Nokkaya-Seṭṭi built Paṭṭana-Svāmī Jinālaya, also called Tirthada-Basadi in AD 1065 in Humcha. He donated to the newly founded temple, the village Kukkudavali, which was in possession of the king. He also donated Molakere to Seṭṭi's temple. The traders also built five reservoirs, namely Santagere, Molakere, Pattana-svamigere, Kukkadavallikere and Tale-vindegere.

BHUJABALA-SANTARA JINĀLAYA (S. 987/AD 1066)

Vīra Santara was succeeded by Taila II *alia*s Bhujabala Santara who founded Bhujabala Santara Jinālaya in Humcha in the Śaka year 987 or AD 1065.[68] He also made some donations to the Tīrtha-Basadi of Paṭṭana-Svāmī as stated in an undated inscription engraved on a *mahāstambha* in front of the Sule-Basadi.[69]

We gather from a stone inscription dated ad 1066 that Bhujabala Santara, who had the second name of Trailokyamalla after his overlord the western Cāḷukya monarch Trailokyamall Deva, constructed a *Jinālaya* called Bhujabala Santara Jinālaya in his capital at Pombucca and granted the village of Haravari to his *guru* Kanakanandideva.[70]

PRAÑCAKŪṬA-BASADI

The finely executed Pañcakūṭa-Basadi attracts even today large number of Jain pilgrims from all parts of India.[71] This is one of the oldest *basadi* in Humcha. It is in front of Dharmaśālā. This is a complex of five temples, hence termed as Pañcakūṭa-Basadi which belonged to the tenth and eleventh centuries AD. This

68. B.L. Rice, *E. Carn.*, vol. VII, No. 58.

69. *Ibid.*, p. 57.

70. B.A. Saletore, *Medieval Jainism* (with Special Reference to the Vijayanagara empire), Bombay, 1938, pp. 90-91.

71. *Mysore Archaeological Report for year* 1929, pp. 6-7.

temple was built by black stones. There are two images of goddess Padmāvatī in this temple complex which are 9 ft in height. It is built in the Cāḷukyan style. It consists of five cells, all in a row with a common *navaraṅga* and an open *mukhamaṇḍapa*. There is a verandah all around the temple. In front of the main structure and a few feet away on either side, there are two small shrines and these are enclosed by a compound with a *mahādvāra*. Between the *mahādvāra* and the main building stand a small *maṇḍapa* and a *mānastambha* which is a magnificent monolithic pillar and is an interesting piece of work having elegant carvings.[72]

The pillar stands on a high platform which has three tiers. The bottom most has four elephants at the four corners and four more at the cardinal points. Lions in different postures are carved in between these elephants. On the face of the next higher tier, there is a procession of the *aṣṭadikpālaka*s with all their retinue and musicians. The column is square in shape to a certain height and then octagonal and finally circular at the top. There is a small pavilion surmounting the pillar with a seated figure facing each of the four directions. There are several inscriptions in the *basadi*.[73]

The art of Vīra Santara's successors, Bhujabala and Nanni Santara strike a somewhat different note. But this again is in keeping with the fashions of the time of the Cāḷukyan monarch Someśvara II (AD 1068-79) and his brother Vikramāditya VI (AD 1078-1126), in whose times the imperial art went "buroque" in spirit and formed the Pañcakūṭa-Basadi at Humcha. There are five seated *jin* images, in its five cells and shelters, three of which still have their accessories in position. Each *jin* figure sits on a *siṁhāsana* with an impressive throne-back terminating at each end by a *vyāla* and a splendid *makara* over whose back the

---

72. *Karnataka State Gazetteer*, Govt. of Karnataka (South Kanara district), p. 735.
73. *Ibid.*

water deities ride. Then there is a triple umbrella and a *caitya* tree behind the umbrella. Again, behind the throne, on either side, stands a flywhisk bearer.[74] There are, besides the figure sculpture, fragments of at least three different *toraṇa*s of differing workmanship. These dates to this collection, except one, which is stylistically the oldest among them. From a later *toraṇa* still in position in Pañcakūṭa-Basadi, which possesses the formal details though not the idiom of what the earlier examples must have been, it is possible to visualize what the older *toraṇa*s were like and how they were positioned.[75]

The next important notice related to the Santara chiefs and their religious deeds has been obtained from the inscription in the Pañcakūṭa-Basadi which belong AD 1077. We have already noted in the later inscriptions that Nanni-Santara was the brother of Bhujabala and the ruling queen, Cattaladevī, a sister of queen Vīra Mahādevī (the consort of Vīra Santara and mother of Bhujabala, Nanni and two more sons) — who was daughter of Arumuli Gaṅgas and wife of the king of Kāñcī and who was then living in Humcha, had founded a Jain temple named "Urvi-tilaka-Jinālaya" also called "Pañcakūṭa-Jin-mandira" in the town in memory of her parents Arumulideva *alia*s Rakkas-Permandi Gaṅga and Gayabbarasi, and sister Viraladevī Gayabbarasi, and sister Viraladevī (Vīra Mahādevī) and Rājādityadeva. She had also got one artificial lake excavated. A village was donated for the worship, maintenance and repair to the temple by Nanni, Santara, conjointly with his brothers, Oddamarasa and Bommadeva (Varmadeva) and sister Cattaladevī. Another inscription of AD 1077 on a pillar to the south of the *toraṇa* refers to the laying of the foundation stone of the Pañcakūṭa-Basadi, when Bhujabala donated a village and his brothers Nanni Santara and Vikrama III (Odduga or Oddamarasa) also granted a village and some land.[76] One more inscription from the same *basadi* and

74. M.A. Dhakey, *op. cit.*, p. 94.

75. *Ibid.*, p. 90.

76. B.L. Rice, *E. Carn.*, vol. VIII, No. 48.

of the same date refers to further donations by the same members of the royal family. And, finally, an inscription on the *mānastambha* in front of the Pañcakūṭa-Basadi eulogizes the royal descendants of Vīradeva, Cataladevī, sister of Vīradeva's wife.[77]

In a later record dated AD 1103, we learn that the same Santara lady, who is called "a cow of plenty to the glorious *jin* congregation" along with her own sons Bhujabala Santara, Nanni Santara, and Vikrama Santara, granted specified lands to the same Pañcakūṭa-Basadi. She and Tribhuvanamalla Santara laid the foundation stone of another *basadi* opposite to the Jinālaya as a memorial for the death of Birabbarasi, pronouncing the name of Vadigharatta Ajitasena Paṇḍita.[78]

There is also an inscription of Vikrama Santara III of the Śaka 1025/AD 1103 from Danasale referring to a donation of a village to Pañcakūṭa-Basadi of Pombucca by Bhujabala Santara. Nanni Santara III had laid the foundation stone of *basadi* in Andanur in memory of Virabbarasi.

Another Santara princess who promoted the cause of the *anekānta-mata* was Pampādevī, the daughter of King Taila and the elder sister of Vikramāditya Santara. Epigraphs highly praise this lady:

> All the world filled with newly raised towers of painted Caityalayas, the ears of all the elephants at the points of the compass filled with the sounds of trumpets and drums in Jina festivals, all the sky filled with flags for Jina worship — Pampadevi shone everywhere with the glory of the Arhad Sasana. Considering the stories of Jinanatha in the well-known *Mahapurana*, her earnings, the bestowal of the four kinds of gifts to Jina *munis*, her bracelets, devotion and praise of Jina Pati, her beautiful necklace. In one month she herself caused to be made Sasanadevate in the same manner as the famous Urvitilakam had been constructed. Pampadevi's foremost

77. *Ibid.*, No. 4.

78. B.A. Saletore, *Medieval Jainism*, p. 160.

desire was the following — the performance of the Asta-Vidharccane, the mahabhisekam, and Caturbhakti.[79]

Pampādevī's daughter was Bacaladevī who was reckoned to be a second Attimabbe. She was a devout and generous lady.

And finally, we may take note of an inscription of Śaka 1069/ AD 1147 of Pampādevī and Śrīvallabha *alias* Vikrama Santara IV on the pillar of the hall of the Pañcakūṭa-Basadi which refers to the setting up of an image of Śāśandevatā in the *basadi* and the extension of the *basadi*'s northern Paṭṭaśālā.[80]

Paṭṭaśālā have been the place of an image of *yakṣa* Dharendra, Śāśandevī, and the Śrutadevatā, a Ssarasvatī which appears to have been executed in the same style as the two large *dvārapāla*s at the central door of the Paṭṭaśālā. At least one of the three can be dated to AD 1147, set-up in that year by Pampādevī, sister of Vikrama Santara IV. A scion of the Santara clan, Jagadeva had for some years worked as the *durgapāla* (master of the keep) of Anahillapatall in the early years of Cāḷukya Jayasiṁhadeva Siddharāja of Gujarat.[81]

Besides major temples mentioned above, the following are the minor temples situated at Humcha.

KṢETRAPĀLA TEMPLE

This temple is in the southern corner of the outer perimeter of the Pārśvanātha temple. The temple is about 15 ft high and 10 l 10 lb approximately. It is built up of stone bricks.[82]

AŚOKA-BASADI

This *basadi* is in the centre of the garden situated in the south corner of the Śrī Maṭha. Here the image of *jin* is in *padmāsana*. This *basadi* is from the ancient period.[83]

79. *Ibid.*, p. 162.
80. M.A. Dhakey, *op. cit.*, p. 82.
81. *Ibid.*, p. 192.
82. Joyess B.D. Sripati, *Atishaya Kshetra Hombuja*, Hombuja, 1997, p. 10.
83. *Ibid.*

CHILDREN-BASADI

This is built with small pieces of rocks. It has the idol of Svāmī Pārśvanātha which is 4 ft. high and seven-hooded serpent is present on the head.[84]

The *dharmaśālā*, *yakṣa* and *yakṣīs*, and also *cavaradhārī* are present in this *basadi*. The *kṣetrapāla* also is present on the outer side of the *mandira*.

KUMUDVATĪ TĪRTHA (HUMCHA KUṆḌA)

This holy lake is at a distance of about 3 km from the Padmāvatī temple. Here the water drops down in a continuous stream. There is always a rush of devotees here for the holy bath.[87] To the south-west of the village, a little inside the hilly woods, is an elegant but partially damaged, square *kuṇḍa* or step-well. Its upper as well as lower inner facings show a series of panels displaying full blown lotuses and demand-shaped floral motifs between the *galapadas*. At the central points of each of the three sides of the *kuṇḍa* descend a stairway flanked at the lower end by totemic elephant pairs. On the fourth side is *pranālā* — conduit through which is conducted a very thin stream of water to collect at the central pool. Five steps continue all around the lower reaches and are pierced only by the three descending stairways, each flanked by a pair of elephants. It is difficult to ascertain the date of *kuṇḍa*, arguably though it could be of a date somewhere in the early years of resurgence of the Santara power, probably built in the sixties of the eleventh century.[85]

The stream of cold water falls in this *kuṇḍa* for 24 hours. It is the birthplace of Kumudvatī river. It is not known as to which place the stream comes from, because there is a hill of soil on this stream. As it is the birthplace of the river, it is called a *tīrtha*. The fresh water from this place was brought everyday for the *abhiṣeka* of the goddess Padmāvatī by the elephant. The people of this village also drew water from this *kuṇḍa*. There is

84. *Ibid.*, p. 11.

85. *Ibid.*

a symbol of *meṣa* (*bakarī* or sheep) present on the lower part of the board pillar. It means that there was a *jin-mandira* in the premises of this *kuṇḍa*. A small lake is also present near the *kuṇḍa*.[86]

MOTĪ TĀLĀB

Motī Tālāb is situated on the left side and near to the Pañcakūṭa-Basadi. The *tālāb* is constructed by the King Jinadattarāya. This inscription of AD 1077 indicates that:

> The mother of King Coggiga Santara alias Nanni Santara reconstructed this Moti-Talab. The length of this talab is about one kilometer and breadth is about 500 to 2000 feet approximately. The water level decreases in summer and increases in rainy season but in summer as it may decrease it should not be dry. The numerous lotus are present in this talab. The great mother had created pearls in this pond to test King Jinadattaraya. Hence it is called the pearl pond or Moti-Talab.[87]

RUINED ROYAL PALACE

The Royal Palace of the Santara king was constructed by the King Jinadattarāya and it is in ruined condition now. The whole palace was made up of wood. This palace was near to the back side of Pañcakūṭa-Basadi and Padmamba High School. Unfortunately this wooden palace had burnt out after some years. Nowadays, if we dig the earth of this place, we will get the carbonized rice and some mud bricks and pieces of tiles. Some statues of *tīrthaṅkaras* were found at the time of construction of the Padmamba High School and are in good condition. The palace at the Humcha city was bounded by a big wall, the monuments of which are even seen today.[88]

Thus, the present Humcha town has the following important Jain temples: the Pārśvanātha-Basadi, Padmāvatī temple,

---

86. Rajamala Jain and Laxmichandra Jain, *op. cit.*, p. 129.
87. *Ibid.*, p. 128.
88. *Ibid.*, p. 129.

Guddada-Basadi, Sule-Basadi, Bogar-Basadi, Paliyakke-Basadi, Tīrthada-Basadi, Bujabala Santara Jinālaya-Basadi and the Pañcakūṭa-Basadi and other minor important *basadis*. These Jain temples are cultural heritage of Karnataka and many Jain devotees used to visit these temples everyday regularly.

In brief, Humcha, the temple city of south Karnataka located in Śimogā district, has been of religious importance since the eighth century onwards. The Santara period of 400 years, from the eighth to twelfth centuries AD, is regarded as golden period in the history of Humcha Santara rulers like Jinadatta, Vikrama-Santara, Chagi-Santara, Vīra-Santara II, Bhujabala-Santara, Vikrama-Santara IV, and their royal ladies spent lavishly their wealth for erecting Jain temples there and thus Humcha became one of the leading Jain centres in south Karnataka. For the development of Jainism in south Karnataka, Humcha like other Jain centres rendered yeomen service and one has to recognize its service without fail.

No doubt, during the Santara period, the Jain community in Humcha had attained a highly developed stage since the eighth century onwards. An old sacred Jain manuscript and canons have been preserved in Humcha library which are important for the student of history.

5

Rise of Jain Centres in South Kanara District

Karkala, Moodabidri and Venur

Karkala Alias Pāṇḍyanagarī: The Political Seat of the Bairarasas Dynasty

LIKE Śravaṇbeḷgoḷa, Humcha, Karkala, Moodabidri and Venur have been famous Jain centres since early medieval period. These places have religious importance even today and a number of pilgrimages and tourist not only from India but all over the world visit these religious places.

Moreover, like Hasan, Śimogā, South Kanara district is full of famous Jain sacred centres which have been responsible for the spread of Jainism in this area. The centre of Jain gravity shifted from Humcha to Karkala in the thirteenth century AD. Hoyasala and other medieval Royal dynasties of south India patronized these centres, built magnificent Jain temples and Jainism was in full swing even though there was menace from Liṅgāyat religion from twelfth century onwards. An attempt has been made in this chapter to bring out the the religious and historical significance and role played by these centres to spread and to protect Jainism in these areas. The following are the noteworthy Jain centres in South Kanara district and subsequent pages are devoted to enumerate the account of these places with help of archaeological and literary sources.

I. Karkala
II. Moodabidri
III. Venur.

Karkala

DESCRIPTION OF KARKALA

Before we study the history of Karkala, it is useful to notice the site and description of the place Karkala. Karkala is unique among the many places of tourist interest in modern Karnataka State. Some have been endowed with nature's bounty, others with ever enchanting creations of the architect, the sculptor or the artist, still others with the seat of modern learning industry or trade. Karkala is an epitome of all of these.

The neat little town of Karkala (13⁰12' N. 75⁰ E) lies 33 miles to the north-east of Mangalore and 24 miles south-east of Udipi. Moodabidri is 10 miles nearer Mangalore on the road to Karkala, while Venur is 12 miles south-east of Moodabidri. A fine asphalted road from Mangalore to Udipi passes through Moodabidri and Karkala; and there are regular bus services plying every 30 to 40 minutes carrying passengers to these places.

Karkala is not only a reputed place of pilgrimage to thousands of Jains coming from all over India, but is also sacred to Hindus and Christians with its famous Church.

BLACK STONE/KARKALA

Cradled in enchanting natural scenery, the town is aptly named Karkala (short for Karikal) black stone — as one can see innumerable black granite formations holding up their imposing heads all around the place. It derives its name from a rock called Karikal meaning black stone which is used for building purposes.[1]

Recorded in epigraphs as Karkala or Karekala, this was the seat of a political power, the Bhairarasas who ruled for 500 years of the kingdom of Karkala, also known as Pāṇḍyanagarī. This region is one of the richest in historical monuments.[2]

---

1. Karnataka State Gazetteer, Govt. of Karnataka, *South Kanara District*, Bangalore, 1973, p. 736.
2. P. Gururaja Bhatt, *Antiquities of South Kanara*, p. 7.

The huge statue of Gommaṭa, the *basadi*s and the temples of Anantaśayana and Veṅkaṭaramaṇa here attract a large number of pilgrims, lovers of art and students of history. These architectural creations, Jain as well as Hindu, are the gifts of the royal family of Bhairarasa Wodeyars.[3] The old palace of this family has been recently renovated.

There is a large colony of gauḍa Sārasvats who came here from Goa. The Jain ruler of the place built the large temple of Veṅkaṭaramaṇa here about AD 1537 to help them to pursue their own method of worship. The Śeṣaśāyī Ananteśvara temple here was built about AD 1567. Every item of the ornaments of the well polished chief idol of this temple is elegantly carved. Viṣṇu rests on the coils of Śeṣa in a serene way. Brahmā rests on the lotus which blooms out of Viṣṇu's navel and Lakṣmī attends on the Viṣṇu near his feet.[4]

Sites of Karkala

GOMMAṬEŚVARA STATUE

The famous gigantic monolithic statue of Gommaṭa, which is 42 ft tall, was installed by Vīra Pāṇḍyadeva, a ruler of the Bhairarasa family of Karkala in AD 1432. About two furlongs from Anekere (it means lake for elephants) this striking statue of Gommaṭeśvara stands on a rocky hillock. It has elongated ears, hawk-nose, curled hairs and half open eyes. It has serenity and awe-inspiring eminence. Of the three Gommaṭa statues in Karnataka, this is second in height and it differs from those at Śravaṅbeḷgoḷa and Venur, as we find a smile on the wonderful lips of its statues while at Karkala it is in a complete meditation.[5]

This statue was not carved out of any rock already standing there. It was carved elsewhere, brought up the hillock and erected. How was this achieved in those days without tractors

3. *Ibid.*

4. Karnataka State Gazetteer, Govt. of Karnataka *South Kanara District*, p. 736.

5. *Ibid.*

and cranes? Here is how Chadura Chandrama describes the feat:

> The King regarded the high hill to the right of his palace as a veritable Kailas, when he went in the Company of his guru, Lalita Keerti Bhattaraka, he found near the hill a stretch of high class granite. The King at once decided to use it for a Gommaṭa statue and with the guru's permission at once performed the preliminary poojas.
>
> Then the King employed clever sculptors to carve the statue, which they began on an auspicious day after the king had again worshipped the stone as directed by his guru.
>
> The sculptors worked hard, day and night. When the required rough hewn statue was complete, it was lifted by ten thousand people and placed on a carriage with twenty wheels. Strong ropes were used to pull the carriage up the hill. The King himself led a concourse of ten thousand persons to pull from the front while the royal elephants pushed it from behind.
>
> Inspite of the herculean efforts of thousands of people, the cart could move up only about two yards a day. Whenever the men tired, the King supplied them with butter-milk and sweet drinks and gave them fruits of various kinds. It was nearly a month's stupendous struggle before the statue reached the crest of the the hill.
>
> A pandal on sixty poles was set-up on the top on the hill and the master sculptor began to give the final shape and polish. It took them over a year to complete the work.
>
> Then the problem was how to set it erect. The hill being covered with grantite, it was not possible to test the ground below. A spot was levelled and the necessary pedestals set-up. Then a thousand wheels and ropes were used to pull up the statue and erect it on the pedestal.
>
> It was the twelfth day of the bright half of Phalguna in the year Virodhikrita. The priests began to chant the holy *mantras*; and the *yatis* chanted the *dasa-bhakthi*. The musicians sang the songs specially composed for the occasion and the ladies recited the ancient auspicious hymns. To the accompaniment

> of deafening bands and bells and the shouts from thousands of throats, the statue was at last erected safe and sound at the appointed hour.[6]

Besides Bāhubali statue, the following are the other historical monuments at Karkala which are worth noticing.

BRAHMADEVARA STAMBHA

The granite pillar in front of Gommaṭa has a Brahmā seated on the top. The small sculpture of Brahmā excels that of Gommaṭa in fine workmanship. The whole pillar is so carved and so polished that one wonders whether it is really granite. This was set-up in the year AD 1437.[7]

CATURMUKHA-BASADI

In the midst of a pond, called Anekere, is a Jain-*basadi*, known as Caturmukha-Basadi with two storeys. It was constructed in AD 1545 by Abhinavapāṇḍyadeva. The celebrated structural temple of the Jains is the Tribhuvana Caityālaya, popularly known as the Caturmukha-Basadi, which is an enduring, soiled and mammoth edifice. It is constructed on a stone boulder, known as *cikka-beṭṭa*. This monument was erected in AD 1586 under the orders of Bhairavendra II of the Bhairarasa family.[8] This *basadi* has four identical looking entrances from the four quarters and hence it is popularly known as "Caturmukha- Basadi." It was completed about AD 1586. It has life size statues of three *tīrthaṅkaras*, besides small images, 24 *tīrthaṅkaras* and Padmāvatī *yakṣī*.[9]

NEMINĀTHA-BASADI AT HIRIYAṄGAḌI

This is second only to Caturmukha-Basadi. This is about 1 km to the west of the Gommaṭa hillock. It was built in AD 1329 in the days of Pāṇḍya.

---

6. D. Puttaswamy, *Karkala a Jain Centre*, Karkala, 1961, pp. 9-10.
7. S.G. Karnataka, Govt. of Karnataka, *South Kanara District*, p. 736.
8. P. Gururaja Bhatt, *op. cit.*, p. 7.
9. S.G. Karnataka, *op. cit.*, p. 737.

The 54 ft high pillar here was carved out of a single piece of granite and was installed in front of the *basadi*. It is an excellent craftsmanship. The Neminātha temple, which is situated amidst enchanting natural scenery at the foot of a hill, was renovated in AD 1946. An oriental school with free boarding and lodging facilities is being run here by the Bhujabali *brahmacarya āśrama*.

The life-size Jain images of Arha, Malli, and Muni Suvr̥tanātha installed in four sides of the altar of the *garbhagr̥ha* are in a contemplative mood. It is a peculiar structure, the style of sculpture being typically Vijayanagara. The two icons of Sūryanārāyaṇa and Venugopāl Kr̥ṣṇa in Anantaśayana and Vanabhojana respectively represent the Hoyasala style. The Veṅkataramaṇa temple in the town of Karkala is of the sixteenth century AD. On the top of the hill, called Parpala, is erected one of the oldest roman Catholic churches of the district.[10]

RĀMASAMUDRA

There is a beautiful lake, called Rāmasamudra, about 1 km from the Gommaṭa hillock. Unlike other reservoirs, this resembles a natural lake. When it overflows through the three different outlets, it is a sight worth-seeing. The sun-setting rays on the wavelets of the lake in the evening enraptures the visitors. This reservoir is said to have been built by Rāmanātha Arasa of the Karkala family who ruled in the last quarter of the fourteenth century AD. The lake offers facilities for boating. A horticultural farm of an area of about 150 acres has recently come up on the eastern side of the lake.[11]

The result of the royal patronage and popular support was beneficial to Jainism as well as to the entire country. It gave a good opportunity to the Jain *ācāryas* to establish various centres of learning and religious studies, monasteries and libraries.

---

10. P.G. Bhatt, *op. cit.*, p. 7.
11. S.G. Karnataka, *op. cit.*, p. 737.

The Jain temples with their *dānaśālās*, i.e., charity-houses for education, food, medicine and retreat became real spots of cultural enlightenment.

This resulted in a vigorous mass awakening, which made the people realize the value of *ahiṁsā* for creating a harmonious atmosphere in human society. The Jain leaders moved freely among the high and low in cities and villages alike imparting the message of *ahiṁsā* and helping the laity to solve its various problems by the right application of it. This brought the Jain *ācāryas* in the direct contact of the people and they were shrewd enough to lay a firm foundation of their hold over the middle and the trading classes in the society. The Jain *ācāryas* worked in a cosmopolitan method and increased the number of followers every year by preaching among the original inhabitants of India.

PATRONIZATION TO KARKALA

These Jain centres enjoyed royal patronage from time to time. Not only royal persons but rich merchants and ladies also extended monetary help to Karkala, making it prosperous and sacred Jain centre since early medieval period in south Karnataka. It rendered valuable service for many years for the spread of Jainism in South Kanara district.

The history of this principality of Karkala is interwoven with that of the Santaras of Patti Pombuccapura on the *ghāṭs*. The first prominent figure in the Santara house was Jinadatta, who, as we have already noted in the previous chapter, is reputed to have brought with him the image of the Jain goddess Padmāvatī.[12] Jinadattarāya founded the Santara kingdom in the ninth century. He, with Patti Pombuccapura as his capital moved down in the same country to Kalaśa (in the Mudgere

---

12. B.L. Rice, *Mysore and Coorg from the Inscriptions*, London, 1909, p. 138.

Tāluka) in the south after extending his kingdom.[13] Here at Kalaśa, the Santara rulers gave expression to their tolerant views. This is seen, for instance, from a record dated AD 1277 of the time of the senior crowned queen Kalala Mahādevī, when on the great days of the gods Kalaśanātha and Jineśvara, a citizen named Mādhava, the son of Kalaseṭṭi made a specified offering of rice and land to the gods.[14]

BHAIRARASA WODEYARS

This dynasty made Karkala as their capital. About eight centuries ago, before the Bhairarasa family made Karkala its capital, the place was only a major village. The Bhairarasa ruled from Karkala for over 500 years, and during this long period, they placed it on the religious map of India. Even the present-day importance of the place is due to the institutions set-up in the days of this great ruler.

Those who admire the architectural and other greatness of Karkala should naturally be eager to know some details of the family which contributed so abundantly to make Karkala famous all over the land; they would like to know who the Bhairarasa were, who have during a period of over five centuries (AD 1300 to AD 1700) strove to make their capital a home of religion, a seat of learning, a centre of art, and a refugee to the oppressed of even other faiths than that of the rulers.[15]

Historians are of firm opinion that Bhairarasa, who first came to Karkala in the fourteenth century, was a descendent of Jinadattarāya who established himself a Hombuchapura in Śimogā district and installed Pārśvanāthasvāmī and Padmāvatī Ammā in that town in the eighth century.[16]

13. B.A. Saletore, *Ancient Karnataka History of Tuluva*, vol. I, Poona, 1936, pp. 224-25.
14. B.A. Saletore, *Medieval Jainism With Special Reference to the Vijayanagara Empire*, Bombay, 1938, pp. 360-61.
15. Lalitakirti Bhattaraka, *Aithishaya kshetra Karkala*, Karkala, 1993, pp. 12-13.
16. *Ibid.*, p. 13.

Prior to the coming of Bhairarasa, a chieftain named Kapittu Heggade used to rule over the sever *Nāḍus* called **"Karkala, Keravase, Padangadi, Arooru, Aidooru, Nalkooru and Mooraru."** There were nearly 770 homes of Jain *śrāvaka*s in his domain whose main occupation was trade. In spite of their rendering to the Heggade, he continued to harasss them. Unable to bear this ill-treatment for long, the *śrāvaka*s sought the protection of Bhairarasa who had come to Moodabidri on pilgrimage. Bairarasarāya immediately summoned an army from Hombucha, defeated the Heggade and took possession of his kingdom.[17] The *śrāvaka*s crowned Bhirarasarāya as their king and Karkala became his permanent abode. Thus began a glorious period of religious, artistic, literary and cultural afflorescence.

It is true, this family had to acknowledge the suzerainty of Vijayanagara for sometime but for most part it was independent. Even when under the overall power of Vijayanagara, the Bhairarasa continued their patronage of religious and cultural activities. It is said that Bhirarasarāya built a palace where we now find the Palace Basadi and also a *basadi* inside the palace, he is reported to have named his town as Pāṇḍyanagara.[18]

KARKALA: SECOND SEAT OF SANTARA DYNASTY

Karkala was another important Jain centre in the country of Tuluva. The early rulers of Karkala were the descendants of one Jinadattarāya, who migrated from Mathurā in northern India to south and founded his kingdom of Santara. Probably at the beginning of the fourteenth century AD the descendants of Śrī Jinadattarāya, i.e., the Santara rulers of Kalaśa, shifted to Karakala and made it their capital.

The Hoyasala feudatory Lokanāthadevarasa, whose possessions included portions of the Karkala Tāluka of South Kanara, was a Jain ruler. His inscription from Hiriyangadi,

17. *Ibid*.
18. *Ibid*., p. 3.

belonging to AD 1334, records grants of lands by a number of donors including the ruler's sisters Bommaladevī and Somaladevī, who were the chief disciple of Bhānukīrti Maladharideva of Mūlasaṅgha and Kranuragana. To the *basadi* of Śāntinātha, built at Karkala by the disciples of the Jain preceptor Kumadacandra Bhaṭṭārakadeva along with Aliappa, the other state officials gave the specified grants. It may be safely concluded from this that Jainism had made gains in South Kanara at least early in the fourteenth century.[19]

Lokanātharasa was a great Santara chief who materially contributed to the spread of Jainism in Tuluva. He was the disciple of Cārukīrti Paṇḍitadeva and exercised some independent sway in the Karkala region.[20]

Lokanātharāja bears the *biruda*s of *samastabhuvanāśraya, śrī-pṛthvīvallabha, mahārājādhirāja,* which were usually assumed only by the independent monarch sway in the Karkala region in the middle of the fourteenth century AD.[21]

Sometimes after him the Karkala rulers came gradually under the influence of the Liṅgāyat faith.[22] But they continued to be warm supporters of the Jain *dharma*. We prove this from records ranging from the middle of the fifteenth century AD to the end of the sixteenth century AD. The credit of turning the mind of the Karkala rulers to the Syādvāda doctrine goes to the Jain *gurus* of Hanasoge. And it was at the instance of Lalitakīrti that King Vīra Pāṇḍya, AD 1418, the Bhairarasa Wodeyar's son went on a pilgrimage to the north. On his way back, he saw the monolithic statue of Śravaṇbeḷgoḷa and was inspired to set-up a similar one at Karkala. When he succeeded his father, the

19. K.V. Ramesh, *History of South Kanara: From the earliest times to the fall of Vijayanagara*, Dharwar, 1970, p. 298.

20. B.A. Saletore, *Medieval Jainism*, p. 361.

21. B.L. Rice, *South Indian Inscriptions*, vol. VII, 247, pp. 124-25.

22. R. Narasimhachar, *Epigraphica Carnatica, Inscriptions in the Shimoga District*, vol. VII, Bangalore, 1902, Mg. 39, 42, 50, 60, pp. 68-70.

Gommaṭa statue was formally installed by him on 13 February, 1432. King Devarāya of Vijayanagara came specially to witness the great event.[23]

There was no separate royal preceptor at Karkala till Hiriya Bhairavadeva's (AD 1462) time. Lalitakīrti Bhaṭṭārakas of Panasoge used to officiate on more important occasions and Cārukīrti of Moodabidri at others times. This king established a branch of Panasoge *pīṭha* at Karkala and the successors to it are also styled Lalitakīrti Bhaṭṭārakas.[24]

It is probably the same *guru* who is mentioned in another inscription dated Śaka 1379 (AD 1457) which records a gift of Paddy to the Hire Nemīśvara *Basadi* at Hiriyaṅgaḍi, one of the suburbs of Karkala. In this record, Lalitakīrti is said to have belonged to the Kalorgana. The same *guru* was likewise responsible for the munificence of the merchants of Hiriyaṅgaḍi, who built a *mukha-maṇḍapa* to the *tīrthaṅkara basadi* of that place in AD 1475-76.[25]

Towards the middle of the sixteenth century, we have the noble lady Kalala Devī, the ruler of the Bagunjisime and the younger sister of the Karkala king Bhairarasa Odeyar. She made special provision in AD 1530 for the continuance of the *jin dharma* in the territory over which she ruled "in her own right." Bagunji itself was a centre of the Bhavyas. The god Pārśva *tīrthaṅkara* of Kalla-Basadi in that principality was the family god of Kalala Devī. It was on the death of her daughter Ramā Devī that Kalala Devī made grants for the daily worship of her family god. But this was done in the constitutional manner of the land. The grant was made in the presence of the former ministers of the Bagunijisime, the brāhmaṇas, the cultivators, the nad representatives, and others. This done, she obtained the sanction

23. D. Puttaswamy, *op. cit.*, p. 5.

24. *Ibid.*

25. R. Narasimhachar, *Epigraphia Caranatica, Inscriptions in the Kadur District*, vol. VI, Bangalore, 1901, KP 47, p. 48.

of the Karkala king for the same, and then had the stone Śāśana engraved. It is interesting to note that on this occasion she added specified lands as gifts to the grant which a boatman name Valiya had made sometime ago to the same Kalla-Basadi.

Kalala Devī's anxiety to endow the Kalla-Basasdi with grants was not merely an expression of outward piety. She was a broad-minded ruler who believed in tolerance. It is this which explains why the charter commemorating her gifts to the same *basadi* begins with an invocation to the Syādvāda doctrine in the usual Jain manner, and also with an obeisance to Ādī Varāha Śambhu.[26]

Along with the rulers of Karkala, the Catholic spirit of *ahiṁsā* of its citizens was more responsible for the spread of Jainism. They were well awakened in the observance of the rulers for spiritual advancement. Some *śrāvakas* of Karkala gave as a gift money in Śaka 1501 (AD 1579) for the study of the scriptures in the Ammanavara-Basadi at Hiriyaṅgaḍi. Jain *ācāryas* thus were ever conscious to help the cause of spiritual welfare of the people and arranged to impart to them the right knowledge of the soul, body and God.[27]

Immadi Bhairvendra Odeyar was another ruler of Karkala who patronized Jainism. The construction of the well-known Caturmukha-Basadi at Karkala was a work of the ruler Immadi Bhairvendra Odeyar, who called himself the ruler of Paṭṭi Pombuccapura. The *basadi* was completed on Wednesday the 10 March, AD 1586.[28] He is evidently the same ruler who granted specified lands for the god Pārśvanātha of the Sādhanā Caityālaya at Koppa in AD 1589. This god had been set-up by a citizen named Pāṇḍya Nāyaka who had himself granted some lands to provide for the offerings to the god.[29]

---

26. *Ibid.*, KP, p. 48.
27. K.P. Jain, *The Religion of Tirthankaras*, Aliganj, U.P., p. 507.
28. B.A. Saletore, *op. cit.*, p. 363.
29. R. Narasimhachar, *E. Carn.*, vol. VI, Kop. 50, p. 86.

Perhaps, the most illustrious name among the many famous Jain rulers of Karkala is that of Immadi Bhairavarāya (AD 1505). Bhairavarāya of Karkala had given his sister, Gomatāmbikā, in marriage to Vīranarasiṁha Banga. The fruit of this alliance was Immadi Bhairavarāya; like Vīra Pāṇḍya, son of Bhairava, this nephew also has left imperishable monuments of his greatness. At a time when people were wrongly fighting over religious differences, this large hearted king set-up an example of religious tolerance and equal patronage to all religions.[30]

In the year AD 1510 hundreds of Gauḍ Sārasvat families had to leave Goa for fear of forcible conversion by the Portuguese. Some of them came to Karkala and received safe refuge in that kingdom; and the Jain king built the temple of Veṅkaṭaramaṇa in AD 1537 to enable them to pursue their ancient mode of worship. It was from the remains of the dilapidated palace of the ancient kings, the parapet walls and the steps leading to the tank in front of the temple were built.[31]

When the head of the Śṛṅgerī Maṭh came to Karkala in AD 1567, he was received with royal honours and was requested to camp there for some weeks. As he would not camp where there was no temple the king offered a newly constructed place of worship and had a magnificent idol of Śeṣaśāyī Ananteśvara installed in it, although the original intention was to make the place a *basadi*.

The royal priest Lalitakīrti Bhaṭṭāraka, of course, objected to this conversion of a *basadi* into a temple to which Bhairavarāya replied with all the dignity at his command that a wise ruler ought to treat all the religions of his subjects with equal reverence.[32]

And to make amends for having displeased his spiritual

---

30. D. Puttaswamy, *op. cit.*, p. 6.
31. *Ibid.*
32. Lalitakirti Bhattaraka, *op. cit.*, p. 5.

teacher, he got Tribhuvana Tilak Caityālaya constructed on the hillock facing on which Gommaṭa stands. As this *basadi* has four identical looking entrances from the four quarters, it is popularly known as "Caturmukha-Basadi." This was completed in AD 1586. There are Arha, Malli, Munisuvrata and *tīrthaṅkaras* installed in it at each of the four sides. Besides, there are 24 *tīrthaṅkaras* on the western side and Brahmā and Padmāvatī *yakṣī* on either side.

LITERARY FAME

During Davani Immadi Bhiravarāya's time (AD 1602), Thimmanna Ajila of Venur wanted to install a Gommaṭa at Venur also. Davani objected to this as he feared that this might diminish the importance of Karkala. This resulted in a battle in which Davani was defeated by Kanta Samant of Naravi, a commander of Thimmanna Ajila Ramanatha Wodeyar (AD 1622). He married the Ajila queen Madhurā Devī.

Vīra Pāṇḍya seems to have objected to Madhurā Devī's proposal to arrange for a *mastakābhiṣeka* to Gommaṭa of Venur. The queen ceded to Vīra Pāṇḍya the Naravi area and bought off his opposition. Very little is known of those who succeeded Vīra Pāṇḍya. There is no representative of the ancient family now.[33]

The Bhairarasas were not only patrons of architecture, sculpture, but also of literature. Some of them were note-worthy poets viz. Pāṇḍya Kṣapati has written *Bhavyānanda Śāstra*, a nosegay of moral aphorisms. Vīra Pāṇḍya wrote *Kriyā Nighaṇṭu*. Sanskrit poets like Lalitakīrti, Nāgacandra and Kalyāṇakīrti and Kannaḍa poets like Ratnākara Varṇī and Chadura Chandrama enjoyed the patronage of the Bhairarasas.[34]

Thus, next to Śravaṇbeḷgoḷa and Humcha, Karkala is the

---

33. D. Pattaswamy, *op. cit.*, p. 7.
34. Lalitakirti Bhattaraka., *op. cit.*, p. 16.

important Jain sacred place where second Bāhubali image is the main attraction for Jain *śrāvakas*.

Moodabidri : A Jain Kāśī of South

ŚRĪKṢETRA MOODABIDRI AND THE LOCATION

Moodabidri is an important Jain centre, next to Karkala in South Kanara district since early medieval times. Moodabidri, popularly referred to as Jain Kāśī of south India is historically *atiśaya puṇya kṣetra*. More than other things, it is famous for its Jain *basadis*.

To the Jains, Moodabidri, a small town nestling in the midst of lively natural setting, is a place of religious pilgrimage and to others it is a centre of architectural treasure. Here are found in the temples, the holy scriptures (*siddhānata*) *Dhavalā, Jaya Dhavalā* and *Mahā Dhavalā,* (The Vedas of Jains) and also a good number of Jain *mūrtis* big and small, made of precious stones.

People from north India mostly call this Moodabidri as "Moolabidri," "Modabadri." But the name Moodabidri which we find in government documents is generally the accepted one. Śravaṇbeḷgoḷa lies 200 km away from Moodabidri. (Generally north Indians refer Śravaṇbeḷgoḷa by the names "Jainbadri" — "Jainbidri" and "Bāhubalijī." However, this holy *kṣetra* is traditionally termed as Śravaṇbeḷgoḷa either in the south India or in any government documents.

Moodabidri and Śravaṇbeḷgoḷa are the two most sacred south-Indian religious pilgrim centres for Jains in India. But some Jain pilgrims finding the similar word "Bidri" in both the holy places came under the wrong impression that the two different names are the name of one place that is Śravaṇbeḷgoḷa. Hence, they visited only Jainbadri (Śravaṇbeḷgoḷa) and returned home without having the *puṇya darśan* of Moodabidri.[35]

---

35. Sri Digambar Jain Math, *Moodabidri Dakshina Kannada District* (I.S.), Moodabidri, 1980, p. 19.

Hence, the pilgrims are to note the following. The other names of Moodabidri are Moolabidri, Moolabadiri and Śravaṇbeḷgoḷa and that of Śravaṇbeḷgoḷa Jainbadri, Jainbidri and Bāhubalijī. Both the places of holy pilgrimage are historically important for tourists and spiritually for the Jains. Each is independent of the other.[36]

LOCATION OF MOODABIDRI

A village in the Mangalore Tāluka of South Kanara district of Karnataka, situated in $13^{0}5'$N and 75^{0}E, is 21 miles east of Mangalore town. Moodabidri lies to the north of and 22 miles away from Mangalore. It is the district headquarters of Dakṣiṇa Kannaḍa district in Karnataka and one of the major ports on the west coast. From Mangalore buses ply, every half an hour to Moodabidri. Tourists, who come down from Delhi to Moodabidri, enjoy the direct route by Delhi-Mangalore Jayanti Janata Express which passes through Agra, Gwalior, Jhānsī, Bina, Bhopal, Iṭārasī, Nāgapur, Jalarpeṭ before it arrives Mangalore. Tourists from Bombay to Moodabidri or back could avail of daily plying tourist luxury buses which are about 4 to 6 in number — 15 miles from Moodabidri is the Mangalore Airport. There is also the Bombay-Mangalore Air Flight and daily service buses are available to cover the 15 miles journey.

OTHER PUṆYAKṢETRAS CLOSE TO MOODABIDRI

Moodabidri-Venur	-	12 miles
Moodabidri-Dharmasthala	-	32 miles
Moodabidri-Śravaṇbeḷgoḷa	-	125 miles
Moodabidri-Karkala	-	10 miles
Moodabidri-Varaṅga	-	26 miles
Moodabidri-Humcha	-	80 miles

36. *Ibid.*, p. 20.

State and private buses are always available to visit these places from Moodabidri at all times on all days.[37]

AN INTRODUCTION TO MOODABIDRI

Moodabidri has yet another name as Jain Kāśī known far and wide. The ancient town is to the north of Mangalore and in Karkala Tāluka of Karnataka State. While Moodabidri is a place of religious attraction for Jains, for others it is a place of cultural and historical attractions. Guru-Basadi or "Siddhānta-Basadi," is the oldest of all temples. It was at one time famous for its glory and excellence, but as time passed, the place was deserted by the Jains owing to the onslaught of either natural calamities or of some strong foreign opposition. As a result, there grew a wild bamboo forest. The temple, later on, became completely covered with thick forest.[38]

The Sanskrit name "Vaṁśapura" or "Venupura" for Moodabidri is derived from Venu (meaning bamboo) Pura (place), referring to the thick forest of the region. The name "Venupura" is mentioned in the local inscription. The Kannaḍa name of the place "Bidri" is probably derived from "Bidiru" (bamboo). Since this "Bidri" is located to the east of Mulki, hence Mangalore and other adjoining places rightly got the name "Moodabidre" which is now popularly recognized by one and all. With a cluster of many holy temples and being inhabited by Jain *vrātika*s, this town come to be known as "Vratapura" in an inscriptions.

Moodabidri is only a small town in Tulunāḍu or South Kanara district. The surrounding landscapes, green patches of paddy fields and the lakes with crystal clear water enrich the beauty of this town. People here grow coconut, *supārī*, banana, cashewnut (*kāju*), pepper, pineapple, etc. Paddy is the main food crop.

---

37. B.A. Saletore, *Ancient Karnataka History of Tuluva*, vol. I, p. 253.
38. *Ibid.*, p. 22.

The palace and the temples here attract the visitors with their architecture, sculpture and delicate carving on wood and stone. The climate being moderate and congenial, there stands a private sanitorium in the outskirts of the town.[39]

It is sanctified by the stay of great saints and poets. Jains from all parts of India come here to worship in the famous 18 Jain *basadis* that are dedicated to the memory of the *tīrthaṅkara*.

SITE OF MOODABIDRI

Moodabidri is a unique place having 18 fascinating Jain temples. Among them Pārśvanātha-Basadi also known as Guru-Basadi is a pretty old one. Thousand pillars temple is another famous *basadi* otherwise known as Tribhuvan Tilaka Cūḍāmaṇi-Basadi. Like these two, the other remaining *basadis*, though small in size, are built of hard stone, each being an architectural treasure in itself. The word *basadi* is derived from the Sanskrit word "VASATI," the meaning being the residences of God.[40]

GURU-BASADIM (SIDDHĀNTA-BASADI)

Formerly, this temple was called Pārśvanātha-Basadi. It is said that at one time, Moodabidri was deserted by Jains and a wild bamboo forest had grown around it. According to a tradition, a Jain ascetic came over to Moodabidri in the eighth century AD and to his great bewilderment, he saw a tiger and a cow drinking water from a common trough while the tiger feeding the calf and the cow the cub.

It was absolutely a strange scene. Guessing that the spot must be sacrosanct, the ascetic had the forest cleared. In the process, he found a large-sized divine image of Śrī Pārśvanātha carved out of black granite. It was sufficiently proved that this image was thousands of years old. The ascetic (Svāmījī) had a *basadi* built at that spot and installed the image in AD 714 with

---

39. K.P. Jain, *op. cit.*, p. 505.
40. Karnataka State Gazetteer, Govt. of Karnataka, *South Kanara District*, p. 750.

Pañcakalyāṇa ceremony. This basadi, built at the instance of the *guru*, is named as the Guru-Basadi.[41]

Another reason for which the *basadi* is called Guru-Basadi is that in Moodabidri one could find an ancient *Guru Maṭh*. His Holiness Śrī Cārukīrti Paṇḍitācāryāvarya Svāmījī is the celebrated Head of this *Guru-Pīṭha*. It is an age long good tradition to celebrate the *Paṭṭābhiṣeka Mahotsava* of this Svāmījī of Jain Guru Maṭha or the *Guru-Pīṭha* found in the outer room of the *basadi*. Since there is a cordial relationship between the *basadi* and the *Guru-Pīṭha*, it became a tradition to call this *basadi* most appropriately by the name Guru-Basadi.

As the holy scriptures (*siddhānta*s) *Dhavalā*, *Jaya Dhavalā* and *Mahā Dhavalā* are found in this *basadi*, it is also called the Siddhānta-Basadi. The ancient palm leaf manuscripts, the only copies of their kind in original found in India are being preserved in a safe custody in this temple. The local *śrāvaka*s confirm the fact that deities brought these *siddhānta grantha*s from Bankapur in Dhārwāḍ and presented them at the holy feet of Śrī Pārśvanātha of Guru-Basadi. It is known from the inscription found on the Siṁhapīṭha of this image that the installation ceremony of the Jinbimba, Śrī Pārśvanātha, took place in the year AD 714.[42]

About 24 images made of diamond, rubies, emerablds, sapphires and many other precious stones (*navaratna*s) are enshrined in this *basadi*. These Jain images, called *navaratna*s and *pratimā*s, are very precious and proud contributions. Their height varies from half an inch to 10 inches. The sight of these images is as holy to the Jains as that of the *siddhānta*s. Thousands of pilgrims from all over India come daily to this *basadi* to sanctify themselves.

The presiding deity in the *sanctum sanctorum* is Lord Pārśvanātha, being made of black granite, the image is remark-

---

41. *Sri Digambara Jain Math, Moodabidri*, p. 26.
42. *Ibid.*, p. 27.

ably large-sized with a sober appearance. Though centuries old it looks so new, as if, it were recently made by the artist. Two climbing cobras each on the back intertwining themselves come upon this 9 ft image of *kāyotsarga* pose, with their raised hood as though holding a *chatram* over the head of the image.

Another inscription speaks well about the outer throne which was erected in AD 1538 by local *śrāvaka*s headed by one Coḷa Shetty. The adjacent *basadi* on the left side is Ammanavara-Basadi. Here are placed 24 *tīrthaṅkara*s on the Hari Pīṭha (*caturviṁśati tīrthaṅkaras*) each 3 ft high. Each sculpture is carved with great physical beauty. The images of goddess Sarasvatī and goddess Padmāvatī are facing each other on either side of these 24 *tīrthaṅkara*s. Both of them are carved out of Chatara stone (black granite) with grace. There are thousands of *jinbimba*s of remarkable beauty on the first floor of the main *basadi* found either in the pose of *kāyotsarga* or *khaḍgāsana*.[43]

HOSA-BASADI, THOUSAND-PILLARS-BASADI, TRIBHUVANA TILAKA-CŪḌĀMAṆI-BASADI

The biggest *basadi* at Moodabidri is the Tribhuvana Tilaka Cūḍāmaṇi-Basadi also known as the "Basadi of Thousand Pillars." Candranātha-Basadi and Hosa (new) Basadi was erected in AD 1429-30 by the devotees of Moodabidri as directed by Devarāya Wodeyar of Nāgamaṅgala of Mangalore kingdom. Later in AD 1462, Bharadevī added the elegant *maṇḍapa* named after her. The image of Candranātha which is 6½ ft in height is made of an alloy of five metals. The monument famous for its beautifully carved pillars have miniature artistic pillars carved upon them.[44]

Bhairava of the same family, on being told by the blessed teacher Vīrasena that such an act would lend to his prosperity in the future, got the third storey of the Tribhuvana Cūḍāmaṇi-Basadi built at the world famed Venupura, roofed with copper-

43. Karnataka, State Gazetteer, *South Kanara District*, p. 750.
44. S.R. Sharma, *Jainism and Karnataka Culture*, Dharwar, 1940, p. 53.

plates. His family-priest is said to have been Paṇḍitācārya (Vīrasena) and his family god Pārśvanātha. He also gave to the temple various kinds of silver plates, vessels, lamp-steads, etc.[45]

Nagaladevī, the queen of Bhairavarāja, erected the *mānastambha* or pillar, a huge monolith of a height of 50 ft, in front of the *basadi*.[46] Likewise his two daughters, Lakṣmīdevī and Paṇḍitādevī, provided for the daily food and special gifts of two Jain ascetics.[47]

Inscription of the Hosa-Basadi related with Bhairavadeva is more than of ordinary interest because of the simple faith it reflects which made Bhairava provide for the forenoon and afternoon worship of the Jinālaya, that he might be a means to the attainment of the highest salvation. It is dated in the Śaka year 1374 or AD 1462.

There are elaborate carvings on the sides of the plinth of the *basadi*, which *inter alia*, has the figures of a giraffe and dragon; this is perhaps indicative that the Jain merchants of those days had extensive trade contacts. No two pillars in the whole *basadi* are alike. They are known for their massiveness, rapturous details, grandeur and exuberance of skill. In spite of granite slab of rough texture, the minute details are gracefully carved with great care. The installed image in this *basadi* is Bhagavān Candranātha found in *khaḍgāsana* posture and is dazzling since it is made of an alloy of *pañca loha*. The pillars in the room, which adjoin the sanctum, have carved figures of *cauri*-bearer, a man beating a drum, a man riding on a gaily caparisoned elephant, a human *garuḍa* with wings, etc.

Nowhere in Karnataka a *basadi* of so grandeur and so magnificence as this could be found. The *basadi* holds mirror to

---

45. *Ibid*., p. 54.

46. *Ibid*.

47. P. Mangesrao, *Inscriptions in the* ***Hosa Basti*** *of Moodabidri*, Karnataka Sahitya Sammelana Report XII, Mangalore, 1923, p. 156.

the glorious Jain tradition of the past dating back 5 to 6 centuries. The *basadi* consists of a line of seven *maṇḍapas*. To begin with, the Bhairavadevī Maṇḍapa in the forefront is raised on the massive pillars. Next in succession are the Citrādevī Maṇḍapa, Namaskāra Maṇḍapa, Tīrthaṅkara Maṇḍapa, Lakṣmī Maṇḍapa, Sukhanāśī Maṇḍapa and the Seventh Garbhagṛha Maṇḍapa. Next to this is Samvasarana Maṇḍapa — the *sanctum sanctorum*, the main shrine where the devotee have the *darśana* of Bhagavān Candraprabha. The *basadi* has two storeyes enshrining a number of rare and valuable *jinbimbas*. The second storey is named as *siddhakūṭa*. This *siddhakūṭa* is perhaps most accurately viewed as a replica of the *siddhaloka*. There are also images of Vedic gods and goddesses on the stone pillars of the Bhairavadevī Maṇḍapa and Citrādevī Maṇḍapa.[48]

BADAGA-BASADI

This beautiful *basadi* lies to the north of the town Moodabidri hence the name Badaga-Basadi. This is 4 to 5 centuries old. The main deity is Śrī Candranātha Svamī, the image being carved out of white marble. The images of 24 *tīrthaṅkaras* of black granite are fascinating. A short but carefully carved *mānastambha* in front of the *basadi* appears to be a *tilaka* on the forehead of a woman. Every year in January, the festival celebrated in this temple attracts people across the world.[49]

SETTARA-BASADI

This is a *basadi* wholly built of granite stone, having entirely a granite slabbed roof. As the name itself denotes the *basadi* came up with the joint dedication of the local Shetty sect. The presiding deity is Lord Mahāvīra — a black granite stone figure of 3 ft. To the left in an adjacent *basadi* are enshrined 24 *tīrthaṅkaras* on the Hari Pīṭha. On either side facing each other are the images of

---

48. Sri Digambara Jain Math, *Moodabidri*, p. 29.
49. Rajamala Jain and Laxmichandra Jain, *Bharat Ke Digambara Jain Tirtha* (Hindi) vol. V, Karnataka Bombay, 1988, p. 168.

two Devīs-Māte-Sarasvatī and Mahāmāte Padmāvatī, each carved out of black granite with exquisite beauty. Both are lovely sculptures in a sitting posture. Special *pūjā*s are offered during Śrāvaṇa *māsa*.[50]

HIRE-BASADI (AMMANAVARA-BASADI)

This is popularly known as Ammanavara-Basadi. Śrī Śāntinātha is the main deity. It is a lovely sculpture of 2½ ft height in a standing posture. In an adjoining shrine to the left are enshrined 24 *tīrthaṅkara*s carved out of clay soil — each image having a face with its child like innocent simplicity. Facing each other one on either side are the sculptures of two Devīs in a sitting posture — Māte Sarasvatī and Mahāmāte Padmāvatī (Ammanavara) — both carved out of clay. The face of each image is calm and free from emotions, exhibiting majestic grace. The dimensions are almost life-size and set an example for a superb art. *Pūjā*s are offered every Friday and hundreds of devotees offer special *pūjā*s during Śrāvaṇa *māsa* to get their mundane wishes fulfilled. Car festival of this *basadi* is spiritually a significant event during February. It is evident from the inscriptions that this is also one of the ancient temples.[51]

BETKERI-BASADI

This *basadi*, facing the Betkeri road, is dedicated to Śrī Mahāvīra Svāmī. The image is in *paryaṅkāsana* posture and 3 ft high. It is made out of white marble. From the far off road below the holy sight of Vīra Jinendra in the *sanctorum* not only attracts the mind but entraps our heart as well.[52]

KOTI-BASADI

This *basadi* was built in AD 1401 by a Jain *śrāvaka*, Koti Setty. The 2½ ft high Bagavān Neminātha carved out of black stone is the

50. *Ibid*., p. 168-69.
51. Sri Digambara Jain Math, *Moodabidri*, p. 29.
52. *Ibid*., p. 30.

presiding deity. Basadi is fairly big and beautiful.[53]

VIKRAMA SETTY-BASADI

This is another *basadi* built of all hard granite. The *basadi* was built by Vikrama Setty, a Jain *śrāvaka* and it is named after him. The main deity is Bhagvān Ādinātha made of black granite and is 2 ft high. The Jinbimba is in a *palyaṅkāsana* posture. The images of 24 *tīrthaṅkaras* made of all bronze are enshrined on a Hari Pīṭha in an adjoining *basadi*. A free standing pillar *mānastambha* of 32 ft high in front of the *basadi* adds to the beauty of the temples.[54]

KALLU-BASADI

This *basadi* appropriately bears the name Kallu-Basadi which is built of only hard rough granite. Its original presiding deity was Śrī Candranātha. Since that image of stone corroded in course of time, it was the past Svamījī of Śrī Jain Maṭha who celebrated in grand scale the *Pañcakalyāṇa Mahotsava* of this *basadi*.[55]

LEPPADA-BASADI

The *basadi* named as Leppada-Basadi have the images of the main deity Bhagvān Candranātha and his attendants Shama Yakṣa-Jwālāmālinī; the two Śāśana-*devatās* in the *basadi* are made of clay (*leppa*). Māte Jwālāmālinī is recognized with a great esteem and a great number of devotees take her *darśana* and offer *pūjā* during Śrāvaṇa *māsa* in the hope of their mundane wishes being fulfilled. A 45 ft high *mānastambha* is very attractively situated on a large plain ground in front of the *basadi*.[56]

---

53. Rajamala Jain and Laxmichandra Jain, *op. cit.*, p. 169.
54. *Ibid.*
55. *Ibid.*, pp. 169-70.
56. Sri Digambara Jain Math, op. cit., p. 31.

DERAMMA SETTY-BASADI

This is fairly a big temple built by Deramma Setty a Jain *śrāvaka*. The shrine made of all hard granite consists of a rectangular *sanctorum* (*garbhagṛha*), Arhanātha, Mallinātha Munisuvratanātha are the main deities found on raised *pīṭhas*. Below are the beautiful images of 24 *tīrthaṅkaras* on a Hari Pīṭha. There is also an upper storey just above the *sanctorum*.

COḶA SETTY-BASADI

The temple built by Coḷa Setty is dedicated to Sumathinātha, Padmaprabha and Supārśvanātha. This is also constructed out of hard granite. Each *paryaṅkāsana* image of Jinendra is found in deep meditation having his sight focused towards the tip of his nose. Two adjoining shrines are found on either side of the main *basadi*. The image of Neminātha seated on a *śaṅkha* found in one of these *basadis* is a rare specimen.[57]

MAHĀDEVA SETTY-BASADI

This *basadi* is so called after the name of its builder, Mahādeva Setty. This shrine is dedicated to Bhagvān Ādinātha. The sculpture carved out of black stone with great physical beauty. The image is 5 ft high and is in *kāyotsarga* posture.[58]

BAIKAṆṬHĪKARI-BASADI

As the name suggests, the *basadi* was built by one Baikaṇṭhīkari, the short name of the *basadi* being Benki-Basadi. Presiding deity is Bhagvān Anantanātha. It is carved out of black stone and is 3 ft in height. The adjacent shrine is dedicated to Mahā-Sarasvatī.[59]

KERE-BASADI

This temple is situated in front of a beautiful tank. Hence, its befitting name Kere-Basadi. Bhagvān Mallinātha is the main

---

57. Rajamala Jain and Laxmichandra Jain, *op. cit.*, p. 170.
58. *Ibid*.
59. Sri Digambara Jain Math, op. cit., p. 31.

deity. The image is made of black stone and is 3 ft high. The *jinbimba* is in *kāyotsarga* posture. Facing this *basadi*, on the other side of the tank, is Vaiṣṇava temple dedicated to Śrī Gopāla Kṛṣṇa — an ideal example for the spirit of religious tolerance of the Jains.[60]

PADU-BASADI

Authentically dated inscriptions reveal that this *basadi* is not only older than Guru-Basadi but also the oldest one. This *basadi* is situated to the west of the town, hence the name Padu-Basadi. The *basadi* is dedicated to Bhagvān Vimalanātha, Anantanātha and Dharmanātha. Each *khaḍgāsana* image is 3 ft in height and artistically carved out of black stone. The central image of Anantanātha, according to an inscription, is older than the other two. As many as 3000 to 4000 palm-leaf manuscripts have been preserved in this temple in a cave like structure of hard granite just above the *sanctorum*. Now they have been removed to Smt. Rama Rani Jain Institute of Śrī Jain Maṭha where they are preserved with great care.[61]

ŚRĪ JAIN MAṬHA-BASADI

The presiding deity here is Śrī Pārśvanātha, a *khaḍgāsana* image, which is 1½ ft high made of black stone. Elaborate form of *devapūjā* ritual is held thrice in a day. Pūjya Svasti Śrī Bhaṭṭāraka Cārukīrti Svāmījī, the Managing Trustee of the group of 18 Jain temples, who looks after the well-being of Śrī Kṣetra, resides in the back apartment house of Jain Maṭha-Basadi. The prayer hall (*mukha maṇḍapa*) of the *basadi* is also being used for *dharmopadeśa* programme.[62]

JAIN PĀṬHAŚĀLĀ-BASADI

Bhagvān Munisuvrata Svāmījī adorns the main *pīṭha* of this *basadi*. The *jinbimba* found in *khaḍgāsana* posture which is 2 ft in height

60. *Ibid.*, p. 32.
61. Rajamala Jain and Laxmichandra Jain, *op. cit.*, p. 172.
62. Sri Digambara Jain Math, *op. cit.*, p. 32.

is carved out of white marble. The belief that the ritual services such as *pañcāmṛta abhiṣeka* or *kṣīrābhiṣeka* offered to Śrī Munisuvrata Svāmī, who is the Ādidevatā of "Śani Gṛha," will fetch great relief to those who are under the evil-influence of "Śani" has gained popularity among the devotees.

It is known from the inscriptions that out of these 18 temples, Padu-Basadi, Guru-Basadi and Ammanavara-Basadi are the most ancient ones and that the remaining ones were built only after the Guru-Pīṭha had been founded.[63]

WORTH-VISITING PLACES OF MOODABIDRI SAMĀDHIS

Besides the 18 *samādhi*s of *maṭhādhipati*s, there are other *samādhi*s of important people like Ambu Setty, Adu Setty and others, in Betkeri. Except a few inscriptions carved on one or two *samādhi*s, nothing is revealed from others.[64]

KODANKALLU (NYĀYA-BASADI)

Temple of Justice : There is a *maṇḍapa* (a small structure of hard granite known as Nyāya-Basadi) about a mile from Moodabidri at a place called Kodankallu. Whenever people demanded, Justice Courts were held here and justice was meted. Nearby, there is a *samādhi* of Śrī Candrakīrti Muni (AD 1637). There was a pious lady who performed *satī* (who let herself be burnt to death on the funeral pyre of her husband).[65]

CHOWTER PALACE

Of the many Jain dynasties that ruled South Kanara at various times, the Chowter of Moodabidri is the most outstanding. Formerly, their capital was at Ullal. At the time when the rulers under Viṣṇuvardhana of Halebiḍu became independent, the Chowters made their independent capitals at Moodabidri and puttige. This Chowter dynasty ruled Tulunāḍu independently

63. *Ibid.*, p. 34.
64. *Ibid.*
65. Rajamala Jain and Laxmichandra Jain, *op. cit.*, p. 172.

for about 700 years (from AD 1160 to AD 1887). The present owners of the old palace and direct descendants of the Chowter enjoy royal patronage. Though the palace is dilapidated in many ways, its ancient grandeur still attracts the visitors. Rare carvings in the Audience Hall, such as the Navanārī Kuñjara (nine women elephant) and the Pañcanārī Thuraga (five women horse) attract the attention of visitors.[66]

PATRONIZATION TO MOODABIDRI

Like other Jain centres, Moodabidri also received patronization from royal persons, feudatories, royal ladies, rich merchants and traders and laity since early medieval period. Therefore, the religious importance of Moodabidri enhanced day by day. Scholars and *śrāvaka*s came to this place to study old Jain manuscripts. This place was responsible for the spread of Jain culture in South Canara.

The history of the spread of Jainism in the fifteenth century confirms the statements that have been made elsewhere relating to its steady popularity in well-known cities of Karnataka like Mattavara, Vanavāsa, Gerasoppe, Moodabidri, etc. Jainism has now a prominent stronghold in these cities. Unlike most of the centres of the fourteenth century, these cities were on the whole, destined to play a decisive part in the history of the Syādvada doctrine.

Moodabidri, one of the cities of Tuluva, was of greater importance than the above seats of Jainism. We have elsewhere traced the advent of Jainism into this city in the reign of the Hoyasala King. Ballāla Deva I (AD 1100-06).[67] The main sources of information for the study of Jainism in Tuluva are the Hindu and Jain tradition, epigraphs, and Jain literature as preserved in the libraries of Jain centres of Moodabidri and Karkala. We have to rely mainly on the Jain and Hindu tradition corroborated

66. B.A. Saletore, *Ancient Karnataka History of Tuluva*, pp. 410-11.
67. B.L. Rice, *Epigraphica Carnataka, Inscriptions in the Shimoga District*, vol. VII, Bangalore, 1902, SK, p. 49.

by the notes of Jainism in epigraphs discovered in Tuluva.

Hindu tradition contains notes of Jain *ṛṣi*s who are said to have introduced Jainism into a part of Tuluva. The wandering of this great teacher Ṛṣabha are given in greater detail in the *Bhāgavata Purāṇa* which contains some details that are of interest of Tuluva history. The Kutaka mentioned above could only have been the Kutakagrāma of Tuluva. Jain advent into Tuluva is to be dated to the early days of Ṛṣabha, the first *tīrthaṅkara.* The activities of the Jains are to be located somewhere in the reign between Kutakagrāma and Hattiangadi. If we are to rely on the story of Ṛṣabha's wanderings, Jainism appears to have been introduced first in the regin of Kundapura and then elsewhere in Tuluva.[68]

But the traditions current in Moodabidri and Karkala, the two strongholds of Jainism in Tuluva, run counter to the above view. The Jain tradition on Moodabidri as well as Karkala, dates the introduction of Jainism into Tuluva to about the ninth century AD.[69] The following may be noted in this context:

In the first place, the Jains of Tuluva have no memories of Paraśurāma unlike the brāhmaṇas, they deny the creation of the Sapta Koṅkaṇas by Jāmadagnya. As Buchanan remarked,

> they merely trace the history of Jainism to Jinadatta Raya who was born, according to them, at Uttara Mathura near the Yamuna. This shows that the Jains came to the district in comparatively later times.[70]

Secondly the Jains of Tuluva themselves admit that the brāhmaṇas of Tuluva were a more ancient people. Buchanan was informed by the Jains that

> the Tuluva Brahmans, who followed Vedas, were first introduced by Mayura-Varma, a Jain Prince who lived at

68. B.A. Saletore, *Ancient Karnataka,* p. 406.

69. Buchanan, *A Journey from Madras through the countries of Mysore, Canara and Malabar,* vol. III, London, 1807, p. 81.

70. *Ibid.*, p. 82.

> Barakura about a thousands years ago. But of these rulers the Jains of Tuluva have no written record.[71]

Hence, the Jains seem to have come to Tuluva in an age when even the traces of Mayūravarmā had grownup.

Thirdly, the oldest *basadi* in Moodabidri is the Gurugala-Basadi. The Jains of Moodabidri reckon this *basadi* to be only 1000 years old. In other words, the Jains of Moodabidri would date the advent of their earliest leaders to the ninth century or thereabouts. Moreover, in that same town the Gaurī temple is admitted by the Jains to be older than the Gurugala-Basadi, thus proving beyond doubt that before the advent of the Jains, Hinduism had already taken roots in that town.[72]

Fourthly, in the same town is a quarter called Hala-varavarga. The Jains of Moodabidri assert that it was the earliest colony of their people in that town. Evidently, the Jains settled in that quarter mainly as traders, and ultimately succeeded in converting the ruler Moodabidri from Hinduism to Jainism. This could only have been in later times when the Alupas had already made Moodabidri one of their provincial capital.

Fifthly, Moodabidri was originally a centre of the brāhmaṇas. Both, the traditions of the Jains and the epigraphs prove this. The Chowters of Moodabidri, who are now Jains, had later changed their centre to Puttige. It was originally a centre of the Hindus, their tutelary deity (*kula devatā*) being the god Somanātha of Villa on the coast. Buchanan relates in his days that there were six *guḍi*s or temples in Moodabidri belonging to the brāhmaṇas, who followed the Purāṇas, and 700 houses mostly occupied by the brāhmaṇas of the two sects.[73]

Sixthly, till AD 1800 when Buchanan visited the Jains of Moodabidri, they were ignorant of the immigration of their co-

---

71. B.A. Saletore, *Ancient Karnataka History of Tuluva*, vol. I, pp. 407-08.
72. Buchanan, *op. cit.*, vol. III, p. 75.
73. *Ibid.*, p. 80.

religionists from northern India to Śravaṇbeḷgoḷa. Instead of tracing their origin to the activities of their own people from northern India, or Śravaṇbeḷgoḷa, the Jains associated their advent with Arabia. Buchanan relates that the Jains "allege that formerly they extended over the whole of Arya or Bharatakanda; and that all those whoever had any pretensions to be of ksatri descent, were of their sect." The Jains came to Tuluva in comparatively recent times. They confounded the Paraśurāma of Hindu tradition with an imaginary Paraso Bhaṭṭāraka whose antecedents are unknown to us. If the Jains, as is maintained by some, had indeed come to Tuluva in the days of Bhadrabāhu, the memory of their advent into the district would never have been forgotten.[74]

Indeed, this assumption of ours is further proved by the following tradition that still prevails in Moodabidri —

Once a Jain sage visited Ballāla ruler whose finger had been cut-off as a punishment by his sovereign. The sage was respectfully served and waited upon by Ballālarāya. But seeing the maimed finger of Ballālarāya, the Jain Sage went away. At this Ballālarāya got angry and destroyed 108 *basadi*s of the Jains and in their place built a tank. Cārukīrti Paṇḍita Ācārya of Beḷagoḷa heard of this disaster that had happened to Ballāla king and cured him of his illness and saved his kingdom. Cārukīrti Paṇḍita Ācārya then travelled onto Nallaru near Karkala. Cārukīrti Paṇḍita realized that it was the right place for building a *basadi*. Accordingly, he built a *basadi* and a monastery (*maṭha*) as well.[75]

It is true that the name Cārukīrti Paṇḍita Ācārya was assumed by many Jain teachers. Thus the earliest Cārukīrti Paṇḍita Deva is represented as the disciple of Municandra Traividya Bhaṭṭāraka, in a record dated in the 12th year of the

---

74. B.A. Saletore, *Ancient Karnataka History of Tuluva*, p. 410.
75. *Ibid*.

Cāḷukya Vikrama era (AD 1096).[76]

The similarity between the tradition of Cārukīrti Paṇḍita Deva in Moodabidri and the story recorded in the above epigraph seem to suggest that it was in the twelfth century AD that Jainism made some headway in Tuluva. It is only in Śaka 1083 (AD 1161-62), however, that we come across a grant made to a Jain temple by a prince called Kumārarāya about whom no detail is available. The patronage extended to Jainism by this prince is definite. The fact that the inscription was found in Kervase suggests that the place had become a centre of Jainism in the middle of the twelfth century AD. It was only in the first quarter of the thirteenth century AD that we come across the inscription of the Alupa kings who had extended their patronage to Jainism. Thus, the defaced stone epigraph found in the Gaurī temple at Prāntya in Moodabidri, dated AD 1215, belonged to the reign of Kulaśekhara Alupendradeva I. The details of the grant to the goddess Gaurī as well as to Pārśvanātha are effaced.[77]

Nevertheless, this record proves that under Kulaśekhara Alupendradeva I, Jainism already received royal patronage in Moodabidri.[78]

The stone inscription found in the Ammanavara-Basadi at Moodabidri of the reign of the Alupa King Kulaśekhara Alupendradeva (III) dated AD 1384, further proves the learning of the Alupa ruler towards Jainism. As we have already narrated, the king is described to be seated on the diamond throne (*ratna siṁhāsana*), obviously in the Pārśvanātha-Basadi itself, of Moodabidri (*kulaśekhara alupendra devaru bidireya . . .* (*pārśvanāthaba*) *sadiyolu ratna siṁhāsana-arudhar. . .*). The defaced inscription

76. B.A. Saletore, *Medieval Jainism: With Special Reference to the Vijayanagara Empire*, p. 352.

77. B.A. Saletore, p. 413.

78. B.A. Saletore, *Ancient Karnataka History of Tuluva*, p. 414.

clearly mentions, however a gift to the Pārśvanāthadeva (*bidireya pārśvanātha devarige nive dyakke*).[79] In the thirteenth century AD Moodabidri possessed the Pārśvanātha-Basadi which received royal patronage from the Alupa kings of Tuluva.[80]

At Moodabidri, which is eulogized in one of the records as (*jin-dharmanadagarām*), there were many exquisitely built Jain *basadis* (*uru-jain-alayaramya-harmya-cāyādim-chelu-adudettampuram*). The earliest epigraphical reference is the Gurugala-Basadi of Chandogra-Pārśvadeva in AD 1390.[81]

Thus Moodabidri record (AD 1430) of Devarāya (II) records the building of the Tribhavana-Cūḍāmaṇi-Mahācaitya by the Jain preceptor Abhinava-Cārukīrti-Paṇḍita with the assistance of the people of Salikenadu, the Chauta ruler and the *aruvaru-ballalugalu* and the financial assistance was granted by the imperial governor Devarāja-Odeya. The extent of the support which Jainism enjoyed in those days in South Kanara is evident from the record that the governor made the grant to the emperor himself.[82]

In AD 1430, Bhairava of the Nagire ruling house provided copper covering (*tāmra-podake*) for the the third storey of the Tribhuvana-Cūḍāmaṇi-Caitya of Candra Jain built by the Halaru at Moodabidri.[83]

The author of another inscription of the same year (AD 1429) and reign describes the young lads of Moodabidri as *balakar* (*illar-udgha-jina-dharmma-rater* and as *anindya-jinodita-sastrasaligal*).[84]

---

79. B.A. Saletore, *Medieval Jainism*, p. 352.
80. B.L. Rice, *South Indian Inscription*, vol. VII, nos. 198 and 299.
81. K.V. Ramesh, *History of South Kanara: From Earliest Times to the Fall of Vijayanagara*, Dharwar, 1970, p. 302.
82. B.L. Rice, *South Indian Inscriptions*, vol. VII, no. 202.
83. *Ibid*.
84. K.V. Ramesh, *op. cit*., p. 301.

Inscriptions of this period from Moodabidri contain many stanzas in praise of the devotion to Jainism by the Kalaśa-Karkala and Nagire rulers of various guilds, and even the common people of all ages. An inscription of AD 1429, of the reign of Devarāya II, which names Moodabidri as Venupura, says —

> *tulu-desakke-visishiam-appa nagaram śrī-venu-nāma puram*
> *vilasach-chri-jin-dharmma-margga-ratarim sat-patra-danamgaclim* ।
> *nalavim-malpa subhavyarim jinakath-alapumgalam sadhu-sam-*
> *kuladim kelva susilasa puruṣarimdoppippad-amta puram* ॥[85]

The Alupa ruler Kulaśekhara III was much influenced by Jainism. An inscription from Moodabidri, belonging to AD 1384, states that he was a worshipper of the Jain preceptor Cārukīrti (*śrīmac-cārukīrti-divya-śrīpādopadam-ārādhaka*), seated on his jewelled throne at a *basadi* (*dame* damaged in the record) at Bidire. The inscription records grants made by the ruler to the Jain-deity Pārśvanātha.[86]

But it was only in the fifteenth century in the times of the Vijayanagara monarchs that it earned fame. A stone inscription dated Śaka 1351 (AD 1429) of the reign of the Emperor Devarāya II (AD 1423-46) relates that Venupura (i.e., Moodabidri) was a city distinguished for its Bhavyas who followed the right path, gladly performed deeds of virtue and who were eager to hear stories relating to the *jin dharma*.[87]

The local ruler Bhairarasa, who was matrimonially connected with the kings who ruled over the Gerasoppe-Nagiri kingdom, made at the instance of his *guru* Vīrasenamuni certain specified offerings in the Candra *jin mandira* at Moodabidri.[88]

---

85. *Ibid.*, p. 298.
86. B.A. Saletore, *Medieval Jainism*, p. 352.
87. B.L. Rice, *South Indian Inscriptions*, vol. VII, pp. 94-98.
88. *Ibid.*, *S.I.I.* vol. VII, no. 197.

In AD 1451, a number of Settis constructed the *mukha-maṇḍapa* of the Tribhuvana-Cūḍāmaṇi-Caitya and carried out numerous repairs.[89]

When the illness of the Nagire ruler Bhairava I had turned fatal in AD 1461, he made grants for worship to the deities Candranāthasvāmī, Supārśva *tīrthaṅkara* and Candraprabha *tīrthaṅkara* of the same Tribhuvana-Cūḍāmaṇi-Caitya.[90]

Moodabidri is described in an inscription found at the place. Among other things, the groups of beautiful Jain temples and houses, ask the poet of the inscription "to sing the glory of Venupura, where women are true to the lords and men are engaged in the study of the Jain *śāstra*s and worshippers find recreation in giving gifts and performing *pūjā*, and where even children are enthusiastic in their adherence to *dharma*." The kind of service and the gifts they made is illustrated by the construction of the Tribhuvara-Cūḍāmaṇi-Caityālaya at Moodabidri.

The inscription states :

> The citizens of Venupura including eight Settikars and others in accordance with a message from Devaraja having given (donations) to Abhinava Carukirti Paṇḍitaa deva, for the construction of the Caityalaya, with the help of other well known persons chief of whom are the counters of Salikenadu in Koteswara erected, the great Tribhuvana-Cudamani-Caityalaya to the wonder of the world.[91]

Then, the public of Moodabidri brought up the beautiful image of Śrī Candraprabhu-tīrtheśvara together with eight great attendants made out of bell-metal, so that people may lift up their hands in prayer. Similarly, when Prauḍha Devarāya was ruling over the entire kingdom and his *ājñādhāraka* loyal servant, Ganapannodeya, was ruling over the kingdom of Mangalore in

89. *Ibid.*, no. 203.
90. S.R. Sharma, *op. cit.*, p. 57.
91. P. Mangesh Rao, *op. cit.*, p. 152.

the Śaka year 1375, Prajotpati, month of Vaiśākha, 7th bright day Thursday, several citizens (*bhavya jana*, lit.: Blessed people) got the *mukha-maṇḍapa* or front bower (Portico) of Caityālaya constructed.[92]

There is another inscription in the Gurugala-Basadi at Moodabidri (in South Kanara district) of the period of Bukkaraya II (AD 1405-06) which records the grant made to the Jain temple.[93]

Similar grants were made to the temples in the same district under Devarāya II (AD 1428-46), perhaps the greatest ruler of the Saṅgama dynasty of Vijayanagara.[94]

Another inscription under the same rulers speak of a gift to Abhinava Cārukīrti Paṇḍitācārya for the construction of the Tribhuvana-Cūḍāmaṇi-Caityālaya (AD 1430) when Devarāja Wodeyar of Nāgamaṅgala was ruling over Mangalura *rājya*.[95]

Under Virupākṣa, son of Devarāya II, the eight *Settigar*s or merchants made a grant to the Jain temple at Bidre for the daily worship, anointment, etc., of Candroga Pārśva *Tīrthaṅkara* Candraprabhu Svāmī and for the gift of *śāstra*s under the direction of Cārukīrti Paṇḍita Deva.[96]

A *mukha-maṇḍapa* called Bhairadeva *maṇḍapa* was built in AD 1451-52 at the Hosa-Basadi during the reign of the Vijayanagara Emperor Mallikārjuna Immadi Devarāya (AD 1446-67), at the time when the Viceroy of Barakuru-*rājya* was Gopana Odeyar. The same *basadi* received a grant of land from the Viceroy Viṭṭharasa Odeyar during the reign of the Emperor Virupākṣa (in AD 1465-86)[97]

---

92. V. Rangacarya, *Inscriptions of the Madras Presidency*, vol. II, Madras, 1919, Sk. 116.
93. S.R. Sharma, *op. cit.*, p. 45.
94. Suryanarain Row, *The Never To Be Forgotten Empire Vijayanagara*, Madras, 1915, Ch. XVI, pp. 331-43.
95. Mangesh Row, *op. cit.*, p. 157.
96. B.A. Saletore, *Medieval Jainism*, p. 352.
97. James Fergusson, *History of Indian and Eastern Architecture*, vol. II, Revised by Burgess, London, 1910, pp. 76-79.

Of the *basadi*s built in the Vijaynagara age, those at Moodabidri deserve a special note. These *basadi*s are much plainer in structures than Hindu temples, with their pillars looking like logs of wood, their angles partially chambered off, suggesting that their originals were built of wood. Fergusson rightly remarks that nothing can exceed the richness or variety with which the temples of Moodabidri are carved. Their ornamentation is almost fantastic and no two pillars are alike in design and beauty.[98]

The eighteen *basadi*s of Moodabidri are specimens of the architectural skill of the Jains of the Vijayanagara age. The *brahmadevastambha*s are best seen at Moodabidri, and *mānastambha*s at Guruvayinakere and Haleangadi. These start from a square at the base, change into an octagon and thence into a polygonal figure approaching a circle with a widespreading capital of the most elaborate design above.

Moodabidri was the seat of a class of political chiefs known as the Chautas. Remains of their palace are still partly intact. They had their first capital at Puttige, now a village 3½ miles to the west of Bidre. The Jain monastery of Bidre is known as the *maṭha* of Abhinava-Cārukīrti Paṇḍita Deva. The place can also boast of the only Veda-Brahma temple at Ladi. The figure may be of the Vijayanagara period.

Tribhuvana Tilaka Cūḍāmaṇi temple in Moodabidri in south district is a testimony to the contribution by three important Jain women. Bhairavarasa's queens namely Citrādevī and Bhairadevī spent lavishly in erecting the *maṇḍapa*.[99]

Nagala Devī, the queen of Bhairava Rāja II, erected the *mānastambha,* a huge monolith of a height of 50 ft, in front of the *basadi*. There are elaborate carvings on the sides of the plinth of the *basadi*, which, *inter alia*, have the figures of giraffe and a

---

98. Jagdishchandra Jain Articles, *Jinamanjari* (Socio-Religious Influences of Early Jainism in its Origin and Growth), April, 1991 U.S.A., p. 20.

99. P. Gururaja Bhatt, *Antiquities of South Kanara*, p. 751.

dragon; this is perhaps indicative that the Jain merchants of those days had extensive trade contacts.[100]

There are also many tombs of Jain priest. Two of them are standing apart from the rest being those of two wealthy Jain merchants. These are lofty erections consiting of several storeys built of carefully cut laterite stones. They were originally ornamented with tall granite finials most of which have now fallen down and have been set-up in the compounds of temples or in private houses as curious things.[101]

The Chautas, a sect of local chiefs, had their capital at this place. Their descendants live in the old palace here. The walls were originally covered with paintings which do not exist at present. The objects of interest in this palace are the four beautifully carved wooden pillars, a handsomely carved wooden ceiling and a wooden screen with fine carvings. There are two excellent panels of carvings on the pillars, namely, the Navanārī Kuñjara and Pañcanārī Turaga. The first one is a composite carved elephant, ingeniously made of the bodies of nine women in various postures, surmounted by a hundred bows and arrows; the second one is also a similar piece of wood carvings depicting five women forming the body of a horse with a rider on the animal. The great Kannaḍa poet, Ratnākaravarṇi is said to have composed his immortal classic *Bharatesh Vaibhava* at this place.[102]

The result of the royal patronage and popular support was beneficial for Jainism as well as the country. It gave a good opportunity to the Jain *ācārya*s to establish various centres of learning and religious studies, monasteries and libraries. This brought the Jain *ācārya*s in direct contact of the people. They were shrewd enough to lay a firm foundation of their hold over the middle and the trading classes of the society.

---

100. *Ibid*.
101. Karnataka State Gazetteer, Govt. of Kranataka, *South Kanara District*, p. 753.
102. Sri Digambara Jain Math, Moodabidri, p. 25.

The Guru-Pīṭha (Maṭha) at Moodabidri was founded by Svasti Śrī Cārukīrti Paṇḍitācāryavarya Svāmījī of Śravaṇbeḷgoḷa in the year AD 1330. Bittideva (AD 1104-41), the king of Dvārasamudra (Halebiḍu), converted himself from Jainism to Vaiṣṇavism and was named "Viṣṇuvardhana." He, then destroyed many Jain temples and killed many Jain house-holders.

Vīraballāla, who ruled this kingdom (AD 1173-1219), approached Cārukīrti Svāmījī of Śravaṇbeḷgoḷa with a request to get rid of this disaster. Cārukīrti Svāmījī came down to Dvārasamudra by his request. He worshipped Pārśvanātha and performed "kalikuṇḍa Ārādhanā" with appropriate rites. He could then make the earth close its mouth with the pumpkins (*kuṣmāṇḍa*) charged with holy *mantra*s.

Cārukīrti Svāmījī then directly came down to "NALLUR" a small village in Karkala Tāluka, south Kanara District, and founded a *maṭha*. Further, he came to Moodabidri in AD 1220 with a view to have Siddhanātha Darśana and founded another *maṭha*. These two *maṭha*s are the branches of the *maṭha* at Śravaṇbeḷgoḷa. The heads of these *maṭha*s came to be known as "cārukīrti." This proves the fact that these *maṭha*s were founded 760 years ago.

The Jain *ācārya*s worked in a cosmopolitan method and increased the number of followers by preaching among the original inhabitants of India.[103]

The pontiffs at Moodabidri were known as Cārukīrti and some of them had the distinguishing prefix of Abhinava. They were highly respected by the Jain disciples, foremost among whom were the rulers of the Kalaśa-Karkala *rājya* from whom the preceptors received such epithets as *rāja-guru* and *kula-guru*. Many *caitya*s in South Kanara were built and repaired during the fifteenth and sixteenth centuries on the advice of these pontiffs.[104]

---

103. K.V. Ramesh, *History of South Kanara*, p. 303.
104. B.L. Rice, *E. Carn.*, vol. I, pp. 19-20.

A number of such inscriptions testify to the growth of Jainism and Jain temples in that city at the hands of the imperial authority, local rulers, local guilds and the commoners.

Thus, Moodabidri was a stronghold of Jainism during medieval period, especially during the Vijayanagara age (AD 1336-1565). Moodbidri is visited by many Jain *śravakas* every year even today.

Venur: Neglected Jain Shrine

Venur, like Karkala Moodabidri, is also an important Jain centre but historians, epigraphists and Jain *śrāvakas* paid little attention to the statue of Bāhubali, which is in existence here since AD 1604. Venur is a Jain centre since the eleventh century.

Venur is a little village in the Karkala Tāluka, figuring as the headquarter of a sect of petty chiefs and at the same time as the seat of Jainism.[105]

Venur, situated at a distance of 9 miles from Moodabidri in the south-east direction and twenty-four miles east of Karkala, is one of the few remaining Jain villages. The original form of Enuru may be Eluru, i.e., seven villages.[106]

This was the citadel of the medieval kingdom known as the Puñjalikeya-rāja or the kingdom of the Ajilas. Venur gives us the earliest dated inscription of the Alupa King Kunda-Kundavarma, i.e., of AD 967. It is this epigraph that informs us of the Alupa emblem — the fish.[107] Venur is rich in historical antiquities. The image of Gommaṭa, the *basadis* and the Mahādeva temple are the historical remains of considerable interest. They must have been a flourishing and splendid centre of the past.

HISTORY OF VENUR

The rulers of Ajila *gotra* were great patrons of Jainism. This dynasty ruled Venur from AD 1154 to AD 1764 and extended

105. P. Gururaja Bhatt, *op. cit.*, p. 25.

106. *Ibid.*

107. Rajamala Jain and Laxmichandra Jain, *op. cit.*, p. 174.

their royal patronage to Jainism. King Somavasī belonged to this dynasty. His successor, Ajila Timmana I (AD 1154 to AD 1180) founded Venur Kṣetra. He considered himself belonging to Gaṅga dynasty and an inhabitant of Gaṅgavāḍī. There is one inscription inscribed on the left side of Bāhubali, which speaks that Timmarāja was the successor of Cāmuṇḍarāya.[108] Some scholars pointed out that this family had relation with Cāmuṇḍarāya as well as Kadamba dynasty. All the rulers of this dynasty were devout Jains and they stayed at Aladhagadi near Venur. Here they built a magnificent seven storey palace. Two huge stone elephants were erected at the entrance of this palace.

One ruler of this dynasty built Śāntīśvara-Basadi in the year AD 1490. Timmarāja Ajila IV of Ajila dynasty ruled this territory from AD 1550 to AD 1610. He was instrumental in erecting the colossal image of Lord Bāhubali at Venur. The installation of Bāhubali icon of Venur was not appreciated by the ruler of Karkala. Hence, this led to a war between Timmarāja and ruler of Karkala. The account of this war is narrated in certain Jain sacred books. Madhurikā Devī (AD 1610 to 1647) the queen of this place, arranged *abhiṣeka* of Gommaṭeśa image. The King of Karkala invaded Venur again in the year AD 1634. This seems to be a cultural conflict between the ruler of Venur and Karkala. Both these rulers were followers of Jainism but they were scrambling for religious hegemony over each other. Because Venur image was a rival image to Karkala image of Bāhubali. Later, a religious-minded queen Padmala Devī reigned here. Subsequently, Haidar Ali annexed this area and after the fall of Ṭīpū Sultān, successor of Ajila dynasty received annual pension from British rulers. Sometimes Venur territory is called as Pujlika.

There is an interesting story about the controversy that occurred at the time of installation of this statue. It seems that

---

108. T.G. Kalghatgi, (editor) Articles (Shubachandra), in *Gommatesvara Commemoration Volume*, "Gommatesvara statues in Karnataka" Śravaṇbeḷgoḷa, Karnataka, 1998, p. 124.

Timmarāja also wanted to become famous like Cāmuṇḍarāya and hence got this statue chiselled in his kingdom. But Bhairavarāya II, who was ruling at Karkala at that time, wanted that no statue similar to the one erected in Karkala should be installed elsewhere. He demanded that the Venur statue should be surrendered to him. Then Timmarāja, a brave warrior, decided to fight. He buried the statue in sand and erected it later after winning the battle. But we have no evidence to corroborate this story either in inscriptions or in literature. This has only a legendary value.[109]

VENUR KṢETRA DARŚANA

This *kṣetra,* known as Śrī Bāhubali Kṣetra, is *atiśaya kṣetra,* i.e., sacred place created by Jains. Pārśvanātha temple is an important historical monument at Venur and a metal image of Pārśvanātha is in a standing posture in this temple. Here is one inscription which is little damaged and not readable. Therefore, it is difficult to fix the period of this temple. The Bhaṭṭārakas of Moodabidri renovated this temple. Very little grant is received from the government now. Adjoining to this temple 35 ft high image of Bāhubali is standing.

Besides Pārśvanātha temple, there are two small Jain temples named as "Binnani" and "Akkanagal" at Venur. There are idols of Śāntinātha in the left side and Candraprabhu at right in Binnani temples.

Akkangal means sister. There is one inscription in this Akkangal temple, which tells us that these two small temples were built by Pāṇḍyakadevī and Mallidevī, who were the queens of King Timmarāja in AD 1604.[110]

1. Bhujabali (Bāhubali)-Basadi
2. Akkangal-Basadi

---

109. Rajamala Jain and Laxmichandra Jain, *op. cit.*, p. 175.
110. M.J. Walhouse, *Indian Antiquary,* vol. IV, Articles "Arachaeological Notes on the two Kanara Colossi" (Feb. 8, 1876) p. 38.

3. Binnani-Basadi
4. Pārśvanātha-Basadi
5. Śāntinātha-Basadi
6. Vardhamāna-Basadi
7. Tīrthaṅkara-Basadi
8. Ṛṣabha-Basadi

Out of these eight temples, Śāntinātha *alias* "Kallu-Basadi" is an old Jain temple built by Timmarāja in the year AD 1490, who was a devout Jain. "Kalla" is a Kannaḍa word and its meaning is stone. This temple is built by black stones which is available on large scale in this area. Therefore, this temple is called as "Kallu-Basadi".

Mūla Nāyaka is Śāntinātha in this temple the 16th *tīrthaṅkara*. A *śāśanam* referring to this temple mentions that the image is that of Śāntiśvara, the 16th *tīrthaṅkara* and that part of its revenues was given over to the service of the great statue, which is styled as the one of Gommaṭeśvara by its setter-up, whose name and date it records. The śāśanam is thus translated :

> Sasanam of the great and holy Jina, the most high: renowned for eloquence; conquereor and master of the three worlds: a Sasanam to all. The work carried out on Sunday the second of Mina of Sobhakrit, 1526 of the Salivahana era (i.e. 1604 AD — this would make the Venure colossus later by 172 years than the one at Karkala, 1432 AD — if there be no mistake). Blessed Vira Timmaraja, the sovereign Ajlar, the beloved disciple of the gods, resplendent with glory, established the royal Gommatesvara on Venur hill and gave over the charitable endowments of the Chaitalya of the holy Shantisvara, on its (Gommatesvara's) right hand to Pandiappa Arasa, the Binnani (minister) of the queen Padileva Devi, whereupon the Binnani built the basadi and devised to the royal Gommatesvara in perpetuity the following to lands producing eighty-two mudas of rice in aggresgate rent; besides forty-nine huns (gold pieces) to be collected from Sanku Narayana, forty-nine huns from Appaji, and hundred and eighty for

> continually anointing the Gumtanatha with milk under the superintendence of the Binnani, to be collected from whoever destroys this bequest shall be guilty of the sin of destroying a multitude of holy cows on the banks of the Ganga.[111]

There is an image of Mahāvīra (Vardhamāna) along with the picture of *yakṣa* "Garuḍa" (eagle) and *yakṣiṇī* on the second storey of this temple. There is a stone image of Candraprabhu on the third storey. There are two inscriptions, in the precinct of Śāntinātha Mandir which shed light on the history of the Venur. There is again a beautiful *mānasthambha*.

Moreover, there is *cauvīsa* Tīrthaṅkara Basadi which is also important and was built by queen Madhurikādevī in the year AD 1621.[112] An epigraph is available in this temple which is easily read by scholars. 3 ft high stone statues of 24 *tīrthaṅkara*s are installed in this temple. The images of goddess Padmāvatī and Sarasvatī are also installed in this temple. Due to this, the temple is also called as *ammāvara* (i.e., mother) temples.

STATUES OF GOMMAṬEŚVARA IN KARNATAKA : A COMPARATIVE STUDY

It is interesting to see the history of erection of major statues of Bāhubali in Karnataka. The statues of Bāhubali at Śravaṇbeḷgoḷa, Karkala, Moodabidri and Venur were installed respectively.

Gommaṭeśvara statues occupy an important place in the sculpture of Karnataka. In fact, Gommaṭeśvara and Jainism have become almost synonymous with the overwhelming fame of Gommaṭeśvara and his images. This image has some special importance in the Digambara sect of Jainism. Gommaṭeśvara's image essentially differs from other *jin* images in one important aspect. All Gommaṭeśvara images can easily be identified as compared to other *jin* images. The presence of serpents and ant

---

111. *Ibid.*, p. 78.
112. T.G. Kalghatgi (editor), Articles (Subhachandra), *op. cit.*, p. 120.

hills near the legs and creepers on the hands-legs of the image confirms that it is Gommaṭeśvara.[113]

The Gommaṭeśvara image of Śravaṇbeḷgoḷa is world famous. It is considered to be one of the wonders of the world. It is an incomparable contribution of Karnataka to Indian sculpture. This statue was installed by Cāmuṇḍarāya who was the minister of Mārasiṁha II and Rachamalla II in AD 984. The biggest statue, Śravaṇbeḷgoḷa, stands about 57 ft in height with a width of 13 ft across the hips, and is cut out of a solid block of genesis, apparently wrought *in situ*.[114]

Next to Śravaṇbeḷgoḷa comes the Gommaṭeśvara statue of Karkala in South Canara district. It was installed on a hill near Karkala town in AD 1432 by Vīrapāṇḍya, son of Bhairavarāja. The statue is 42 ft tall.

The other Gommaṭeśvara statue is in the Venur, South Canara district. This statue, which is 35 ft tall, was erected by chief Timmannjila in AD 1604. These "Colossal monolithic nude Jain statues . . . are among the wonders of the world." These are undoubtedly the most remarkbale of the Jain statues and the largest free standing statues in Asia. . . . All three, being set on the top of eminences, are visible for miles around and in spite of their formalism, command respectful attention and dignified expression by enormous masses.[115]

The three images are almost identical, but the one at Venur has the special peculiarity of the cheeks, being dimpled with a deep grave smile, which is considered to detract from the impressive effect. This illustrates the extreme conventionalism of the Jain art.

---

113. S.C. Ghoshal, *The Sacred Books of The Jains: Original Texts and Commentaries*, vol. I, Arrah, 1917, p. Introd. XXVI.

114. *Ibid.*

115. V.A. Smith, *A History of Fine Art in India and Ceylon*, Oxford, 1911, p. 268.

DESCRIPTION OF BĀHUBALI STATUE OF VENUR

As mentioned, a gigantic image of Gommaṭa was set-up in AD 1604 at Venur, at the orders of Timmarāja, the brother of a ruler called Pāṇḍya of the family of Cāmuṇḍarāya and on the advice of Cārukīrti Paṇḍita of Beḷgoḷa.[116]

This statue is placed on an elevated terrace on the south bank of the Gurpur river, which meets and unites with the more southern river, the Netravatī, at its mouth, so that the two rivers half enclose and separate the town of Mangalur by a broad wateryway girdle from the sea-beach. Venur is some 40 miles in land, and the river is a swift clear stream about 20 yards broad running over a rocky bed. Approaching from the west, over an undulating well-wooded country, the first glimpse of statue is very striking. One sees rising in the distance a gentle tree-clad slope on which a huge dark giant seems to stand, towering full height above the tree tops, that just conceal the terrace. The terrace rises about 50 ft above the river's bed and the image is enclosed by a square wall, 7 or 8 ft high, with massive covered entrance, forming a good-sized quadrangle, in the midst of which it stands on a stone plinth of two stages placed on a platform, 4 or 5 ft in height. The people only knew it by Vulgar name of Gumtarāja or Gommaṭeśvara.[117] Two fine black-steel bearing long inscriptions stand in one corner of the quadrangle. The salient characteristics of all these colossi are the broad square shoulders and very massive at the setting of the arms. Perhaps from the exigencies of the material, the thickness and remarkable length of the arms.

The forehead was medium in the Venur image, neither high nor retreating, the nose slightly hooked, with broad nostrils; the lips full, especially the upper, and the cheeks remarkably broad widening towards the bottom, the chin moderate. The neck is short and thick with three creases across it, the same

---

116. B.A. Saletore, *Medieval Jainism*, p. 363.

117. J.A.S. Burgess, *Indian Antiquary*, vol. II, p. 129.

across the belly. All the colossi are distinguished by crispy, close-curled hair and pendulous ears and their entire form and aspect appeared unlike anything Hindu.

The Venur giant like its brother at Karkala, looks eastward towards the prodigious slopes of the Kudire Mukh mountain, the highest part of the Western Ghāṭs, which rises abruptly more than 6000 ft about 12 miles in front.

The natives say that this statue was cut and brought at a spot 3 or 4 miles distant from where it now stands on the other side of the river. Both, this and the Karkala image are traditionally said to have been sculptured by Jakkanachari, a kind of Hindu Wayland Smith around whom numbers of legends have gathered and to whom remarkable works in stone are popularly ascribed. He was probably a workman of extraordinary excellence.[118]

The legend goes that a bitter dispute had arisen between him and his son regarding respecting an image in a temple at Venur. He and his wife committed suicide and became *bhūta*s or demons; and to this day, under the appellation of Kalkatti (i.e., stone mason), he is the most powerful, dreaded, and malignant *bhūta* in South-Kanara where the principal popular cult is really *bhūta*-worship.

There are two or three Jain temples in the village of Venur, which are neither big nor specially distinguished for architecture or sculpture. One temple, without any enclosure, contains a life-sized brass image, erect, and enshrined in burnished silver and brass work variegated with red ornaments. There is a large black marble image further down the village, in another temple, about 8 ft and its head surrounded with a broad golden aureole, precisely like the glories depicted round the heads of saints.

There is a small building or sacellum, adjoining this, containing the 24 *tīrthaṅkara*s, in a row, all of the same size, each

---

118. *Ibid.*, p. 38.

resembling the other, about 2 ft high, cut in black stone, and each under a horse-shoe-shaped arch elaborately wrought from the same material. This long dark row of doll-like figures has a curiously quaint appearance. The building containing them is poorly maintained with a thatched roof, but the entrance is a wonder of exquisite and beautiful workmanship set in a common rough stone wall. The doorway is square-headed, its sides and top framed with long narrow slabs of black serpentine, of almost steel like hardness and lustre, carved with a luxuriance and delicacy of an ornament, absolutely marvellous. A band of most elegant wavy foliage is succeeded by another bearing a line of rosettes bordered and separated by tasteful beadings and several other bands rich with foliage; moulding and rossette-work fill up the deeply recessed entrance. There is a line of six seated figures with hands laid on their laps in the wall over the doorway. There sits a cross-legged image of Ādīśvara, the primal god, grave, clan and earnest looking opposite to it, in a small plain covered shrine.[119]

In front of the temple stands one of those wonderful Jain pillars, which are typically peculiar to South Kanara, where about 20 such pillars exist. There rises a monolithic shaft about 30 ft high, on a pedestal formed by four stages, exclusive of capital, quadrangular at the base and for nearly a third of its height, each face bearing a different design of such intricate inter-placement as only Jains contrive and execute.

Above this, the shaft rises in four sections — the first octagonal, the next sixteen-sided, the fourth plain, with arabesque enrichments on every alternate, third, or sixth side, and as ornamental band between each section over the fourth section, the shaft passes into a bell-shaped necking, reeded and enriched with elaborate mouldings, the upper one spreading out circularly with downward curving edge — toothed with pendants and supporting a square abacus on which a stone

119. *Archaeological Survey Reports*, vol. I, p. 92.

canopy ending in a flame-like finial — rests on four colonnetters. The canopy covers a square block bearing in relief on each side a long armed, curly-headed *tīrthaṅkara*. Four (grasdas) griffin-like monsters stretch upward, from a moulding below the capital, meeting each corner of the abacus with their heads. The whole capital and canopy area wonder of light and elegance, highly decorated stone work and nothing can surpass the stately grace of these beautiful pillars, whose proportions and adaptation to surrounding scenery are always perfect, and whose richness of decoration never offends. The Jains delight in making their images of all substances and sizes, but always with the same features and attitude.[120]

A slab has been set-up to the right of the entrance of the *maṇḍapa* in front of the Śāntīśvara-Basadi. A record, dated AD 1411, mentions of a Saumya chief of Puñjaliṅgarāja.[121]

Another slab is set-up close to the west wall of the Gurugala-Basadi near the same village. The inscription of Lokanātha Devarasa (son of Bomnndevarasa and Siddhaladevī)[122] is on the right side of the colossal statue of Gommaṭa. The hill records, dated AD 1525 in Śobhakṛt, describes the setting up of the image of Bhujabali by Timmanrāja of the family of Cāmuṇḍarāya at the instance of Cārukīrti, the family teacher.[123] A slab has also been found in the south-east corner of the *maṇḍapa* in front of the Śāntīśvara-Basadi. Records the consecration of 24 *tīrthaṅkaras* in *basadi*[124] in Hemalambin, 1459.

In brief, Jainism rose to great heights during this period and remained the religion of a large section of the people and of many of the local ruling families, especially during the fifteenth and later centuries.

---

120. *Ibid.*, pp. 92-93.
121. *Epigraphia Jainica*, p. 59.
122. *Ibid.*
123. *Ibid.*, p. 57.
124. *Ibid.*

Many trade guilds and local assemblies renovated the buildings of old and new Jain *basadi*s all over the region, particularly in the Jain strongholds of the Karkala Tāluka. It was during this period that Karkala, Moodabidri and Venur became great centres of Jainism, while it was not the case with the other parts of the Tulu country. Jainism became the principal faith in these populous townships situated in the Karkala Tāluka. The large number of Jain *basadi*s, which are masterpieces of architecture, stand even today in silent witness to the heyday of Jainism in these towns during the fifteenth and sixteenth centuries. Devotion of Jainism was a common zeal among many ruling houses and their services to their faith were done without any reference to the territorial limitations of their own tiny principalities.

To sum up, South Kanara has a rich Jain antiquity such as Karkala, Moodabidri and Venur. These Jain centres played vital role in spreading Jainism in Western Karnataka area. The rich libraries at these places preserve the old Jain canons and books and thus it is a treasure house to posterity. Even now many Jain scholars used to go to Moodabidri and study these holy books and old manuscripts. The dynasties like Santara, Bhairavas, Añjali Vaṁśa, rendered great service in medieval period for spreading Jainism in South Karnataka along with the rulers of Gaṅgas, Tuluvas, Alupas, Hoyasala, etc.

6

Bhaṭṭāraka and Jainism in South Karnataka

Śravaṇbeḷgoḷa, Humcha, Moodabidri and Karkala

THOUGH Jainism was founded and nourished by 24 *tīrthaṅkaras*, *kevalis* and *ācāryas*, the credit of spreading Jain culture all over India go to Bhaṭṭārakas, which is a unique and indispensable religious institution in the Jain system. Bhaṭṭārakas were the religious rulers who devotedly protected the Jain sacred literature. Generally, Bhaṭṭārakas were erudite scholars of Jain literature and the spreading Jainism was there main aim. Moreover, the Bhaṭṭārakas from the concerned places, built various Jain temples, *mānastambhas* and *maṭhas*. Again, some Bhaṭṭārakas themselves were author of many Jain works and composed various treatises on Jainism. The credit of protecting *Śraman* culture during the Muslim period (i.e., medieval period) go to the Bhaṭṭārakas. These Bhaṭṭārakas strongly advocated and propagated non-violence and vegetarian principles which are the cardinal tenets of Jainism. This institution came into existence generally from the eighth century AD onwards. There are Bhaṭṭāraka's *pīṭha* in north India as well as in south India.

The Bhaṭṭārakas of Śravaṇbeḷagoḷa, Humcha, Moodabidri and Karkala are important institutions in south India that possessed large landed estate as well as *maṭhas*. Fortunately the persons, who became *bhaṭṭāraka* are well read, cultured and well versed in Jain canons and sacred literature.

There was a serious menace to the Jain religion in medieval times from the Muslim iconoclasts, who were the rulers of India, and the duty of protecting the Jain religion came upon these Bhaṭṭārakas. These Bhaṭṭārakas also run free feeding centres and maintained respective *maṭha*s and good libraries of sacred Jain literature.

Therefore an attempt is made in this chapter to study the role of Bhaṭṭārakas hailing from Śravaṇbeḷagoḷa, Humcha, Moodabidri and Karkala for spreading Jainism in southern Karnataka by utilizing source material available in their old libraries.

BHAṬṬĀRAKA TRADITION

The Bhaṭṭāraka tradition is a very well-established tradition of sufficiently long duration and prestige found among the Digambara Jains of different parts of India. The Bhaṭṭāraka was a special type of religious authority evolved by the Digambara Jains during the early part of the medieval period as a policy of survival to meet the severe challenges created by the advent of Muslim rule in India. As the Muslim rulers looked down upon the practice of nudity observed by the Digambara Jain ascetics, it became extremely difficult for these *sādhu*s or ascetics to move freely on foot in different regions according to the rules of conduct prescribed for them and to exercise their influence on the proper behaviour of the *śrāvaka*s or the lay followers of the religion. The memebrs of the Digambara Jain community also faced disintegration due to uncertainty and insecurity prevailing at that time. In these peculiar and pressing conditions, the system of Bhaṭṭārakas was slowly formed to save the religion and its followers from utter distraction.

A special functionary known as Bhaṭṭāraka was created to perform certain important religious and social duties in the interests of the community and he was placed above the laymen and below the ascetics with a view to helping the Bhaṭṭāraka in the discharge of his duties in an orderly and continuous manner. A new organization known as *maṭha* was also constituted.[1]

In this way, the tradition became popular in different parts of the country. It is thus clear that the system of Bhaṭṭārakas was not established on a particular day but it was slowly evolved during the medieval period. That is why, we get stray references about the Bhaṭṭāraka tradition from the eighth century onwards and continuous references from the thirteenth century onwards to the present day.

THE MEANINGS OF THE WORD "BHAṬṬĀRAKA"

It is interesting to see the meaning of word *bhaṭṭāraka*. The word Bhaṭṭāraka is a title given to a highly venerated Jain monk or priest of the Digambara Jain tradition, equivalent to the Jagadguru, Mahanta or Maṭhādhīśa of the Hindu tradition and also to the "Jāti tradition" or the "Pūjya tradition" (*paramparā*), of the Śvetāmbara Jains. Such a priest enjoy a highly revered place in society.[2]

Bhaṭṭāraka is a term applied to a particular type of Jain ascetics. Unlike a *muni* or *yati*, these ascetics assumed the position of religious ruler. They managed large estates donated to some temple and enjoyed supreme authority in religious matters. Their tradition is very much similar to that of Śaṅkarācāryas.[3]

EXTENT OF THE TRADITION

As the Bhaṭṭāraka was a religious preceptor of the Saṁgha or Gaṇa or Gaccha, i.e., religious division of the Jains, of a particular region or locality, the seats of Bhaṭṭārakas increased in number and were found in different parts of India during the medieval

1. T.G. Kalghatgi (editor), Articles (A. Sangave), *Gommatesvara Commemoration Volume* (*A.D. 981-1981*) (Bhaṭṭāraka tradition), Śravaṇbeḷagoḷa, 1981, p. 62.
2. Śrī Bhaṭṭāraka Cārukīrti Paṇḍitācārya Svāmījī Moodabidri (Personal letter).
3. H.V. Joharapurkar, *Bhaṭṭāraka Sampradāya* (in Hindi), Introd., Nagpur, 1958.

9.	Karnataka	Bhaṭṭakalaṅka	Swadi (Dist. North Kanara)
10.	Karnataka	Lakṣmī Sena	Narasiṁharājapur (Dist.Cikmaglūr)
11.	Tamil Nadu	Lakṣmī Sena	Melasittamur (Dist. South Arcot)

It is evident from the above list that out of 11 existing seats of Bhaṭṭāraka as many as six are in Karnataka, three in Maharashtra and one each in Rajasthan and Tamil Nadu.[7]

In fact, that Bhaṭṭāraka was a religious preceptor of a *saṁgha* or a *gaṇa*, i.e., religious division of the Jains. But when the Jains adopted the caste system from the Hindus, with whom they were in intimate contact for centuries, it was considered that a particular seat of Bhaṭṭāraka belonged to a specific caste only. Accordingly, the Bhaṭṭāraka got special powers also to control the affairs of the caste which was associated with him.

In this way an intimate link was established, especially in Maharashtra and Karnataka, between the seat of Bhaṭṭāraka and the members of a specific caste.

NAME OF THE CASTES AND PLACE OF THE BHAṬṬĀRAKA OF THAT CASTE

The list of the names of such castes and their seats of Bhaṭṭārakas at present is given below :

	Name of the caste	*Name and place of the Bhaṭṭāraka of that place*		
1.	Narasiṁhapura	Yaśakīrti	-	Pratāpgarh
2.	Saitavāla	Viśālakīrti	-	Lāṭūr
3.	Pañcama	Lakṣmī Sena	-	Kolhāpur
4.	Caturtha	Jina Sena	-	Nandani
5.	Bogara	Devendrakīrti	-	Humcha

7. V.A. Sangave, *Jain Community* (*A Social Survey*), Bombay, 1959.

6.	Upādhyāya	Cārukīrti	-	Moodabidri
7.	Vaiśya	Cārukīrti	-	Śravaṇbeḷgoḷa
8.	Kṣatriya	Lalitakīrti	-	Karkala

Even though each Baṭṭāraka is linked with a particular caste, it may be specially noted that according to religious precepts every Bhaṭṭāraka belongs to all Jains irrespective of the distinctions of caste and locality. The Bhaṭṭāraka is technically above all caste considrations.[8]

The general opinion seems to be in favour of retaining the institution because a religious preceptor is considered necessary to look after the spiritual life of the people. It is suggested that if the Bhaṭṭārakas, who are well educated, who wish to renounce life after fulfilling their worldly desires, are appointed and recognized not as the heads of particular castes but as organizers, propagators and preceptors of the Jain community.

GENERAL DUTIES OF BHAṬṬĀRAKAS

The Bhaṭṭāraka has to perform a number of duties of religious and social nature. In the field of religion, he was not only to direct and control the religious behaviour of these followers but also to encourage and help the undertaking and completion of various religious projects and activities.

DHARMARAKṢAṆA

The principal duty of Bhaṭṭāraka is *dharmarakṣā*, that is, protection of religion. The protection is to be achieved by repulsing the attacks of other religionists and by making his people more religious-minded by means of preaching and educating the people. He has to perform a social duty also along with the religious duty. He has to help them in social matters by giving them advise or by cementing their quarrels or by regulating

8. T.A. Kalghatgi, *op. cit.*, p. 332.

social relations, institutions, customs and manners according to the rules of conduct prescribed by the Jain books from time to time. Thus, the nature of his duties is spiritual as well as temporal.[9]

ŚIṢYA-PARAMPARĀ (DISCIPLE TRADITION)

In general, the procedure is that of *śiṣya-paramparā* in which the existing Bhaṭṭāraka always selects his successor from his disciples. When the predescessor nominates his successor, the latter has to be installed by the people of the caste concerned. There is also an another way of appointing a Bhaṭṭāraka. In this method, the successor is chosen from among the disciples by the caste members through their representatives known as *pañcas*. This is the common practice among the saitavāla, caturtha, pañcama, upādhyāya, bogara, vaiśya and kṣatriya caste. Once a Bhaṭṭāraka is appointed, he cannot be removed from his position even though he fails in his duties or misuses his authority.[10]

A Bhaṭṭāraka is not required to lead the life of a strict ascetic. Though he has to maintain celibacy throughout his life and to live according to the religious principles, he has been allowed to possess property. Generally, a Bhaṭṭāraka possesses both movable and immovable property and utilizes it according to his own will. The property consists of contributions and gifts from his followers and sympathizers and grants from the state. It is gathered from the replies that the financial position of all Bhaṭṭāraka is sound.[11]

As the Bhaṭṭārakas have been enjoined upon to look after the religious and social welfare of their people, they were endowed with powers to exercise some control over their members in certain matters like exacting contributions, enforcing

---

9. V.A. Sangave, *op. cit* , p. 332.
10. H.V. Joharapurkar, *cp. cit.*, p. 11.
11. V.A. Sangave, *op. cit* , p. 333.

decisions, etc.[12]

It is his responsibility to provide religious education to students and others by various means like conducting *pāṭhaśālās*, i.e., religious schools, maintaining *śāstra-bhaṇḍārs*, i.e. religious scripture houses, delivering *dharma-pravacanas*, i.e., religious discourses, publishing and distributing *dharma-granthas*, i.e., religious books, training persons in the performance of *dharmavidhis*, i.e., religious rituals, arranging *dharma-sammelanas*, i.e., religious conferences, etc.

Further, it is his main work to supervise and direct several religious functions like *mūrti-pratiṣṭhā*, i.e., installation of images in temples and various *dharma-samārambhas*, i.e., religious ceremonies. Again, he has to officiate all kinds of *pūjās*, i.e., worships and especially the great *vrata-udyāpana-pūjās*, i.e. the special worships arranged at the completion of vows. On the same lines, he is required to perform, personally or through others, important *dharma-saṁskāras*, i.e., religious sacraments, at the time of birth, marriage and death. Moreover, it is his major concern to look after the management of *tīrthakṣetras*, i.e., holy places and at times to arrange for long *tīrthayātrās*, i.e., pilgrimages, with a large number of followers.

Furthermore, it is solemn work to encourage and help his followers in carrying out religious activities like construction of new temples, renovation of old temples, grant of donations, publication of books, provision of education, medicine and shelter to the needy, etc.[13]

STATUS OF BHAṬṬĀRAKAS

The Bhaṭṭārakas occupy a very distinctive position in society. A Bhaṭṭāraka is a special type of religious functionary in society. In the "Caturvidha Jain Saṁgha," i.e., fourfold division of Jain social organization, consisting of *śrāvakas* (male laity), *śrāvikās*

---

12. *Ibid.*, p. 334.

13. T.G. Kalghatgi (editor) Articles (V.A. Sangave), *op. cit.*, Bhaṭṭāraka Tradition, p. 61.

(female laity), *sādhus* (male ascetics) and *sādhvīs* (female ascetics), he is placed above the laity but below the ascetics. As such, he combines the characteristics of both. He possess property and moves anywhere and uses all means of transportation. At the same time like ascetics, he leads a celebrated and higher state of religious life, stays at one place during the *cāturmās*, i.e., the four months of rainy season, wears sparse clothing and carries *piñchi*, i.e., a tuft of peacock feathers.

In fact, it is reported that in the beginning the *nirgrantha sādhus*, i.e., the usual naked ascetics of the Digambara sect, used to work as Bhaṭṭārakas but with the increase in property and extension of activities of social nature, instead of *nirgrantha sādhus*, special persons similar to *sādhus* were appointed as Bhaṭṭārakas. That is why even today the Bhaṭṭāraka is expected to enter, even though for a very short period, the *nirgrantha sādhu* stage of the Digambara ascetic order at the the time of his death.[14]

Further, a Bhaṭṭāraka holds a distinctive position in society because he is regarded as a religious ruler. In this sense, all the attributes, accessories and paraphernalia of a king are associated with the Bhaṭṭāraka. His *maṭha*, i.e., central place of residence, is termed as *saṁsthāna*, i.e., state and his ceremonial place of sitting is termed as *gaddī*, i.e., throne. Like a king, he maintains huge property, wears luxurious dress, lives in a palatial building, uses articles made of gold or silver, goes in a procession led by elephants and horses, moves in a special palanquin and is entitled to use accessories like *chatra*, *cāmara*, *abadagiri*, etc. On ceremonial occasions, he gives honorific titles to distinguished persons, issues proclamations and orders with his own seal, settles caste-disputes, resolves enquiries, conducts court proceedings, gives judgements, prescribes punishments of fine, expiation or ex-communication, and collects contributions or taxes from his followers. At the same time, he enjoys certain privileges like

14. *Ibid.*, pp. 66-67.

going in a procession with his palanquin facing the road, using lighted torches during day-time in procession, and exemption from paying certain taxes and duties of a state.

Of course, the Bhaṭṭārakas have ceased to use these royal honours, accessories and privileges with the liquidation of the princely states in India.

CONTRIBUTIONS OF BHAṬṬĀRAKAS

The Bhaṭṭārakas, throughout their long history, contributed a great deal to the advancement in various fields of culture of region. Their lasting contribution can be seen in the development of several arts like architecture, sculpture, painting, music, dance and drama.

CONTRIBUTION TOWARDS ART AND ARCHITECTURE

Installation of various images was considered to be the main work of a Bhaṭṭāraka. These ceremonies presented a good opportunity for large religious and social gatherings and to establish one's prestige in the society. Various titles such as *saṁghapati*, *seṭh*, etc., were conferred upon chief donors of the ceremony. They encouraged their rich followers to construct new temples in large numbers and they personally officiated at the image installation ceremonies of these temples. According to tradition, Cāmuṇḍarāya, after erecting the colossus on the larger hill, appointed his *guru* Nemicandra as the head of *maṭha* at Śravaṇbeḷagoḷa.[15] This Gommaṭa statue is 57 ft high. The famous gigantic monolithic statue of Gommaṭa, which is 42 ft high, was installed by Vīrapāṇḍyadeva, a ruler of the Bhairarasa family of Karkala, in AD 1432. He took the permission of his Guru Lalitakīrti and thenafter performed the preliminary *pūjās*.[16] Venur has mentioned of a gigantic image of Gommaṭa to have been set-up in AD 1604, at the orders of Timmarāja family of Cāmuṇḍarāya, on the advice of Cārukīrti Paṇḍita of Beḷgoḷa.

---

15. B.L. Rice, *E. Carn.*, vol. II, Śravaṇbeḷagoḷa, Bangalore, 1989, p. 31.
16. Karnataka State Gazetteer, *South Karnataka District*, p. 756.

This statue is 35 ft high.[17]

LITERARY CONTRIBUTION OF BHAṬṬĀRAKA

The contributions of Bhaṭṭārakas have been really impressive in the field of literature. Their main literary works have been in the forms of epics, stories and texts for worship.

The creation, development and preservation of the sacred texts of the Jains was a notable achievement of the new monastic life in Karnataka. Free from the worries of constant movements, the monks developed a sense of religious solidarity and devoted much time and energy to the study and exposition of the Jain scriptures.

The rise of *kāvya* and Purāṇic literature and the development of regional languages may be attributed to the Jain monks and preceptors who lived in the monasteries. They mastered the various south Indian languages besides Sanskrit and Apabhraṁśa for the propagation of the Jain faith among the people and enriched the different branches of learning such as philosophy, ethics, grammar, logic, mathematics, etc.

Pūjyapāda, who was the preceptor of the Gaṅga King Durvinīta, wrote several important Sanskrit works. The *Śabdāvatāra* on the *sūtras* of Pāṇini, the *Sarvārthasiddhi*, and the *Jainendra Vyākaraṇa* are all attributed to him. Ravisena, who composed *Padma Purāṇa*, flourished during the sixth-seventh centuries. Besides, the Jain *ācāryas* such as Vīrasena, Guṇabhadra and Somadeva cultivated Sanskrit with great vigour.[18]

Literary contribution in Sanskrit, Prākṛt, Apabhraṁśa, Hindī, Marāṭhī, Gujarāti and Rājasthānī, Kannaḍa and Tamil languages by Srutasāgar Sūri are noteworthy. By their valuable literary works the Bhaṭṭārakas contributed not only to the enrichment of literature but also to the growth of different regional

17. B.A. Saletore, *Medieval Jainism* (with Special Reference to the Vijaynagara empire), Bombay, 1938, p. 363.
18. P. Singh Ramabhushan, *Jainism in early Medieval Karnataka*, Delhi, 1975, p. 108.

languages.

CONTRIBUTION OF LEARNING

The Bhaṭṭārakas made monumental contributions in the field of learning. By various means they turned their *maṭha*s into the central seats of learning in the region. They used their *maṭha*s as *grantha-bhaṇḍāra*s, i.e., book-houses, which were virtually treasure-houses of knowledge. They assiduously preserved a large number of manuscripts in these *bhaṇḍāra*s written on paper or palm leaves by both the Jain and non-Jain scholars and in different languages on various religious and scientific subjects. In addition to preservation of knowledge, they also helped in the spread of knowledge by making specific arrangements to copy the manuscripts and to distribute the manuscripts to several places.

Further, the *maṭha*s were used at schools where permanent provisions were made to impart regular training to Jain priests and general instructions to all students.[19]

ORIGIN AND GROWTH OF JAIN MONASTERIES (MAṬHAS) IN KARNATAKA

Jain monarchism means the collective life of the monks and nuns organized at a fixed place where they live together under one authority for spiritual liberation. It appears to be the most important development in Karnataka during earlier medieval times.

The earlier Jain monks led a wandering life throughout the year except the four months of the rainy season when they lived at a fixed abode. The earlier texts of both Śvetāmbara and the Digambara frankly recommend solitary life for the Jain ascetics, who aspired to attain salvation. The former states that the monk should stay in a deserted house or under a tree or on burial grounds or in caves.[20] It further advises to avoid such places as were especially built for them and were likely to arouse their

---

19. T.G. Kalghatagi, *op. cit.*, p. 68.

passions[21] and present obstacles in the path of spiritual liberation.

The transition from solitary wandering to settled life in Jain monasteries and Jain *basadis* was a striking development in the history of Jainism in Karnataka. The Jain epigraphs, which record donation for the erection of monasteries and temples, show that the practice of permanent settlement of the Jain monks in monasteries had begun in the last quarter of the fourth century.

From the fifth century onwards, numerous epigraphs show that the Jain monasteries were built on the side of the Jain temples in the different parts of Karnataka by the pious Jain devotees. They displayed great enthusiansm in donating large tracts of land and villages for the proper maintenance of those monasteries and the monks and nuns living therein.

The relation between the Jain monasteries and the Jain temples should be made clear at the very outset. The Jain monasteries in Karnataka were generally a composite structure incorporating the Jain *maṭhas* and the Jain temples within its fold. We have only a few separate Jain *maṭhas* serving exclusively as residences of monks and nuns; generally they were attached to the Jain temples.[22]

The *maṭhas* of Bhaṭṭārakas carried out various social functions. This provided an occasion for preservation of various arts. According to the Joharapurkar, the institution of Bhaṭṭāraka came into existence from the second century AD but this institution acquired importance only in medieval period because during this period some royal dynasties like Gaṅgas, Rāṣṭrakūṭas, Śilāhāras, etc., patronised Jainism. There was decline of Hindu dynasty in medieval period and all Indian subcontinent was overpowered by an iconoclast Muslim ruler. Therefore, there was decline of Jain religion also. However, the institution of

20. S.B. Deo, *History of Jain Monarchism from Inscriptions and Literature*, Poona, 1960, p. 342.
21. *Ibid.*
22. R.B.P. Singh, *op. cit.*, p. 101.

Bhaṭṭāraka proved to be crucial at this juncture in safeguarding Jainism. Thus, it would be clear that the Bhaṭṭāraka tradition played an important part in the history of medieval Jain society.

In course of time, some Jain monasteries came to assume authority over other religious establishments. An inscription speaks of such a monastery at Śravaṇbeḷagoḷa in the Hassan district of Mysore. The foundation of the Humcha *maṭha* is in existence in the Nagar Tāluka of the Śimogā district. The Karkala and Moodabidrī *maṭha*s are existing in South Kanara district.

The Main Maṭhas and Gurus

ŚRAVAṆBEḶGOḶA — CĀRUKĪRTI BHAṬṬĀRKA

The principal seat of the Jain faith in former Mysore state now Karnataka, is at Śravaṇbeḷagoḷa in Hassan district. This *maṭha* was founded in 982 by Cāmuṇḍarāya, the military general of the Gaṅga King Mārasiṁha II, who is said to have erected in the following year the famous colossal statue of Gommaṭeśvara on the Vindhyagiri hill.[23] It became the chief centre of the Jain pontiffs, which claimed authority over the Jains throughout south India.[24] The Jains extended their religious activities in the different parts of Karnataka from here. The shrine continues to be important even now not only for the Jains of south but also of northern India. He established a *maṭha* and other religious institution with liberal endowments.

According to a list from the *maṭha*, the following was the succession of *gurus*.[25] They were of the Kunda-Kundānvaya, Mūlasaṁgha, Deśī-Gaṇa and Pustaka-Gaccha.

Nemicandra Siddhāntācārya appointed by Cāmuṇḍarāya — *c.* 983

Kunda-Kundācārya appointed by Vīrā Pāṇḍya — *c.* 983

---

23. B.L. Rice, *Ep. Carn.* vol. II, Śravaṇbeḷagoḷa, 122, p. 50.
24. *Ibid., E. Carn.*, SB 175, p. 89.
25. *Ibid., op. cit.*, Introd.

Siddhāntācārya appointed by Kuna Pāṇḍya	*c.* 983
Amalakīrtyācārya appointed by Vinayāditya	*c.* 1050
Somānandyācārya appointed by Vinayāditya	*c.* 1050
Tridama Vaibhubanyācārya appointed by Hoyasala	*c.*. 1070
Prabhācandra Siddhāntācārya appointed by Ereyaṅga	*c.* 1090
Guṇacandrāya appointed by Ballālarāya	*c.* 1102
Śubhacandrācārya appointed by Bitti Deva	*c.* 1110

All the *gurus* bear the name of Cārukīrti-Paṇḍitācārya from AD 1117 and endowments have been granted to the *maṭha* by all succeeding kings. There are about a dozen inscriptions printed in the *Epigraphic Caranatica* II (Śravaṇbeḷagoḷa), revised edition, which gives succession lists of Jain *gurus*.[26]

ORIGIN AND FOUNDER OF ŚRAVAṆBEḶGOḶA MAṬHA

It is interesting to see the early history of Śravaṇbeḷagoḷa monastery which was for the first time founded by Bhadrabāhu in fourth century BC. The year 300 BC saw the eighth successor of Tīrthaṅkara Mahāvīra. Śīrutakevali Bhadrabāhu Muni attained *sallekhana samādhi* at Śravaṇbeḷagoḷa. Emperor Candragupta Maurya, Muni Bhadrabāhu's disciple, who accompanied him as a monk from the north, also attained *samādhi* here. The *dharmācārya pīṭha,* established then, has remained dedicated to the task of protecting the holy place, religion and society and patronizing literature and the arts.

Śravaṇbeḷgoḷa has since been recognized as an important centre of learning of Jain philosophy, religion and practice. After Bhadrabāhu and Candragupta, amother great ascetic Ācārya Kundakunda was also associated intimately with Śravaṇbeḷagoḷa.

Muniśrī Nemicandra Siddhānta Cakravarty was the *ācārya* when Cāmuṇḍarāya came to Śravaṇbeḷagoḷa along with his

---

26. B.L. Rice, *Inscriptions in Śravaṇbeḷagoḷa,* vol. II, Bangalore, 1989, p. Introd.

mother on a pilgrimage. As desired by his mother, Cāmuṇḍarāya the general of Gaṅga King Rachamalla got the 57 ft tall idol of Bāhubali sculptured in the year AD 981. He established a *maṭha* (monastery) and requested *ācārya* Nemicandra to be the pontiff.

Later, when Muni Śubhacandra was the *ācārya* during the reign of the Hoyasala dynasty, the title "Cārukīrti Svāmījī" was conferred upon him by the king for his able guidance during a turbulent period. The title Cārukīrti Svāmījī continued as the name of the succeeding *ācārya*s of the *dharmapīṭha* of Śravaṇbeḷagoḷa *maṭha*.

Very naturally, such great *ṛṣi*s of Beḷgoḷa, who were the great examples of the higher life, in time, came to be worshipped even by kings and in due course became *rājaguru*s, *mahāmaṇḍalācārya*s and *jagad-guru*. Of such *ṛṣi*s, who thus worked their way to power and influence through their learning, character and other attainments, have been referred in the Śravaṇbeḷagoḷa inscriptions.

(a) "Siddhānta yogī. . . whom, though his lotus feet were ever tinted with the rays from the crows of bending kings, no substance and no women, no clothing and no youthful pride, no strength and wealth coat tempt."[27]

(b) "After him, Hulla, the minister of king Narasimha, his guru was the Jagadguru Kukkutasana Muladhari deva."[28]

(c) "Maghanandi Siddhanta Chakravarti, Rajaguru to the Hoyasala King."[29]

(d) "Mahamandalacharya Deva Kirti Paṇḍita Deva."[30]

If Jainism or the Jain culture is again to influence the Indian

---

27. R. Narasimhachar, *E. Carn*, vol. II, Śravaṇbeḷgoḷa No. 108 (dated AD 1433).

28. *Ibid.*, No. 37 (dated AD 1160).

life in modern times, it should concentrate, as did its ancient *ṛṣis* in south India. On the practical teaching of its spiritual discipline, its *dīkṣās* and *śikṣās* to one and all, men, women and children, high and low, rich and poor, the mass mind may be illumined and the mass life ennobled and freed from the bondage of ignorance and sense desire.[31]

The following interesting account of the the history of this place is furnished by the local *Sthala Purāṇa.*

> Camundaraya repaired the ruined temples, and among other ceremonines had that of sprinkling of the god performed. He appointed Siddhantacharya as Guru of the *maṭh* to conduct the daily, monthly, annual and other procession. He established in the *maṭh* a *chatram* where food, medicine and education were provided for pilgrims. He appointed men of his caste to receive with due respect the devotees and pilgrims of all the three castes who resort to this place from Delhi, Kanakadri Svitapura, Sudhapura, Papapuri, Jayanagara, etc. For this purpose certain villages, giving an annual revenue of 1,96,000 *pagodas*, were made over to the temple. He fixed *sila sasanas* in the four directions in the chaitra month of the year Vaibhava-605 of Kaliyuga or the 1215th year after the death of Vardhamanasvami. This endowment was maintained by his descendants for 109 years.[32]

Afterwards, from the Śaka year 444, Prajotpatti Pāṇḍu Rāya and his descendants appointed Kundakundācārya to manage the affairs of the temple and continued the charitable endowments for 90 years.

Again from Śaka year 564, one Vīrapāṇḍyarāya and his son appointed Siddhāntācārya to the temple for 80 years. They also gave *ināṃ* lands to the temple.

Then followed Kuna Pāṇḍu Rāya, who appointed Amalakīrti

---

29. *Ibid.*, No. 129. (dated AD 1283).
30. *Ibid.*, No. 89 (dated AD 1258)
31. Seshagiri B. Rao, *JA*, (Articles) *Ancient South Indian Jainism*, p. 10.
32. J.S.F. Mackenzie, *JA*, Articles, (Śravaṇbeḷagoḷa), Delhi, 1872, p. 130.

Ācārya to the temple. This king, however, changed his religion and destroyed the charities established by his predecessors. He and his family were ruined. At this time, certain princes belonging to the family of Cāmuṇḍarāya, who governed the provinces of Halebiḍu, Bilikere, Kaḍanahalli, Aukanaballi, etc., built small temples at Gommaṭeśpura Bilikere, Biliulli, Halebiḍu and set-up an image Gommaṭeśvara, of the height of two men, on the hill of Gommaṭapura, and gave the villages called Śravaṇahalli, Jinnahalli, Gommaṭapura and Padenahalli for the maintenance of worship. They also gave eight other villages and appointed Amalakīrti Ācārya to manage the affairs in the hope that the discontinued worship at Śravaṇbeḷagoḷa might be renewed and continued. This they continued for 67 years.[33]

> From the Saka year 777, Bhava, this country fell into the hands of the Hoyasala Ballala Kings who were Jain kshatriya ruling over the country of Hoyasala. Aditya, a descendant of this house, having heard of the excellence of the place and the beauty of the idol, paid a visit to it and had the ceremony of sprinkling the god performed. He gave villages (out of those that had been given by Chamundaraya) yielding a revenue of 96,000 *pagodas*, and appointed Somanandyacarya to carry out the worship properly.

Afterwards, Amalakīrti Ballāla made over lands yielding 5,000 *pagoḍā*s to the temple and appointed Tridāmavibudhānandyācārya as head of the *maṭha*. This continued for 49 years.

Another Ballāla king named Ango Rāja continued the same for 56 years and appointed Prabhācandra Siddhānatācārya to manage the affairs. After this Pratāpa Ballāla nominated Guṇacandrācārya to manage the affairs. This continued for 64 years. Udayāditya Ballāla, Vīra Ballāla and Gangarāya Ballāla each continued the worship by granting lands yielding 5,000

---

33. *Ibid.*, p. 131.

pagoḍās. Bettivardhana Ballāla gave an *ināma* of land yielding 50,000 *pagoḍās* and continued the worship for 31 years under the management of Śubhacandrācārya.[34]

According to a tradition Cāmuṇḍarāya, after erecting the colossus on the larger hill, appointed his *guru* Nemicandra as the head of the *maṭha* at Śravaṇbeḷagoḷa. It is also stated that there was a line of *gurus* at the place even before this period. One of the *gurus* of this *maṭha*, Cārukīrti Paṇḍita, is said in some inscriptions [Nos. 254 (105)] of AD 1398 and [258 (108)] of AD 1432 to have cured the Hoyasala King Ballāla I (AD 1100-06) of a terrible disease and have thence acquired the title of Ballāla Jīvarakṣaka.[35]

EPIGRAPHICAL ACCOUNT REGARDING BHAṬṬĀRAKA

Some inscriptions from Śravaṇbeḷagoḷa and other places, furnished the following account regarding Bhaṭṭārakas and their service to Śraman culture.

Among the Mārasiṁha Guttiya Gaṅga, Nolambakulāntaka, who reigned from AD 961 till AD 974, was a very fervent Jain. The Kuge Brahmadeva pillar inscription on the Cikkabeṭṭa at Śravaṇbeḷagoḷa, dated AD 974, gives a detail of the meritorious work of the Mārasiṁha Guttiya Gaṅga on behalf of the Syādvāda doctrine. He maintained the doctrine of Jain, and caused to be erected at various places the *basadis* and *mānastambhas*. According to the same record, King Mārasiṁha:

> having reverently carried out works of piety, one year later, he relinquished the sovereignty and observing the vow for three days with the rites of worship in the presence of the holy feet of Ajitasena Bhaṭṭāraka at Bankapura, accomplished Samadhi.[36]

Tribhuvanamalla Ereyaṅga, ruling the Gaṅgamaṇḍala, granted

34. *Ibid*.
35. Hayavadana C. Rao, *Mysore Gazetteer*, vol. V, Delhi, 1984, pp. 1063-64.

to this great Jain logician, Rachamalla and the Beḷgoḷa 12 for the repairs of the *basadi*s of the Beḷgoḷa.[37] Since the king was ruling the Gaṅgavāḍī, and the royal endowment affected all the *basadi*s in the holy place around the Candragiri hill at Śravaṇbeḷagoḷa, it is said in the epigraph that Gopanandī caused the *jin dharma* to prosper through the wealth of the Gaṅga kings. In an earlier context, we have had an occasion to describe all the celebrated colleagues of Gopanandī, as given in the Kattle-Basadi record dated about AD 1100. This inscription dated AD 1094, we may incidentally add, repeats the praise given to Gopanandī. King Ballāla I, the eldest son of King Ereyaṅga, succeeded the latter and ruled from AD 1100 till AD 1106. The *guru* of this ruler was Cārukīrtimuni. Two stone inscription dated AD 1398 and AD 1432 respectively prove this. These are the Siddheśvara-Basadi records of Śravaṇbeḷagoḷa, which will be styled here as the I and II of that name. The I Siddhesvara-Basadi inscription dated 1398 relates the following about Cārukīrti Paṇḍitadeva. He was the disciple of Śrutakīrti Deva, a great disputant and an accomplisher of everything that had to be accomplished. This remarkable *guru* (Cārukīrti Paṇḍitadeva) was proficient in medicine as well. The *guru* of King Vinayāditya II was Śāntideva. This is proved from the two stone inscriptions, one of them being the Pārśvanātha-Basadi record found at Śravaṇbeḷagoḷa, dated AD 1129. This inscription informs us that King Vinayādita Hoyasala's *guru* Śāntideva having performed the rites of *saṁnyāsana*, as a reward of his faith, attained to the realm of *nirvāṇa*. The king and the company of townsmen erected the monument on the departure of their *guru* Śāntideva.[38]

What King Vinayāditya did as a Jain, obviously on the advice of his *guru*, is described in the another record found in the Gandhavaraṇa-Basadi at Śravaṇbeḷagoḷa, dated AD 1131. He has been described to have gladly made a number of tanks and

---

36. B.A. Saletore, *M.J.*, pp. 26-27.
37. B.L. Rice, *Ep. Carn.*, vol. V, Cn. 148, pp. 189-90.

temples, Jain shrines, a number of *nāḍus*, villages and subjects.[39] The credit of maintaining the *anekāntamata* was also shared by the wives of the great Jain Generals. Foremost among them was the wife of the celebrated Jain General Gaṅga Rājā Lakkale or Lakṣmīmati. She was styled Lakṣmīmati Daṇḍanāyakīti and was the disciple of Śubhacandra who is described as "a *siddhanandī* in philosophy." Lakṣmīmati is described in a record assigned to AD 1128 as "the lady of police in business" and "the lady of victory in battle." She caused a new Jinālaya to be built in Śravaṇbeḷagoḷa in about the same year.[40] It was some of these *jina* temples erected by her that, as we related in an earlier context, were granted liberal endowments.[41] As for example, her husband Lakṣmīmati bestowed the gifts of food, shelter, medicine and learning and acquired thereby the name of being a mine of auspiciousness.[42] The same year, however, Lakṣmīmati Daṇḍanāyakīti adopting the *saṁnyāsana* ended her life by *samādhi*, and her husband as an act of reverence, set-up an epitaph (at Śravaṇbeḷagoḷa) and consecrated it with great gifts and worship.[43]

Gaṅgarāja had an elder brother whose wife was Jakkanabbe. Jakkanabbe was also the disciple of Śubha-candradeva. She was the mother of general Boppa. After observing the vow known as *mokṣatilaka*, she caused the god to be carved on the boulder of Nombare and had it consecrated at Śravaṇbeḷagoḷa in about AD 1120. The same year, a tank was built there by her[44] for which she was praised in very high terms.

To this period belongs the saintly figure Santaladevī, the queen of the Hoyasala King Viṣṇuvardhanadeva. An inscription

---

38. B.L. Rice, *Ep. Carn.*, MG. 17, p. 61.
39. B.A. Saletore, *op. cit.*, pp. 73-74.
40. B.L. Rice, *Ep. Carn.*, vol. II, No. 130, pp. 57-58.
41. B.A. Saletore, *op. cit.*, p. 162.
42. B.L. Rice, *E. Carn.*, vol II, No. 127, p. 56.
43. *Ibid.*, *op. cit.*, vol. II, No 128, p. 56.

dated AD 1123 praises her beauty in two exquisite verses. Her *guru* was Prabhācandra Siddhāntadeva, the disciple of Meghacandra Traividyadeva, of the *pustaka gaccha* and the *deśīya gaṇa*. Queen Santaladevī's work to promote the cause of the *jina dharma* was lasting. She was the cause of the elevation of the four *samayas* (or creeds) and she delighted in gifts of food, shelter, medicine, and learning and in the narration of stories relating to Jainism. It was she who had the image of Śānti Jinendra made at Śravaṇbeḷgoḷa in AD 1123.[45]

In the same year, she caused to be erected the Savati-gandhavaraṇa-Basadi in the same holy place and with the permission of King Viṣṇuvardhana, she granted the village of Mottenavile to her *guru* for the worship of the god and food for ascetics in the same *basadi*. To this gift was added in the same year specified lands of the Gaṅgāsamudra.[46]

In the succeeding generations too, it was the ladies of the higher rank who set the example. The senior Herggaditi Acaladevī was the wife of the Śaivite General Candramauli. She had become pre-eminent for the four traditional gifts she gave. The learned Nayakīrti was her *guru*. She had a fine Jinālaya dedicated to Pārśvanātha constructed in Śravaṇbeḷgoḷa and it was to this temple, as we saw in an earlier context, that on the application of Candramauli the King Ballāla gave the village of Bammeyanhalli. And the merchants together with the representatives of the *nāḍu* and the *nagara* likewise granted specified money for the maintenance of the temple. These gifts were received by Nayakīrti's disciple Bālacandradeva in AD 1182. In the same year, the Hoyasala king added the village of Bekka to the above gift.[47]

Nagara Jinālaya temple was erected in AD 1195 by the minister Nāgadeva, a lay disciple of Nayakīrti Siddhānta-

44. *Ibid., op. cit.*, pp. 160-61.

45. B.A. Saletore, *op. cit.*, p. 165.

46. B.L. Rice, *op. cit.*, vol. II, Nos. 132, 133, pp. 60, 75.

Cakravartī, and the Pattanasvāmī of the Hoyasala king Ballāla II (AD 1173-1220). The temple was named Nagara Jinālaya because the *nagara* or merchants were its supporters.[48]

Samaladevī was the wife of the devout Jain minister called Ecan. She too had a *basadi* erected in AD 1207 in Belagavattināḍ for the worship of which she granted specified lands.[49]

We may mention a word about General Hulla and his *gurus*. The Mangayi-Basadi record dated AD 1159 tells us that Hulla rejoiced in bowing at the feet of Mālādhārīsvāmī,[50] while one of the inscriptions on the Doddabetta dated about AD 1175 explicitly states that he was the lay disciple of Nayakīrti Siddhāntadeva.[51] The former was also known as Kukkuṭāsana Mālādhārīdeva and was merely his *vrata guru*.[52] Inscriptions dated AD 1159 to AD 1163 tell us of the manner in which he strengthened the cause of the *jina dharma* in these three well-known places.

Purchasing land and freeing it from all obligations and bestowing it with charitable endowments for the Jain institutions was noteworthy feature of the times. Having purchased specified lands at Mattiyakere from the Mahāmaṇḍalācārya Nayakīrtideva's disciple Candra-prabhadeva, Śambhūdeva and the three others (named) granted the same and the milk offerings to Gommaṭadeva and the 24 *tīrthaṅkaras* at Śravaṇbeḷgoḷa in AD 1273 in the reign of the Hoyasala King Narasiṁha III.[53] Likewise in AD 1280, in the reign of the same monarch, all the farmers of Arakottara having freed the *basadi* of that locality from all the obligations of money payments, granted the water-rate, alms, house-tax, poll-tax, the *nicandi* and other dues for the same

47. *Ibid.*, pp. 136, 139 and 140.
48. K.A. Nilakantha Sastri, *A Guide to Sravaṅbeḷgoḷa*, Mysore, 1981.
49. B.A. Saletore, *op. cit.*, p. 170.
50. B.L. Rice, *op. cit.*, vol. II, p. 153.
51. *Ibid.*, p. 103.
52. *Ibid.*, p. 148.
53. *Ibid.*, 246, p. 104.

basadi.[54]

The same procedure was adopted in AD 1282 when all the jewel merchants (*māṇikya nagaraṅgal*) of Śravaṇbeḷgoḷa desired to make some endowments. Together with the royal *guru* Nemicandra Paṇḍita's disciple Bālacandradeva, these merchants, who belonged to the Balātkāragaṇa, and who were the disciples of the Mahāmaṇḍalācārya Māghanandī, purchased wetland from Bālacandradeva and gave it along with other lands for the worship of the god Ādi of the Nagara Jinālaya.[55]

It is interesting to note in this connection that the impulse to support the cause of the *jina dharma* came from the queens of Vijayanagara, one of whom was a Jain herself. Inscription No. 337 states that the Śāntinātha statue was caused to be made by Bhīmā-Devī, a lay disciple of Paṇḍitācārya and the queen of Devarāya Mahārāja in about AD 1410 at Śravaṇbeḷgoḷa.[56] Inscription Nos. 339 and 341 state that the Mangayi-Basadi built in about AD 1325 by Mangayi of Beḷgoḷa, a disciple of Cārukīrti-Paṇḍitācārya and crest jewel of royal dancing girls, was named Tribhuvana-Cūḍāmaṇi.[57]

This versatile statesman was the minister of King Harihara-rāya II in AD 1403. But he continued to serve also in the reign of King Devarāya II. The Śravaṇbeḷgoḷa inscription dated AD 1422 cited above inform us that in that year General Irugappa, in the presence of the Jain *guru* Śrutamuni, granted the village of Beḷgoḷa for the worship of Gommaṭeśvara.[58]

PRESENT LIVING BHAṬṬĀRAKA SVĀMĪJĪ : HIS HOLINESS JAGADGURU KARMAYOGĪ CĀRUKĪRTI BHAṬṬĀRAKA SVĀMĪJĪ ŚRAVAṆBEḶGOḶA MAṬHA

The benevolent and socio-cultural activities are being carried

54. B.A. Saletore, *op. cit.*, p. 183.
55. B.L. Rice, *op. cit.*, Ch. 84, p. 10.
56. B.A. Saletore, *op. cit.*, p. 299.
57. R. Narasimhachar, *E. Carn.*, vol. II, Śravaṇbeḷagoḷa, p. 2.
58. B.A. Saletore, *MJ*, p. 306.

out even today by the present Cārukīrti Bhaṭṭāraka Svāmījī of Śravaṇbeḷgoḷa *pīṭha*. Therefore, it is perfectly in order to see his life and work in brief in the following pages.

The present pontiff was born on May 3, 1949 at Varaṅg in Karnataka as Ratnavarmā. He became a monk at an early age on December 12, 1969 and was ascended to the *Dharmācārya pīṭha* at Śravaṇbeḷgoḷa *maṭha* on the 19 April, 1970 and thereby also became the Chairman of S.D.J. M.I. Management Committee, i.e., the Management Committee of Śravaṇbeḷgoḷa shrine.

H.H. Svamījī's studies have not been limited only to the Jain philosophy in Prākṛt, Sanskrit and Kannaḍa, rather he is also M.A. in History (Mysore University) and M.A. in philosophy (Bangalore University).

More than 30 temples at Śravaṇbeḷagoḷa have been renovated and arranged for daily *pūjā*. The credit for organizing the highly successful holy journey of the *dharmacakra* across the length and breadth of southern India in commemoration of the 2500th anniversary of Bhagvān Mahāvīra's *nirvāṇa*, goes mainly to H.H. Svamījī. The well organized 1000th year consecration and Head Anointing (*mahāmastakābhiṣeka*) ceremonies of Bhagvān Bāhubali speak a volume about H.H. Svamījī's acumen. The then Prime Minister, late Smt. Indira Gandhi, in appreciation of his dedication and selfless service, honoured H.H. Svamījī with the title *karmayogī*.

H.H. Svamījī is also deeply involved in the causes of society and education. During the 1000th year celebrations, 1000 people benefitted from the free eye camp organized at Śravaṇbeḷgoḷa. Ten villages in the vicinity of Śravaṇbeḷgoḷa were also adopted for development. These villages are now provided with school buildings, drinking water, new tanks, community centres, roads and street lights. The service projects are not restricted to any one community but care for the public at large.

In the field of education, H.H. Svamījī has established Pre-Primary, Primary and High Schools, a College of Pharmacy and a Polytechnic. Gommateshvara Vidyapitha is instrumental in producing scholars in religious studies. Svamījī had established the Prakrit Jñānabharati Education Trust at Bangalore in order to make the treasure of knowledge in Prākṛt available to the common man. National Prakrit Conferences are held once every two years under the auspices of this trust. "Prakrit Jnanabharati Awards" are also presented to ten scholars selected for their notable contribution in the field of Prākṛt, every year.

Numerous *dharmaśālā*s and guest-houses providing all amenities for the large number of pilgrims and tourists have been constructed under the able guidance of H.H. Svāmījī. Beautiful gardens now add to the beauty of the place. Generaous donations from devotees have been applied in fruitful developmental projects. An āyurvedic hospital and a clinical lab are in service. A mobile hospital has been launched for the benefit of the rural areas.

H.H. Svāmījī has command over Hindi, English and Kannaḍa languages. His discourses in simple and lucid style leave the listeners spellbound. He has often been invited to deliver enlightening speeches and steer several social organizations like Vishwa Dharma Shanti Sammelan Samiti (World Religion Space Conference Committee) in their projects and has toured abroad on several occasions (Singapore 1976, U.S.A. 1979, Kenya, U.K. and Europe in 1984 and 1988). The consecration of the Jain temple of Leicester, England in 1988 was performed with traditional rites under the able guidance of H.H. Svāmījī.

H.H. Svāmījī has adopted a much required progressive outlook about the practice of religion in the present context. He has simplified religion for the layman and opened several avenues where the preachings of the *tīrthaṅkaras* could be practised.[59]

Thus the "Śravaṇbeḷgoḷa Bhaṭṭārakas" played important role in preserving and spreading Jain culture throughout south India since early days. Not only this, the Bhaṭṭārakas also extended monetary help to various social and educational institutions which would build the personality of new generation. They also provided civic amenities to twelve adjoining poor villages by giving light, constructing roads and providing water facility. Therefore, this Bhaṭṭāraka Institution is relevant to modern time also and would be required in future too.

Humcha : Devendrakīrti Bhaṭṭāraka

Like Śravaṇbeḷgoḷa, Humcha is also a seat of Bhaṭṭārakas since eighth century AD. It has a cherished history. Some Bhaṭṭārakas of Humcha were celebrated and learned men. They rendered yeomen service to the cause of Jainism and protected Śramaṇ culture.

The foundation of the Humcha *maṭha*, which is still in existence in the Nagara Tāluka of the Śimogā district, was laid by Jinadattarāya during the eighth-ninth centuries, who carved out the kingdom of the Santaras in the south.[60] The *gurus*, as given in the following list, were of the Kundakundānvaya, and the Nandisaṁgha from Jayakīrtideva were of Sarasvatī *gaccha*. The descent is traced in a general way from Bhadrabāhu, the Śrutakevali, through Viśākhamuni, the Daśapūrvī his successor, through Umāsvāti, author of the *Tattvārthasūtra* and then the following :

Sāmantabhadra, author of *Devāgama-stotra*; Pūjyapāda, author of *Jainendra Vyākaraṇa*, of a *nyāsa* on Pāṇini called *Śabdāvatāra*,

---

59. I took personal interview of Bhaṭṭāraka and also utilized biodata supplied by Śravaṇbeḷagoḷa Maṭha itself.

60. B.L. Rice, *E. Carn.*, inscriptions in the Shimoga district, vol. VIII, Bangalore, 1904, No. 35 (1077 AD).

and of a *Vaidya Śāstra*. Siddhāntakīrti, *guru* to Jinadattarāya. About AD 730 Akalaṅka, author of *Bhāṣya* on the *Āptamīmāṁsā* and also of *Ślokavārttikālaṅkāra*. Māṇikyanandī Prabhācandra, author of *Nyāya Kaumudī Chandrodaya*, and of a *nyāsa* on Śakaṭāyana Vardhamāna Munīndra, by the power of whose *mantra* Hoyasala subdued the tiger AD 980-1040. His successors were *gurus* to the Hoyasala kings. Vāsupūjyavartti, *guru* to Ballālarāya (AD 1040-1100).[61]

Śrīpāla - Śubhakīrtideva
Nemicandra - Padmanandī
Abhayacandraguru - Maghanandī
Carama Keśavarāya - Siṁhanandī
Jayakīrtideva - Padmaprabha
Jinacandrarāya - Vasunandī
Indranandī - Meghacandra
Vasantakīrti - Vīranandī
Viśālakīrti - Dhanañjaya

Dharmabhūṣaṇa, *guru* to Devarāya (AD 1401-51), Vidyānanda, who debated before (AD 1451-1508) Devarāya and Kṛṣṇarāya and maintained the Jain faith at Bilige and Karkala.

His sons were : Siṁhakīrti, who debated before AD 1468-82, in the court of Mohammad Shah; Besides, Sudarśana, Merunandī, Devendrakīrti, Amarakīrti and Viśālakīrti, also debated before AD 1465-79.

Sikander, Virupākṣarāya and Nemicandra, debated in the court of Kṛṣṇa and Acyutarāya in AD 1508-42.[62]

The present *guru* is now named Devendrakīrti Bhaṭṭāraka.

---

61. B.L. Rice, *E. Carn.* vol. I, No. 35 (1070).
62. *Ibid.*, No. 35 (AD 1070).

EPIGRAPHICAL ACCOUNT REGARDING THE BHAṬṬĀRAKA

Fortunately, there are a number of epigraphs which furnish the following account regarding Bhaṭṭārakas.

Vikrama-Santara made grant to Siddhānta-Bhaṭṭāraka and the inscription of AD 1077 runs as follows:

Tolapuruṣa Vikrama Santara, who in AD 897 had a *basadi* made for *muni* Siddhānta Bhaṭṭāraka of the Kundakundarāya and endowed it with certain lands.[63] He was the same Vikramāditya Santara who constructed the Guddada-Basadi at Humcha and had it dedicated to Bāhubali in the next year i.e. AD 898.

Bhujabala Santara, had the second name of Trailokyamalla after his overlord, the western Cāḷukya monarch Trailokya-malladeva. We gather information from a stone inscription dated AD 1066 that he constructed a Jinālaya called Bhujabala Santara Jinālaya in his capital at Pombucca and granted the village of Haravari to his *guru* Kanakanandideva.[64] His brother Nanni-Santara (AD 1077) is said to be "a worshipper of the feet of *jina*"[65] who also made the charitable endowments to *jina*.

The following inscription provides information about the long penance performed by one Bhaṭṭāraka named Lakṣmīsena who was famous in the Śrī-Mūla-Saṁgha and Pustaka *gaccha*. Lakṣmīsena-Bhaṭṭārakadeva, a Bhaṭṭāraka's disciple performed penance for long time at sunrise, Lakṣmīsena-muni attained the higher state[66] in AD 1098.

The following information is important regarding Śrīvijaya Bhaṭṭāraka. Cattaladevī undertook the task of making the Pañca-Basadi in AD 1077. Santara queen's other meritorious work were the following: the construction of tanks, wells *basadis*, temples,

---

63. *Ibid.*, and B.A. Saletore, *op. cit.*, No. 60 p. 154.
64. B.L. Rice, *Ep. Carn.*, vol. VIII, No. 35, p. 137.
65. *Ibid.*, No. 59, p. 154.
66. *Ibid.*, No. 42, pp. 45 (AD 1098).

watersheds, sacred bathing places, *śāstras*, groves and bestowing gifts of food, medicine, learning and shelter. We may observe here that Cattaladevī's preceptor was Śrīvijaya Bhaṭṭāraka, also known as Paṇḍita Pārijāta, who was proficient in all the Śāstras and Āgamas, and who was head of the Nandi *gaṇa* of the Aruṅgulānvaya of the Nidambare *tīrtha* of the Tiyan-gudi. He was also the *guru* of Rakkasa Gaṅga, the father of Cattaladevī, of Bīradeva and Nanni Santara.[67]

We learn from a later record dated AD 1103 that the same Santara-lady, who is called "a cow of plenty to the glorious *jina* congregation," granted specified lands to the same Pañca-Basadi along with her own sons Bhujabala Santara, Nanni Santara and Vikrama Santara. She and Tribhuvanamalla Santara laid the foundation stone of another *basadi* opposite to Jinālaya in Ananpur as a memorial of Bīrabbarasi and pronounced the name of Vadigharatta Ajitasena Paṇḍita.[68]

The following inscription is important which mentions the names of disciples of Ajitsena. It runs as follows :

> These three being lay disciples of Ajitsena-Paṇḍita-deva known as Vadibhasimha of Dravila Sangha, Nandi-gana and Arungalanvaya. They had the northern *pattasale* of Pancha-Basadi made. Consecrating the northern Pattasale, Srivallabha-deva, washing the feet of Vasapujya-Siddhanta-deva, made a grant, during his and Pampadevi's rule.[69]

Another Santara Princess who promoted the cause of the *anekāntamata* was Pampādevī, the daughter of King Taila and the elder sister of Vikramāditya Santara. She herself made Śāśanadevatā in one month in the same manner as the famous Urvitilakam had been constructed. She and her daughter Bacaladevī, so we are informed in the inscription dated AD 1147,

67. *Ibid.*, No. 35, pp. 137-38, Nos. 39, 40, pp. 143-44.
68. B.A. Saletore, *op. cit.*, p. 160.
69. B.L. Rice, *op. cit.*, Nr. 37 (1147 AD), p. 142.

were the disciples of the illustrious Vadibhasiṁha Ajitasena Paṇḍita. They and Vikrama Santara had constructed the northern *pattasale* of the Urvitilakam.[70]

Inscription on a stone set-up to the south in the enclosure of Pañca-Basadi temple in Humcha in Kannaḍa of size 4' × 1' records.

> Chokisetti, a disciple of Dharmbusana Bhaṭṭāraka — a repairer of Jain temples, mention of Amarkirti as junior disciple to Dharmabhusana Bhaṭṭāraka of Mula Sangha. Balakaragana — later revered by King Devaraya. Amarkirti, a contemporary of Laxmisena-Manasena and a disciple of Laxmisena of 15th century.[71]
>
> The another inscription at the village on a slab near the northern wall in the enclosure of Padmavati temple in Kannaḍa, size 2' × 1'-4" records the death of Samadi Bammgavuda a disciple of Siddhanta Yogindra on 17 March, 1295, and also mention of Gunsena Muni.[72]

The following small inscription furnishes information about Gunsena Siddhānta Bhaṭṭāraka:

> Gunsena-Siddhanta-Deva's beloved and lay-disciple of Yadagavuda gained the world of gods in AD 1296 by the rite of samadhi.[73]

Purpasena and Akalanka performed *sallekhana* and gained the path of *mukti*. The following inscription gives interesting account about the *sallekhana*. The *mahāmaṇḍalācāryas* and *rājagurus* Purpasenadeva and Akalaṅkadeva expired practicing the *saṁnyāsana* and obtained *mukti*. Fixing his mind on the thoughts of the supreme spirit, repeating the five words, which are the

---

70. *Ibid., E. Carna.*, vol. VIII, Nr. 37, pp. 141-42.
71. *Archaeological Survey of Mysore Annual Report*, Bangalore, 1934, pp. 175-76.
72. *Ibid.*, p. 177.
73. B.L. Rice, No. 143, p. 145.

sources of eternal happiness, a bee at the lotus feet of Vādirāja Muni — Purapasena gained the fruit of *mukti* with great desire. He handed over the Pañca-Basadi to the chief *muni* Guṇasena-Siddhānta with joy, while the men applauded his achievement of *mukti*. Akalaṅkadeva gained *mukti* on the date specified. Was it right for Brahmā to take away Akalaṅkabratī, publisher of the *jin-dharma*, and distinguished for good works, and so learned in the doctrine?

Purpasena-Yatipati, a disciple of Vādiraja Muni, who possesed a great wisdom of logic and grammar and was a gem of the *nandi anvaya;* he was a thunderbolt to the opponent speakers and held the glory of the Jain Saṁgha, in AD 1255.[74]

The following inscriptions give the information about female Soyi-Devī who took *samādhi* and was a disciple of Bālacandra Bhaṭṭāraka. It runs as follows :

> Mother of . . . lay disciple of Dutraividya-deva of the Sri-mula Sangha and Desi-gana, Balachandra deva's female lay disciple Soyi-Devi, expired by the rite of samadhi and gained by force the world of gods. Her mother was Kamambika, her father Madhav, her daughter Somambika.[75]

Divākarnandī and Candrakīrti Bhaṭṭārakas were two great Bhaṭṭārakas and the following inscription give information about them:

> Vīra Santara's eldest son Tailabadeva, known as Bhujabala Santara, having assumed the crown for the Tīrthada-Basadi erected by the Paṭṭanasvāmī, made a grant to Bijakanabayal temple. The *arhat* Parameśvara Parama Bhaṭṭāraka, who is possessed of the fame *mahādāna* and the eight *mahāpratihārya* and adorned with thirty-four *atiśaya* filled with pure wisdom cleansed in the water of the ocean of nectar the *siddhānta*. His disciple was Divākarnandī Siddhāntadeva. The Santara kings

74. *Ibid.*, No. 44 (AD 1255), pp. 145-46.
75. *Ibid.*, No. 53 (AD 1235), p. 152.

> of the Pomburcca *kula*, their heads on the feet of *jin*. They were making gifts of food, shelter, medicine and learning the source of widespread fame and ocean of good character, and was the Paṭṭansvāmī Nokayya-Setti, praises of him and their *guru* Bīradeva was successful.

The Bhaṭṭāraka Divākaranandī Siddhānatadeva, whose fame spread across the compass, was the *guru* of the brave Vīra Santara and his father Ammana Santara. Cārukīrti-Bhaṭṭāraka, a chief disciple of Divākaranandī Sūri, who was the disciple of Siddhānta-Ratnākara Sakala-Candra-Munināthа, of whom Pitāmaha (Brahmā) has written on the tusks of the elephants at the points of the compass that in all the world he is supremely worthy.[76]

Thus, the above information is gleaned from the inscriptions available in Humcha which threw light on the relations between Bhaṭṭārakas of Humcha and ruler's queens of the Santara dynasty.

The present Bhaṭṭāraka is continuing the glorious past tradition and has maintained *maṭha* in good condition. *Pāṭhaśālā* has also been preserved as good old library and many other social works have also been conducted. The following is a brief account of his life and work.

THE PRESENT BHAṬṬĀRAKA OF HUMCHA

The honourable title of the present Bhaṭṭāraka is Paramapūjya Śrīmadjagadguru Bhāratgaurava Bhaṭṭāraka Ratna Śrī Padmāvatī-labdhavar, Prasanna Syādavāda Kesarī, Svastiśrī, Śrī-Śrī-Śrī-105 Śrīmad Devendrakīrti Bhaṭṭāraka Paṭṭācārya Mahāsvāmījī of Śrī Jain *maṭha* of Humbuja.[77]

At present, the seat of Bhaṭṭāraka is occupied by Paramapūjya Svasti Śrī Bhaṭṭāraka Devendrakīrti Paṭṭācārya Mahāsvāmījī, who is a son of the soil, born in a famous family of

---

76. *Ibid.*, No. 57 (AD 1077), p. 153.
77. Joyess B.D. Sripati, *op. cit.*, p. 1.

scholar. Pūjya Svāmījī was born on 25-5-1949 at Multi village. The name of his parents are Shri M. Dharmapalayya and Sou. Maghamalamma. The early name of the Svāmījī was "Vinayacandra." Svāmījī had completed his primary and high school education in his own village. Then he had taken B.Sc. degree from Shimoga University.

Once upon a time, he had visited Hombuja for the *darśana* of goddess and Maṭhādhipati. The former Svāmījī of this *maṭha* had observed his honesty, patience and obedience of Vinayacandra. This person was very much like the former Svāmījī in nature and hence he appointed Vinayacandra as the Bhaṭṭāraka of this Hombuja *maṭha* later. The former Svāmījī had given him the name "Hemaratha Sāgar" *alias* Vinayacandra. Vinayacandra had taken *dikṣā*, on 20-3-1971 after the death of early Svāmījī and he became "Devendrakīrti Bhaṭṭāraka Svāmījī" on 29-10-1971.[78]

The present Bhaṭṭāraka Mahārāja had completed M.A. and Ph.D after taking *dikṣā*. He is also expert in Tulu, Kannaḍa, Hindī, English, Sanskrit and Marāṭhī. He is also the Bhaṭṭāraka Head of Warang-Maṭha of D.K. District, Malakhed Jain *maṭha* of Gulbargā district, and the Jain *maṭha* of the great holy place Sammedaśikharajī. Kundakandadri and Hattiyangadi Kṣetra are also controlled by this Svāmījī.

Kundakunda Vidyāpīṭha Brahmacaryāśrama of Hombuja, Vardhamāna Nilaya of Śimogā, Śrī Sanmati Digambara Jain Boarding of Sāgar, and elementary school of Warang are being run and controlled by this honourable Svāmījī. The Svāmījī is the main editor of the *Gurudeva Dhārmika Patrikā* and also *Siddhāntakīrti Granthamālā*.[79]

The present Bhaṭṭāraka is doing the work of protecting and promoting Jain culture. He has been undertaking the task of

---

78. *Ibid., op. cit.*, p. 31.
79. *Ibid.*, p. 32.

propaganda and publicity in regard to Jainism for several years not only in India, but also abroad, in a laudable manner. In this way, he has popularized the Jain codes of conduct. Śrī Svāmījī is good at delivering religious lectures in a simple, impressive, logical and attractive way; he is considered a good speaker both in the country and abroad.

Pūjya Svāmījī has travelled all over India and also in the foreign countries for 21 times. He toured England, U.S.A., Canada, Belgium, France, Italy, West Germany, Holland, Greece, Singapore, Thailand, Nepal, Japan, Switzerland, Bhutan and preached Jainism to the people of these countries.[80]

Svāmījī is also a good writer. He had written some *grantha*s and religious papers. Also he had established the statue of Lord Pārśvanātha on the hill, which is 21 ft high. This statue is made up of marble. The *Pañcakalyāṇa Mahotsava* was also celebrated at the time of establishment of the icon of Lord Pārśvanātha. Svāmījī has worked hard for the progress of Jain *dharma* and its *śāstra*. The experts of the other religion have also congratulated Svāmījī for his works. The people from the Jain and other communities have given him several titles like "Jagadguru," Bhaṭṭāraka Ratha," "Siddhānta Jyoti," "Saddharma Parama Jyoti," "Rājayogī," "Charity Cūḍāmaṇi," "Bhārata Gaurava," "Yuga Puruṣa," "Samyakatva Cūḍāmaṇi," "Jain Samāja Dīpaka," etc.[81]

His Holiness Svāmījī is also a member of the Jain Dharma Canvassing Committee, Haridvār; Jain Tīrtha Kshetra Samiti; Candraprabhu Religious Trust of Kerala; Vishwa Shanti Dharma Sammelan of India; Vishwa Bauddha Sammelan of Japan; Vishwa Yuva Janotsava of Singapore; Ahimsa Anekanta Trust of London; Vishwa Hindu Sammelan of Nepal, etc. He occupies an eminent position in these Trusts. The Svāmījī is the President of All India Bhaṭṭāraka Sangha.[82]

---

80. *Ibid.*, p. 32.

81. *Ibid.*, pp. 32-33.

82. *Ibid.*, p. 33.

Svāmījī is the member and guide to the Vishwa Sahakari Sanstha (the world of vegetarians of USA). He has made donation for the construction of an ancient Jin Mandir. The Mahavira Bhavan of Hassan is the proof of this donation. He also gave donations to the research fellows. Many *Pañcakalyāṇa Pūjā*s have been performed under his guidance.[83] The people of all the community wish and pray to the goddess to render Svāmījī a long life and good health. At present, he is at the age of 51.

Thus, the Bhaṭṭāraka tradition is occupying unique place in the history of Jainism and the present Bhaṭṭāraka of Humcha is rendering yeomen service to spread and protect the Jain monuments and Śramaṇ culture not only in south India but even abroad, besides running Humcha *maṭha* itself.

MOODBIDRI : CĀRUKĪRTI BHAṬṬĀRAKA

Next to Humcha, Moodabidri is renowned for its old library and Bhaṭṭāraka *pīṭha* is the Jain sacred place. It is regarded as "Dakṣiṇa Kāśī" and the old Jain monuments and temples exist here. But Bhaṭṭāraka tradition is old and protecting and spreading Jain culture in South Kanara.

During the third century BC, Ācārya Bhadrabāhu lived in Śravaṇbeḷgoḷa along with 12,000 apostles including Candragupta Maurya, the Emperor. Some of his disciples scattered all over the areas where Tamil, Telugu, Kannaḍa and Tulu were spoken. These disciples considerably spread the Jain religion. The Jains, who thus migrated and settled in the south built Jain temples and *maṭha*. They also traded with distant countries through the ports on the western coast and amassed a lot and came to be called as Śreṣṭhis" (Setty).

But a bad time came and the town once rich and crowded, became deserṭed with all its Jain temples ruined and surrounded by thick forests of bamboo trees. According to the traditional

83. Interview of the P.A. to Swamiji (Humcha).

source of information in the eighth century AD, a Digambara Jain monk coming from Śravaṇbeḷgoḷa, one day, happened to see, on his way to the forest, a tiger and a cow drinking water from a common source and licking each other with mutual affection at a place where "Guru-Basadi" stands at present.[84]

It was absolutely a strange scene. Guessing that the spot must be sacrosanct, the ascetic had the forest cleared and a search made. He found a large-sized divine image of Śrī Pārśvanātha carved out of black granite. It sufficiently proves that this image is thousands of years old. The ascetic (Svāmījī) had a *basadi* built at that spot and installed the image in AD 714 with *Pañcakalyāṇa* ceremony. This *basadi*, built at the instance of that *guru*, is named the Guru-Basadi.

Another reason for which the *basadi* is called Guru-Basadi is that in Moodabidri one could find an ancient Jain Guru Maṭha. His Holiness, Śrī Cārukīrti Paṇḍitācāryavarya Svāmījī is the celebrated Head of this Guru Pīṭha. It is an age long tradition to celebrate the *Paṭṭābhiṣeka Mahotsava* of this Svāmījī of Jain Guru Maṭha on the Guru Pīṭha found in outer throne room of the *basadi*. Since there is a cordial relationship between the *basadi* and the Guru Pīṭha, it became tradition to call this *basadi* most appropriately by the name Guru-Basadi.[85]

This Guru-Basadi is also called "Siddhānta-Basadi" because the old Āgama scriptures of Jains namely the *Dhavalā*s are preserved here with utmost care. These *Dhavalā*s of some 850 years ago were handwritten in old Kannaḍa scripts on palm-leaves with colourful paintings on them. The practice of carving religious-scriptures on palm leaves with a pointed needle and spreading ink on them prevailed in the south then, while paper was used in the north for writing scriptures. The installation ceremony of the *jin bimba*, Śrī Pārśvanātha, took place in the

---

84. Sri Digambara Jain Math (Moodabidri), Dakshina Kannada District (Karnataka State), pp. 22-23.

85. *Ibid.*, p. 26.

year AD 714 from the inscription found on the Siṁha Pīṭha of this image.[86]

The Guru Pīṭha (Maṭha) at Moodabidri was found by Svasti Śri Cārukīrti Paṇḍitācāryavarya Svāmījī of Śravaṇbeḷagoḷa in the year AD 1330. Bittideva (AD 1104-41), the king of Dvārasamudra (Halebiḍu), converted himself from Jain religion to Vaiṣṇavism and was named "Viṣṇuvardhana." He then, destroyed the main Jain temples and killed many Jain house-holders. This caused a great disaster and the result was the sudden appearance of chasm in his city, into which many people and animals were buried.

Vīraballāla, who ruled his kingdom (AD 1173-1219), approached Cārukīrti Svāmījī of Śravaṇbeḷagoḷa with a request to get rid of this disaster. Cārukīrti Svāmījī came down to Dvārasamudra at his request. He worshipped Pārśvanātha and performed "Kalikunda Adhana" with appropriate rites. He could then make the earth close its mouth with the pumpkins (*kuṣmāṇḍa*) charged with holy *mantra*s.

Cārukīrti Svāmījī, then directly came down to Nalluru, a small village in Karkala Tāluka, South Kanara District and founded a *maṭha*. Further, he came to Moodabidri in AD 1220 with a view to have Siddhānta Darśana and founded another *maṭha*. Thus, these two *maṭha*s being the branches of the *maṭha* at Śravaṇbeḷagoḷa, its Heads came to be known as "Cārukīrti." This proves the fact that these *maṭha*s were founded about 760 years ago.[87]

The inscriptions from Moodabidri furnished the following account regarding Bhaṭṭāraka and *maṭha*:

> Once a Jain sage visited a Ballala ruler whose finger had been cut off as a punishment by his sovereign. The sage was respectfully served and waited upon by the Ballala Raya. But seeing the maimed finger of the Ballala Raya, the Jain sage went away. At this the Ballala Raya got angry and destroyed

86. *Ibid.*, p. 26.

87. *Ibid.*, p. 25.

> 108 basadis of the Jains and in their place built a tank. A whirlpool arose because of this impious deed. Charukirti Paṇḍita Acarya of Belgola heard of this disaster that had happened to the Ballala King and cured him of his illness and saved his kingdom. Carukirti Paṇḍita Acarya then travelled to Nalluru near Karkala. On coming to Nalluru, the Jain teacher's elephant and his seat made up of sandalwood (Candana mane) refused to move. Carukirti Paṇḍita realised that it was the right place for building a basadi which he accordingly did. A monastery (*maṭha*) was built there by him. Both the iron chain used for binding the back and the neck of the elephants and the sandal-wood seat can still be seen at Nalluru.[88]

The Śravaṇbeḷagoḷa Jain pontiffs were called Abhinava Cārukīrti Paṇḍita Ācāryas, and not merely Cārukīrti Paṇḍita Ācāryas.[89] The other detail of Ballālarāya having had his finger cut of by his sovereign may also be dispensed with. But, all the same, the main part of the story that a Cārukīrti Paṇḍitadeva cured Ballāla king of his illness, may be made to square with the known facts of history. It is true that the name Cārukīrti Paṇḍita Ācārya was assumed by many Jain teachers. Thus, the earliest Cārukīrti Paṇḍitadeva is represented as the disciple of Municandra Traividya Bhaṭṭāraka, in a record dated the 20th year of the Cāḷukya Vikrama era (AD 1096).[90] A later record, dated AD 1398, informs us that Cārukīrti Paṇḍitadeva cured Ballāla of a terrible disease.[91] The similarity between the tradition of Cārukīrti Paṇḍitadeva in Moodabidri and the story recorded in the above epigraph seems to suggest that it was in the the twelfth century AD that Jainism made some headway in Tuluva.

Even the Late Bhaṭṭāraka of Moodabidri was a celebrated luminary in the Jain culture. He preserved the old Jain canon

88. B.A. Saletore, "Ancient Karnataka," *History of Tuluva*, vol. I, p. 410.
89. *Ibid.*
90. *Ibid.*, p. 411.
91. B.L. Rice, *E. Carn.*, vol. II, No. 254, p. 105.

and spread the Jain culture in south Karnataka. The following paragraphs gives his life-sketch in brief which would inspire the present generation.

LATE BHAṬṬĀRAKA SVĀMĪJĪ H.H. SVASTI ŚRĪ BHAṬṬĀRAKA CĀRUKĪRTI PAṆḌITĀCĀRYAVARYA SVĀMĪJĪ: ARCHITECT OF MODERN MOODABIDRI (1975-98)

The sacred tradition of the Bhaṭṭāraka seat is as ancient as Moodabidri itself. This ancient religious seat is a thing of worship, devotion and veneration for all the Jains of India and was occupied by Parama Pūjya Svasti Śrī Bhaṭṭāraka Cārukīrti Paṇḍitācāryavarya Svāmījī from 1975 to 1998. He was a son of this soil born in a famous family of scholars who had great respect for old values and tradition.

Śrī Svāmījī had his early education in Moodabidri. Later he accepted the "life of celibacy" in order to devote himself heart and soul to the study of *Jain-darśana*, spiritualism, culture, and literature and he went to the north for this purpose. Śrī Svāmījī obtained his studies in various institutions such as Sri Gopal Das Sanskrit Jain Mahavidyalaya, Murena (MP); Sri Ganesha Varni Sanskrit Jain Mahavidyalaya Sagar (MP); Sri Syadvad Jain Mahavidyalaya, Varanasi (UP); Rajasthan University, Jaipur (Rajasthan); and this enriched his knowledge. He also quenched his thirst for knowledge by getting post-graduate degree in Hindī and Sanskrit literature and a research degree (Ph.D.) in Jainism. He also received the titles or degrees like Sāhityaśāstrī, Siddhāntaśāstrī and Upādhyāya. Then he was awarded the religious seat of "Bhaṭṭāraka" (the religious head) on 30-4-1975. This event opened a new chapter in the history and destiny of this Jain centre and it brought about a rejuvenation to this holy place, and enabled it to shine in its old glory and grandeur. There had been a reawakening in the field of religion, education, economy and spiritualism. It will not be exaggeration if Śrī Svāmījī is called the architect of modern Moodabidri. Śrī Bhaṭṭāraka Svāmījī was the Saviour, President and Managing Trustee of this sacred institution.

Svāmījī had shouldered the responsibility of protecting and promoting the ancient Jain culture. For several years he had been undertaking the task of propaganda and publicity in regard to Jainism, Jain culture and the spiritual side of Jainism not only in India, but also abroad in a laudable manner; Śrī Svāmījī was good at delivering religious lectures in a simple, impressive logical and attractive way. He is considered a good speaker both in the country and abroad. He had enriched the "Paryuṣana-Parva" of the Śvetāmbara Jain and the "Daśalakṣaṇa Parva" of the Digambara Jain by means of his discourses for 18 days in various cities of USA. For several years Pūjya Svāmījī travelled in USA, Canada, London, West Germany, Japan, Hong Kong, Singapore, Malayasia, Holland, delivering religious discourses and thus popularized Jainism in these countreis.

Therefore, the Jains in various states such as Karnataka, UP, MP, Assam, Nagaland, Manipur, Delhi, Calcutta had been felicitated by Svāmījī on various occasions. The number of four different organizations (Caturvidha Saṁgha) honoured him by conferring the title of "Jñanayogī" on him at Śravaṇbeḷagoḷa in 1981. Besides, the Jain society honoured him by conferring on him the title of "Dharma Ratna," "Syādvada Kesarī," "Vāṇībhūṣaṇa," and "Samāja Ratna" on different occasions.

In 1991, the Mayor of Hagstrem (USA) and the Governor of the State of Ohio (USA) honoured Pūjya Svāmījī in recognition of his goodwill mission to USA. He was also accorded respectful welcome to participate in the religious rites called *Pañcakalyāṇa* religious ceremonies, and installations in almost all the Jain temples built abroad and he has thus enriched the sanctity of such ceremonies through his deep knowledge in relgious rites like religious offerings, installations, *Pañcakalyāṇa, Gṛhavastuśānti, Bhāk Vidhāna* and *tāmara Śānti Vidhāna*. He had enriched the purposes of these ceremonies by adhering to the rites exactly laid down by the Jains scriptures and Jain monks. With his specialized knowledge in Astrology, Palmistry and other science typically known as as "Yantra-Mantra-Tantra" (occult-hymns-techniques) he had set free thousands of people from their distress, difficulties and problems. He had also participated in several conferences called "Sarva Dharma Sammanvaya," "Vishwa Dharma Sammelan." As an official representative of the Jain religion, he participated in the "World Conference on Religion for Peace" in Princeten in 1979. He also made his presence at "World Religious Parliament Centenary" valedictory function held at Ulm-New-Ulm in West Germany. Svāmījī's favourite topic of interest was the deep and comparative study of Jainism with other great religions.[92]

Certain hints in regard to things, people should give attention to in relation to Moodabidri — the great sacred place.

The worthy and generous donations of the pilgrims who visit Moodabidri help the trustees to carry out the daily activities in a smooth manner. Generous donations had helped the donors feel a sense of contentment for having done something virtuous towards a noble cause. What you give will be, in a sense justifiable and righteous. What you donate towards this fund entitled "DHRUVA NIDHI" will be utilized for various activities of this religious centre, such as, mass-welfare-fund, renovations, construction and maintenance of choultries, preserving of the great words of Jain (Jinvāṇī), maintenance of the free hostels for students (Jain Gurukula), daily religious rites at 18 Jain temples, special religious rites, free food, medicine, free teachings in scriptures (*śāstra-dāna*), collecting, editing and publishing the great words of *jin*, promoting kindness to animals. The local *maṭha* had taken up the mammoth task of construction of huge structure called "Dhawala Paragama Mandira" at a cost of 80 lakh rupees and it was the intention of the *maṭha* to inscribe on marble the entire text of the holiest Jain scripture *Śatkhaṇḍa Gāma Dhavalā, Jaya Dhavalā, Mahā Dhavalā* — that has decked the book case in the *maṭha*. Your kind attention is being drawn towards

92. A letter or bio-data of ex-Bhaṭṭāraka sent by Moodabidri Maṭha itself.

the noble take of either donating to the daily *cathurvidha dāna*s or the *pūjā* programme of a day in all the 18 Jain temples if you so desire. He is a linguist and under his able leadership this centre of pilgrimage is progressing rapidly. He had been responsible for taking up a number of activities during the very short period after his ascending to the *gaddī*. All the local temples and the precious images of *navaratna*s are in his safe custody. He is the Managing Trustee and the Director of the *kṣetra*.

PRESENT BHAṬṬĀRAKA OF MOODABIDRI

Parama Pūjya Jñānayogī Svasti-Śrī-Bhaṭṭāraka Cārukīrti Paṇḍitācāryavarya Svāmījī is the present *Bhaṭṭāraka* of Moodabidri. He is a son of the soil born in the famous family of scholars. Pūjya Svāmījī was born on 29-3-1970 at Bajagoli Tāluka Karkala district, Dakṣiṇa Kuṇḍa of Karnataka state. The name of his parents is Śubra Śāstrī and Lalitā Devī. The early name of the Svāmījī was Arvind Heggade. He had completed primary and high school education at Bajagoli in Karkala district. Svāmījī obtained M.A. degree with Economics from the Mangalore University. He also did Civil Engineering from the Mangalore University. Then he took *dīkṣā* as a seventh *pratimādhārī brahmacarya* in October 1992 at Bījāpur. Although he took *śulka dīkṣā* after seven years only on 8 October, 1999, at Śravaṇbeḷagoḷa. This Svāmījī was selected as a Cārukīrti Bhaṭṭāraka Svāmījī to the *maṭha* of Moodabidri after the sad demise of H.H. Bhaṭṭāraka Svāmījī of the Moodabidri *maṭha* on 15-1-1998. The *paṭṭābhiṣeka* of the Svāmījī was celebrated on 29 August 1999, and from that time a *maṭha* is being run under his guidance. Many *pañcakalyāṇa pūjā*s had taken place under the guidance of H.H. Svāmījī. Svāmījī had also given donations to the Jin Mandir and schools. So the people of all the community wish and pray to the goddess Padmāvatī to bestow Svāmījī a long life and good health.[93]

93. I took the interview of present Bhaṭṭāraka and also utilized bio-data supplied by Moodabidri Maṭha itself.

The present Svāmījī is 30 years old and continuing the noble tradition, as his predecessors, of protecting and spreading Jain culture in south Karnataka.

The Moodabidri seat of Bhaṭṭāraka is an old one and the one thousand pillars of the Jain temple as well as the library containing the old manuscripts are still attracting scholars and laymen.

KARKALA: LALITAKĪRTI BHAṬṬĀRAKA

Karkala was another important and sacred Jain centre in the country of Tuluva; now it is south Canara district. The sacred tradition of the Bhaṭṭāraka seat exists since medieval period. This *pīṭha* has been working under the jurisdiction of Moodabidri Bhaṭṭāraka since its existence.

The early rulers of Karkala were the descendants of one Jinadattarāya who migrated from Mathurā in northern India to south India and founded his kingdom of Santara at Humcha. Probably, at the beginning of the fourteenth century AD, the descendants of Śrī Jinadattarāya, i.e., Santara rulers of Kalaśa, shifted to Karkala and made it their capital.[94] One of the chiefs, who materially contributed to the spread of Jainism in this age in Tuluva was Lokanātharasa. He was the disciple of Cārukīrti Paṇḍitadeva, who had, among other titles, that of Ballālarāyacitta Camatkāra and exercised some independent way in the Karkala region.[95] During the regime of Lokanātharasa in Śaka 1256 (AD 1334), his elder sisters Bommaladevī and Somaladevī along with some prominent state officials among whom figured Allappa Adhikārī, gave specified grants to the *basadi* to Śāntinātha at Karkala which had been built by Kumudacandra Bhaṭṭārakadeva, the chief disciple of Bhānukīrti Mālādhārīdeva of the Mūla Saṁgha and the Kranur *gaṇa*.[96]

---

94. Kamta P. Jain, *The Religions of Tirthankaras* (An Allround Survey and Valuation of Jainism), p. 306.
95. B.A. Saletore, *MJ*, p. 361.
96. B.L. Rice, *SII*, vol. III, pp. 124-25.

Sometime after him, the Karkala rulers came gradually under the influence of the Liṅgāyat faith. But they continued to be warm supporters of the *jin dharma*. We prove this from records ranging from the middle of the fifteenth to the end of the sixteenth century AD. The credit of turning the mind of the Karkala rulers to the Syādvāda doctrine goes to the Jain *gurus* of Hanasoge. It was at the instance of Lalitakīrti Mālādhārīdeva Bhaṭṭāraka of Hanasoge that King Vīra Paṇḍya, the son of Bhairavendra, caused to be constructed and set-up the colossal image of Gommaṭa at Karkala, to which reference has already been made.[97]

Abhinava Pāṇḍya Deva (AD 1458) is probably the same *guru* who is mentioned in another inscription dated Śaka 1379 (AD 1457-58) which records a gift of paddy to the Hire Nemīśvara-Basadi at Hiriangadi one of the suburbs of Karkala. In this record, Lalitakīrti is said to have belonged to the Kalorgaṇa.[98] The same *guru* was likewise responsible for the munificence of the merchants of Hiriangadi, who in AD 1475-76 built a *mukhamaṇḍapa* to the Tīrthaṅkara-Basadi of that place.[99] He granted a munificent donation to Neminātha-Basadi at Hiriangadi.

There was no separate royal preceptor at Karkala till the time of Hiria Bhairavadeva (AD 1462). Lalitakīrti Bhaṭṭārakas of Panasoge used to officiate on more important occasion and Cārukīrtis of Moodabidri at other times. This king established a branch of Panasoge *pīṭha* at Karkala and the successors to it are also styled Lalitakīrti Bhaṭṭāraka.[100]

In AD 1567, when the Head of the Śṛṅgerī Maṭha came to Karkala, he was received with royal honours and was requested

97. B.L. Rice, *E. Carn.*, vol. VII, p. 109.

98. B.A. Saletore, *MJ*, p. 362.

99. K.P. Jain, *op. cit.*, p. 306.

100. Rajaguru Swastshri Shri Bhaṭṭāraka Lalitakirti Maharaj, *Atishaya Kshetra*, Karkala, 1993, p. 14.

to camp there for some weeks. As he would not camp where there was no temple for his stay, the king offered a newly constructed place of worship and had a magnificent idol of Śeṣaśāyī Ananthеśvara installed in it, although the original intention was to make the place a *basadi*.

The royal priest, Lalitakīrti Bhaṭṭāraka, of course objected to this conversion of a *basadi* into a temple. Bhairavarāya replied all his subjects of different religions with equal reverence. And to make amends for having displeased his spiritual teacher, he got constructed the Tribhuvana Tilaka Caityālaya, on the hillock facing that on which Gommaṭa stands. This *basadi* has four identical looking entrances from the four quarters which is popularly called "Caturmukha-Basadi."

But much of the importance of Karkala was due not only to the patronage of its rulers but to the large-heartedness of its citizens as well. In Śaka 1501 (AD 1579) some *śrāvaka*s of Karkala gave as a gift money for the study of the scriptures in the Ammanavara-Basadi at Hiriangadi. Lalitakīrti Bhaṭṭāraka is said to have been the *vicāra-kartā* (superintendent) of the charities. This *guru* could not have been the one mentioned above, but probably one of the pontiffs at Karkala itself who bore the title of Lalitakīrti.

Immadi Bhairvendra Odeyar was ruler of Karkala who patronized Jainism. He caused to be built the famous Caturmukha-Basadi temple at Karkala in AD 1586 under the guidance of Lalitakīrti Bhaṭṭāraka.[101]

NIṢIDHI

There is Niṣidhi within the precincts of Guru-Basadi; such remains have not been elsewhere in these parts. We can find there sculpted images of Nemināthа, Pārśvanātha and Vardhamāna Svāmī. We may also read the names of the *muni*s Kumudacandra, Hemacandra, Cārukīrti, Pūjyapāda Svāmī

101. B.A. Saletore, *op. cit.*, p. 363.

Vimala Sūri, Śrī Kīrti Siddhāntadeva, Cārukīrtideva, Mahākīrti and Mahendrakīrti.[102]

The Catholic spirit of *ahiṁsā* of its citizens was more responsible for the spread of Jainism them the rulers of Karkala. They were well awakened in the observance of the rules for spiritual advancement. Thus, the Jain *ācārya*s were ever conscious to help the cause of spiritual welfare of the people and arranged to impart to them the right knowledge of soul, body and god.

The result of the royal patronage and popular support was beneficial for Jainism as well as the country. It gave a good opportunity to the Jain *ācārya*s to establish various centuries of learning and religious studies, monasteries and libraries. The Jain temples with their *dānaśālā*s, i.e., charity-houses for education, food medicine and retreat became real spots of cultural enlightenment. This is a vigorous mass awakening which made the people realize the value of *ahiṁsā* for creating a harmonious atmosphere in human society.

The Jain leaders moved alike among the high and low in cities and villages imparting the message of *ahiṁsā* and helping the laity to solve its various problems by its application. This brought the Jain *ācārya*s in the direct contact of the people and they were shrewd enough to lay a firm foundation of their hold over the middle and the business classes of the society. The Jain *ācārya*s worked in a cosmopolitan method and increased the number of followers ever by preaching among the original inhabitants of India.

Present Karkala Bhaṭṭāraka is also looking after *pāṭhaśālā*, and protecting Jain culture. Karkala has a very good library and the structure of Bāhubali on the hill is the main attraction to the visitors. Karkala Bhaṭṭāraka has cordial relation with Moodabidri Bhaṭṭāraka.

---

102. Bhaṭṭāraka Lalitakīrti Maharaja, *op. cit.*, p. 120.

To sum up, Bhaṭṭāraka institution in Jain community came into existence as a need of time in early medieval period when iconoclast Muslim rulers had established political hegemony over India. This institution exists even now and is useful to the progress and development of Jain community in south Karnataka. Not only this, but all the Bhaṭṭārakas from Śravaṇbeḷagoḷa, Humcha, Moodabidri and Karkala rendered great service in the spread and protection of Jain culture in south Karnataka. They not only erected many new Jain temples, but also renovated and repaired the old ones. In addition, they arranged religious functions, delivered religious discourses, maintained good libraries, printed sacred canons, created habits of reading Jain literature among *śrāvaka*s and *śrāvikās* through holding *mahāmastakabhiṣeka* ceremonies. They also arranged *pañcakalyāṇa pūjā*s and thus gave impetus to Jain religion. The present Bhaṭṭārakas of these places are spreading and protecting Jainism not only in India but abroad also like Europe, America, etc., like their predecessors. Bhaṭṭārakas are the religious leaders, organizers, propagators and preceptors of the Jain community even today.

7

Epilogue

JAINISM stands for peace and non-violence since inception. To save the succeeding generations from the scourage of war — peace is required. Even the chief objectives of the United Nations are to maintain international peace and national security, to promote economic and social welfare of the people of the memebrs states, to remove threats to the peace of the world by suppressing acts of aggression and other breaches of peace; to settle the international disputes through peaceful means so that these may not disturb the peace of the world.

Nowadays conflicts, wars, unrest, unhealthy competitions, scramble for power are going on everywhere in the world. Human race is in danger due to production of modern sophisticated weapons, like nuclear, atom bomb and various missiles.

Therefore, "Peace" has no alternative and the motto of Jain religion, propounded by Lord Mahāvīra and his predecessor *tīrthaṅkaras* was *ahiṁsā* and "Live and Let Live."

Modern statesman and politicians, even of UNO, knew the importance of peace in the survival of human race. Peace is essential and it can be observed only if a nation observes non-violence.

It is rightly pointed out that more than any other creed, Jainism gives absolute religious independence and freedom to man. The scriptures make it abundantly clear that nothing can intervene between a human being's actions and the fruits of such actions. No God or his prophet, deputy or beloved can interfere with human life. The soul alone is reponsible for all that it does.

The Jains recognize divinity in man and godhood for them is the attainment of purity and perfection inherent in every soul. The Jain idea of God is that of a pure soul, possessed of infinite faith, knowledge, bliss and power. These qualities are inherent in the soul itself, either destroyed or veiled by our *karmas*.

Historically speaking, the Jains have always been a small religious community and yet have believed that their religion is truely a "world religion" (*viśva-dharma*) because it is available to all aspirants, and is beneficial to all beings, including those of the animal world and the vegetable kingdom. Throughout their history, the Jains have been associated with the ideal of *ahiṁsā* (non-violence) both as a means as well as end, both in the temporal as well as spiritual life.[1]

The Sublime Message of Mahāvīra

The place and contribution of Jainism and Bhagvān Mahāvīra is a most fascinating subject in the history of Indian culture and civilization. So seminal has been the influence of Jainism and its teachings on ancient Indian thought as propounded by the 24 Jain *tīrthaṅkaras* — to the path of liberation — right from the first *tīrthaṅkara*, Ṛṣabhanātha, to the 24th *tīrthaṅkara*, Mahāvīra.

It would be a mistake to suppose that Jainism originated in the sixth century BC with the advent of Bhagvān Mahāvīra. The genesis of Jainism can be traced to the deepest antiquity, and it was a wholly indigenous and characteristically ethical outcome of the Indian environment is now recognized by scholars, both Indian and foreign.

Jainism is also a pioneer in the evolution of human ethics by reason of the tremendous discovery of the principle of *ahiṁsā* or non-violence.

Excelled as a teacher, Mahāvīra was also a great organizer of Jain ascetics and the laity. The estalishment of the *saṁgha* is again a clear confirmation of his systematic thinking. He classified his disciples into four sections: *muni, āryikā, śrāvaka* and *śrāvikā* of which the first two belonged to the monastic order while the last two were of the laity. Mahāvīra was not only "the most versatile thinker we know of in ancient India" but also was a bold religious innovator and a fearless reformer.

The great contribution of Mahāvīra's teachings was its stress on the sanctity and equality of all life, it was logical, therefore, that Mahāvīra should have simultaneously emphasized the cardinal importance of self-control and tolerance. In other words, he declared that deeds and not birth make a man what he is, that all life should be protected and the material possession should be limited. It was a revolutionary assertion in the context of the times.

Mahāvīra admitted into the Jain asceticfold, men and women, regardless of caste considerations. He taught that every man was entitled to salvation without the intervention of any authority.[2]

The message of Lord Mahāvīra is valid for all castes, creeds and communities and is relevant in every era. *Ahiṁsā* and *anekānta* are conductive in inculcating virtues such as kindness, fraternity and benevolence. *Anekānta* can help to cultivate tolerance, respect and fraternity amongst the nations, whereas *ahiṁsā* is the key to world peace and stability. Spreading the message of Lord Mahāvīra shall diminish the hostilities in the world. Thus Lord Mahāvīra's message is essential for global peace even today.

Jainism is an ancient religion of India and, right from hoary antiquity to the present day, it has continued to flourish along with other religions in different parts of India. Jains, the followers of Jainism, are, therefore, found all over India since ancient times. *Ahiṁsā*, vegetarianism, controlled way of life and the concept of *aparigraha* constitute the main tenets of Jainism.

This religion has spread over the different parts of the country from the times of Bhagvān Ṛṣabhdeva till today. Although the great personalities — *tīrthaṅkara*s of Jainism were born in Bihar and the northern provinces of the country but the religion preached by them has also blossomed and flowered in Karnataka.

Jainism was founded by 24 *tīrthaṅkara*s from Ṛṣabhanātha *alias* Ādinātha to Vardhamāna Mahāvīra. All these *tīrthaṅkara*s flourished in north India and due to their endeavour Jainism as a heterodox religion came into existence. The last two *tīrthaṅkara*s, Pārśvanātha, belonging to the eighth century BC, and the 24th *tīrthaṅkara* Mahāvīra belonging to the sixth century BC are regarded as historical personalities.

In fourth century BC, Jainism penetrated into the south during the period of Candragupta Maurya and Karnataka become the second home of Jainism. Fortunately, Jainism received royal patronage from royal dynasties like Kadambas, Cāḷukyas, Rāṣṭrakūṭas, Hoyasalas, Gaṅgas and Vijayanagara rulers who ruled over Karnataka area from time to time. Even today, there are a number of sacred Jain places like Śravaṇbeḷagoḷa, Humcha, Moodabidri, Karkala which are located in southern Karnataka. Rich archaeological and literary sources are available to study the spread of Jainism in south Karnataka.

South Karnataka consisted modern district of Hassan, Mysore, Śimogā and South Kanara which are rich in Jain antiquities and monuments. Therefore, the temple complexes of Śravaṇbeḷagoḷa (Dist. Hassan), Humcha (Dist. Śimogā), Moodabidri and, Karkala (Dist. South Kanara) played a very vital role in spreading Jainism in south Karnataka since ancient period. Development of Jainism in southern Karnataka up to AD 1565 is studied with a help of the activities that took place at Śravaṇbeḷagoḷa, Humcha, Moodabidri and Karkala because these were the centres of Jain activities. Many *ācārya*s, Jain saints, *śrāvaka*s and *śrāvikā*s stayed at these religious places and developed them as a leading Jain centre. The year AD 1565 was a turning point in the history of Karnataka because in that year, Vijayanagara, the last great Hindu empire, had collapsed and Muslim rule was established all over Karnataka and south India.

The ancient Hindu dynasties like Maurya, Sātavāhana, Kadamba, Rāṣṭrakūṭas, Cāḷukyas, Gaṅgas, Hoyasalas and Vijayanagara had extended patronization to Jainism in Karnataka. Therefore, it can be said that the Jain religion blossomed from fourth century BC to AD 1565. Rich archaeological material is available of this period, which will help to reconstruct the development of Jainism in Karnataka from fourth century BC to AD 1565. Again Jain scholars produced valuable Jain literature during this period, which are helpful to fill up the gaps of the epigraphical records and complete the story of development of Jainism. The following were the important Jain *ācārya*s and scholars during the period: Bhadrabāhu Svāmī, Jinasena, Kundakunda, Sāmantabhadra, Somaladeva, Pūjyapāda, Akalaṅka, Vādirāja, Wādibhasiṁha, Guṇabhadra, Vīrasena, and Puṣpadanta.

There are traditions even on Mahāvīra's visit to south India from the *Jīvandharacarita* of Bhāskara. It is known that Jīvandhara, who was the ruling chief of this region at that time, was a Jain. He cordially received Mahāvīra and became an ascetic after obtaining *dīkṣa* from him. Jīvandhara seems to be an imaginary name. In fact, there was no such ruler whose kingdom extended to and comprised southern India during this period.

Legends and beliefs apart, the earliest historical evidence for the advent of Jainism in south India is the visit of the saint Bhadrabāhu, the eighth teacher in succession after Mahāvīra, along with the Magadhan monarch, Candragupta Maurya of Śravaṇbeḷagoḷa in Mysore State. The event forms the subject-matter of a persistent legend in the Kannaḍa country and the southern sects of Jainism invariably trace their descent from Bhadrabāhu.

Sammedaśikharjī and Pāvāpurī are important sacred Jain *tīrtha*s in north India and Śravaṇbeḷagoḷa occupies important place in the history of Jainism in south India. The development of Śravaṇbeḷagoḷa as a Jain centre took place in two phases. The first phase of development forms the period between fourth century BC to ninth century AD and the second phase started from AD 981 onwards, in which year the installation of Bāhubali image by Cāmuṇḍarāya took place and Śravaṇbeḷagoḷa developed in rapid scale as a Jain centre in the second phase.

Number of Jain temples erected after the fourth century BC by the nobles, royal and rich persons in and around Śravaṇbeḷagoḷa which developed powerful centre of Jainism in south India. Śravaṇbeḷagoḷa, the most ancient and prominent sacred place of the Jains in south India, has got a unique combination of many distinctive features which are rarely found elsewhere in the world. Śravaṇbeḷagoḷa is the most important *tīrtha* (sacred place) of the Jains in south India and at the same time it is a place of great cultural significance in south Indian history. Śravaṇbeḷagoḷa is famous in the world not only for its religious sanctity but also for its natural beauty, historical antiquity and architectural superiority.

In the first phase of the development of Śravaṇbeḷagoḷa, a number of Jain temples were erected on the Vindhyagiri hill *alia*s Doddabetta viz: Śāntinātha-Basadi, Supārśvanātha-Basadi, Pārśvanātha-Basadi, Kattle-Basadi, Candragupta-Basadi, Candraprabhu-Basadi, Cāmuṇḍarāya-Basadi, Śāśana-Basadi, Majjigaṇa-Basadi, Eradukatte-Basadi, Savāti Gandhavaraṇa-Basadi, Terina-Basadi, Śāntīśvara-Basadi, Kuge Brahmadeva pillar, Mahānavamī Maṇḍapa, Bharateśvara, Irue Brahmadeva temple, Kanchinadone, Lakkidone, Bhadrabāhu cave, and Cāmuṇḍarāya's rock. Moreover, some inscriptions prior to the ninth century AD are also found in this hill.

The Mauryas, Sātavāhanas, Cāḷukyas, Rāṣṭrakūṭas, Kadambas, extended royal patronage to Śravaṇbeḷagoḷa and many land grants were given to this place during this period. Rāṣṭrakūṭa period is regarded as the golden period for the development of Jainism in south India. Jainism was a state religion during reign of Amoghavarṣa, the emperor of Rāṣṭrakūṭa dynasty. Emperor Amoghavarṣa's great commander-in-chief called Bankeya was a staunch follower of Jainism. Gaṅgas of Talakaḍ was the next dynasty which extended full support to Jainism.

There are a number of references regarding the persons, who ended their life by observing Jain rites of *sallekhanā*, i.e., fast unto death on Candragiri hill. The name of this hill is associated with Candragupta Maurya itself, who died on Candragiri hill by observing *sallekhanā*. So up to the ninth century, Candragiri hill is more important than the Indragiri hill. Śravaṇbeḷagoḷa is not only a religious centre of the Jains but also a nucleus of social and cultural tradition of India.

The installation of Bāhubali statue on Vindhyagiri hill in AD 981 by Cāmuṇḍarāya was a turning point and landmark in the history of Śravaṇbeḷagoḷa, because this statue is one of the wonders of the world and many Jain as well as other pilgrims visit this place. The rapid development of Śravaṇbeḷagoḷa started from AD 981, which became the second phase of the development of this place. This excellent and enormous statue installed by Cāmuṇḍarāya is the best and most important ancient monument in the field of Indian iconography in general and Jain iconography in particular. The *Cāmuṇḍarāya Purāṇa* (AD 978) does not mention about the statue but Nemicandra Siddhāntacakravartī, the teacher of Cāmuṇḍarāya refers to it as the *Gommaṭasāra* (AD 993). This means that the statue was installed between AD 978-93. Govinda Pai, Dr. Nemichandra Shastri, Dr. Jyoti Prasad Jain and others have come to the conclusion that the Bāhubali statue was installed on Sunday, the 5th day of Caitra Śukla in AD 981. In the second phase, Vindhyagiri hill acquired more importance than Indragiri due to the image of Bāhubali. Bāhubali was a son of the first *tīrthaṅkara* Ṛṣabhanātha and acquired a place next to Jain *tīrthaṅkara* in Jain pantheon. There are a number of legendary accounts of Bāhubali composed by Jain authors after AD 981. But Cāmuṇḍarāya and his overlord Gaṅga king Rachamalla II became memorable due to the installation of Bāhubali image. No single individual could be given a credit for building Śravaṇbeḷagoḷa, for it was built over a millennium and half by a number of pious saints, rulers, chieftains, merchants, artists, scribes and pilgrims. The men who contributed materially to strengthen and enhance its spiritual, artistic and historical value are, however, recognized as early as the twelfth century. Among them:

1. Cāmuṇḍarāya (974-84AD)
2. Gaṅgarāja (1108-1132 AD)
3. Hullarāya (1142-1173 AD)

are considered to be the greatest.

Among these three benefactors of Jain religion, however, the contributions of Cāmuṇḍarāya are by far the most outstanding, inspiring and lasting nature. By his rich personal accomplishments and varied achievements in different fields, Cāmuṇḍarāya has made a permanent mark and there is hardly any other personality of his stature and competence in the history of Karnataka.

Cāmuṇḍarāya was a faithful minister, a loyal general, a profound scholar, a great patron of Jainism, a brave soldier, a devout Jain and still a more honest man Karnataka has ever seen. Gaṅgas of Talakaḍ and Vijayanagara rulers extended royal support to this Bāhubali image. Some of the Vijayanagara rulers like Harihar II, Kṛṣṇadevarāya issued land grants to Śravaṇbeḷagoḷa and other Jain temples. A number of inscriptions are found in the Vindhyagiri hill and on the feet of Bāhubali image itself. It is interesting to note the first Marāṭhī inscription, that is श्री चामुंडराजे करवियले, श्री गंगराजे सुत्ताले करवियले is found on the feet of Bāhubali. Cāmuṇḍarāya made an outstanding contribution to world culture by erecting Bāhubali's image at Śravaṇbeḷagoḷa,.

Humcha, next to Śravaṇbeḷagoḷa, is a political seat of Santara dynasty and abode of goddess Padmāvatī. It played a very important role in spreading Jainism in south Karnataka since eighth century AD onwards. Fortunately, Humcha was patronized by one political dynasty and that was Santara dynasty. Jinadatta was the founder of this dynasty, who built Padmāvatī temple and Pārśvanātha temple at Humcha.

Śravaṇbeḷagoḷa is famous for Bāhubali image while Humcha is famous for goddess Padmāvatī. Generally a pious Jain *śrāvaka*s and *śrāvikā*s believe that blessings of goddess Padmāvatī is essential for any important work. Therefore, Jains from all over India go to this place every year to receive the blessings of this Goddess.

So, Humcha became famous and nuclear of Jain activities the eighth century onwards. A great number of buildings, palaces, Jain *basadi*s and temples, were erected between eighth to fourteenth centuries AD at Humcha and a small village became a famous city of temples. Side by side, Bhaṭṭāraka Pīṭha was established here and Śramaṇ culture was spreading from this place. Among the secondary deities of the Jain pantheon chosen for individual adoration as in independent goddess, Padmāvatī, the *yakṣiṇī* of Pārśvanātha, stands foremost, being the most popular and widely invoked goddess in Karnataka.

Following temples are important and have a historical value at Humcha: Pārśvanātha-Basadi, Padmāvatī-Basadi, Bogara-Basadi, Sule-Basadi, Pañcakūṭa-Basadi, Guddada-Basadi, Aśoka-Basadi, Kṣetrapāla-Basadi, etc. Every temple has an image of Jain *tīrthaṅkara*. Moreover, some temples, pillars and walls possessed old Canarese inscriptions. In all, we find 22 inscriptions of Santara dynasty at Humcha belonging between eighth to fourteenth centuries AD. All these inscriptions have been read and published with English translation by B.L. Rice, Director of Archaeology, Mysore State, in his *Epigraphica Carnatica* volume nos. VI, VII and VIII. These inscriptions provide many useful material to the students of history.

The Santara period of 400 years from eighth to twelfth centuries AD was regarded as the golden period in the history of Humcha. Santara rulers like Jinadatta, Vikrama Santara, Chagi Santara, Vīra Santara II, Bhujabala Santara, Vikrama Santara IV and their royal ladies spent lavishly their wealth for erecting Jain temples and Humcha became one of the leading Jain centre in south Karnataka. Humcha, like other Jain centres, rendered yeomen service for the development of Jainism in south Karnataka and one has to recognize its service without fail.

Even today, the library at Humcha *tīrtha* is preserving old Jain canons and sacred books and occupying an important place in the Jain Humcha *maṭha* which is preparing new Jain scholars, who spread the gospel of Lord Mahāvīra and other *tīrthaṅkara*s. Karkala, Moodabidri and Venur flourished as the Jain centres in South Kanara district since early medieval period.[4] The centre of Jain gravity shifted from Humcha to Karkala in the thirteenth century AD. In Vijayanagara, Hoyasala royal dynasties of south India patronized these Jain centres, built magnificent Jain temples and Jainism was in full swing even though there was menace from Liṅgāyat religion and iconoclast Muslim rulers from twelfth century onwards. The huge statue of Gommaṭa, the *basadi*s and the temples of Anantaśayana and Veṅkataramaṇa at Karkala attract a large number of pilgrims, lovers of art and students of history. These architectural creations, Jain as well as Hindu, are the gifts of the royal family of Bhairaras Wodeyars. The famous gigantic monolithic statue of Gommaṭa at Karkala, which is 42 ft tall, was installed by Vīra Pāṇḍyadeva, a ruler of the Bahirarasa family of Karkala in AD 1432. Besides, Gommaṭa statue of

Caturmukha-Basadi, Neminātha-Basadi, Rāmasamudra are important temples at Karkala which attract the Jain people. Like Humcha, Karkala is also patronized by Santara and their successor rulers viz, Bhairarasa Wodeyars dynasty. Even Vijayanagara rulers extended their patronization to Karkala and granted land to this place. Karkala is also the famous seat of Lalitakīrti Bhaṭṭārakas since fifteenth century onwards. Karkala is visited even today by a number of Jain people who pay reverence to Gommaṭeśvara statue.

Next to Karkala, Moodabidri is another important Jain centre in South Kanara district. Since early medieval times, Moodabidri, popularly referred to as Jain Kāśī of south India is historically an *atiśaya pūṇya kṣetra*. Here are found the holy scriptures (*siddhānta*), *Dhavalā* (The "Vedas" of Jains) in the temples. Guru-Basadi or Siddhānātha-Basadi is the oldest Jain temples. There are more then 18 Jain *basadi*s at Moodabidri. Another famous *basadi* known as "Tribhuvan Tilaka Cūdāmaṇi" *basadi* is known for its 1000s of pillars. It is known from inscriptions that out of these 18 temples, Padu-Basadi, Guru-Basadi and Ammanavara-Basadi are the most ancient ones and that the remaining ones were built only after the Guru Pīṭha had been founded. Moodabidri is also famous for Bhaṭṭāraka Pīṭha and old library which housed a number of old Jain manuscripts and canons that are useful to historians studying Jain history. Bhaṭṭāraka is also rendering great service to the cause of spreading Jainism. He also run one *paṭṭaśālā* and free feeding centre there. Moodabidri is famous for Navaratna temple, i.e., Jewel temple. Like other Jain places, Moodabidri also received patronization from royal families, rich merchants and Jain traders. Even today, Moodabidri is worth seeing and is spreading Jain culture in that area.

The third important Jain place known for the Bāhubali statue, which is located in South Kanara district is Venur. Venur is also important Jain centre but historians, epigraphists and Jain *śrāvaka*s paid little attention to the statue of Bāhubali.

which is 35 ft in height and erected by Timmarāja in the year AD 1604. Venur is rich in historical antiquities. The image of Gommaṭa and the *basadi*s and the Mahādeva temple are the historical remains of considerable interest. Now very small but must have once been a flourishing and splendid culture.

Unfortunately, Venur is a neglected place. At present, Venur is a small hamlet. Therefore, little attention is paid by visitors as well as Jain *śrāvaka*s. There is also one Jain temple. There may be many old Jain monuments and inscriptions which may not have been studied yet.

However, Karkala, Moodabidri and Venur situated in South Kanara district, protected and preserved Jain culture since early medieval times to present day.

At present there are eight Jain temples at Venur, namely, Bhujabali (Bāhubali)-Basadi, Akkangal-Basadi, Binnani-Basadi, Pārśvanātha-Basadi, Śāntinātha-Basadi, Vardhamāna-Basadi, Tīrthaṅkara-Basadi and Ṛṣabha-Basadi.

However, South Kanara was very active in extending patronage to Jainism during this period. Karkala, Moodabidri, Venur and other places became centres of Jain art. The Alupa, Bhairarasa Wodeyar, Chouter and other chiefs ruled in this area. Not only they built many monuments but also gave a large number of grants to them.

The role of Bhaṭṭārakas from Śravaṇbeḷagoḷa, Humcha, Moodabidri and Karkala was important for promoting Jain culture in south Karnataka. Even the present Bhaṭṭārakas, are also playing vital role in protecting and spreading Jainism in their respective areas. Bhaṭṭārakas possessed large estate and raised funds from *śrāvaka*s. They utilized these funds for erecting the Jain temples, arranging *pañcakalyāṇa pūjā*s, publishing sacred Jain literature, distributing Jain literature on cheaper rate to Jain *śrāvaka*s, running *pāṭhaśālā*s in their *maṭha*s, provided religious training to Jain lads, who will be future Upadhyas and finally running free kitchen and hospitals for orphanage and poor people. This institute is useful even today.

The history of the Bhaṭṭāraka institution is interesting and fascinating. Bhaṭṭārakas is regarded as religious ruler of Jain community. The creation, development and reservation of sacred task was a notable achievement of these Bhaṭṭārakas. Free from the worries of constant movement, these Bhaṭṭārakas developed sense of solidarity and devoted much time and energy to the study and explosion of the Jain scriptures. The Bhaṭṭāraka made monumental contribution in the field of learning. By various means, they turned their *maṭha*s into the central seats of learning in their region.

The Bhaṭṭārakas conduct *pāṭhaśālā*s, i.e., religious schools, maintaining *śāstra-bhaṇḍār*s, i.e., religious scripture houses; delivering *dharma-pravacana*, i.e., religious discourses; publishing and distributing *dharma-grantha*s, i.e., religious books; training persons in the performance of *dharma vidhi*s, i.e., religious rituals; and arrange *dharma-sammelana*s, i.e., religious conferences, etc.

The Bhaṭṭārakas, throughout their long history, contributed a great deal to the advancement in various fields of the culture of the region. Their lasting contribution can be seen in the development of several arts like architecture, sculpture, painting, music, dance and drama. Installation of various images was considered to be the main work of a Bhaṭṭāraka. They encouraged their rich followers to construct new temples in large numbers.

The general opinion seems to be in favour of retaining the institution because a religious preceptor is considered necessary to look after the spiritual life of the people. It is suggested that if the Bhaṭṭārakas, who are well educated and wish to renounce life after fulfilling their worldly desires, are appointed not as a recognized heads of particular castes but as organizers, propagators and preceptors of the Jain community.

The seats of Bhaṭṭāraka from Śravaṇbeḷagoḷa, Humcha, Moodabidri and Karkala are treasure house of knowledge. These rich libraries will promote Jainism among posterity for years to come.

Jainism has made a profound influence on the lives and culture of this country. It made a substantial contribution to the philosophy and culture of this country and specially of Karnataka.

Thus, the result of the royal patronage and popular support was beneficial for Jainism as well as for the country. It gave a good opportunity to the Jain *ācārya*s to establish various centres of learning and religious studies, monasteries and libraries. The Jain temples, with their *dānaśālā*s, i.e., charity houses for education, food, medicine and retreat became real spots of cultural enlightenment.

The influence of Jainism in Karnataka has been profound. For nearly twelve hundred years, Jainism has played a prominent part in social and political life of the people of Karnataka. There was royal patronage for Jainism. Jainism flourished under the Gaṅga rulers and also received the royal patronage of the Kadambas and Rāṣṭrakūṭa kings. Cāḷukyas also gave patronage to Jainism. Jainism was an influential force during the Hoyasala period too.

Peace is required to save human race on this globe. The cardinal principles of Jainism namely *ahiṁsā* and "Live and Let Live," are required to protect humanity and to maintain peace. So the study of the development of Jainism in southern Karnataka, no doubt, is useful to the modern student of history.

The present work, hopefully, will open a new vista to the study of the contribution of Jain centres in other parts of India and would be universally useful to the students of history in future.

Glossary

Ahiṁsā	Non-violence
Ācārya	Teacher
Atiśaya kṣetra	Sacred place created by Jains
Avasarpiṇīkāla	The descending half arc of time
Bhāratavarṣa	The land of Bhārata
Brahmacārī	Chastity
Basadi	A Jain temple
Cāturmās	Four months of rainy season
Cakra	Circle of states
Daṇḍanāyaka	Officer in the army
Darbār	Court
Dharma	Religion
Dharma-pravacana	Religious discourse
Dharma-grantha	Religious book
Dharma-vidhis	Religious rituals
Dharma-sammelanas	Religious conferences
Dṛṣṭi-yuddha	Looking at other without winking
Gadyana	Coin
Gaḍhā	Cavity
Horse's bit	The part of the bridle in horse's mouth
Jin	The spiritual conquerors
Jala-yuddha	Throwing water on each other's face
*Jāti-pañcāyata*s	Caste councils
Kevali	Omniscience
Mūrti-pratiṣṭhā	Installation of images in temples
Maṭha	Monastery
Mokṣa / *Nirvāṇa*	Salvation

Piñchi	Tuft of peacock
*Pūjā*s	Worship
Ṛṣigiri	The hill of sage
Seṭṭi	Merchant
*Śrāvaka*s	Male laity
*Śrāvīka*s	Female laity
Sādhu	Ascetic
*Sādhvī*s	Female ascetic
Saṁsthāna	State
Śramaṇ	Jains ascetic
Śrutakevali	Master of knowledge
Saṁgha or *Gaṇa*	A religious division of the Jains
Sallekhanā	Fast unto death
Statue	Image
Tīrtha	Sacred place
Tīrtha-kṣetra	Holy place
*Tīrtha-yātrā*s	Pilgrimages
Tīrthaṅkara	An ideal man of perfection and founder of Jains
Vṛtti	Share of land revenue generally in an *agrahāra*

Appendix

B.L. Rice (1837-1927)

His father Benjamin Holt Rice was a Christian missionary. He came to Bangalore in order to preach religion. B.L. Rice was born in Bangalore and he spent the early days of his boyhood in Karnataka. He received higher education in England. He became proficient in Kannaḍa, Telugu, Tamil and Sanskrit. He rendered good service in the field of education, study of history, epigraphy and oriental literature.

He became the Headmaster of Central High School in 1860 and devoted himself to the cause of education. Later on the school grew up into the famous Central College. After five years of service, he became the Inspector of Schools for Mysore and Coorg Districts. Three years later, he became the Director of Public Institution and the first Secretary of Education for the Mysore State. He travelled all over the state and collected many inscriptions connected with ancient history. He had collected nearly 9000 inscriptions which today throw a lot of light on the heritage and glory of the country. Thereby, he inspired others to study the ancient history of this land. We can imagine the hard ships that he might have faced during his extensive travels as there was no better means of transportation; and besides this, his valuable service compared to our own has put us to shame. Whenever he went outside on official or private tour, he used to collect relevant material pertaining to ancient history. His collections include copper-plates, palm-leaves, inscriptions, etc. It is said that there is no place that he has not visited in Karnataka. When the Oriental Research Institute in Mysore was started, he became its first Director. He retired in 1906 and till his end devoted himself to the historical research.

The Hunter Commission of India appointed Rice as its Secretary to bring reforms in the educational field. He served for sometime as the Secretary in the Police Department too. The British Government conferred upon him the title of C.I.E. (Commander of the Indian Empire). The Madras Government honoured him with the degree of the Doctor of Philosophy. The following are his achievements in the fields of Research:

1. *Mysore Inscriptions* — Its year of publication — 1877.
2. *Mysore Gazetteer.*
3. *Epigraphia Carnatika* volumes, 1986.
4. *Sravanbelgola Inscriptions* volume.
5. *Inscriptions from Mysore and Coorg.*
6. *Finding of Ashoka's Brahmagiri Inscriptions.*
7. *Bibliothica-Karnataka* Serial.
8. Editing *Pampa Bharata* or *Vikramarijana Vijaya, Nagachandra's Pampa Ramayana, Kavi Raja Marga, Kavyavalokana, Amarakosha* and innumerable research articles.
9. *Imperical Gazetteer* (Editor)

He returned to England after his retirement in 1906. Although he settled at Harrow, he often thought of Kannaḍa state. He had to bring out ten more volumes of inscriptions. The Gazetteers, published by him, were later on revised by Sri C. Hayavadana Rao. It is rather a surprise that a foreigner could devote his entire life to the cause of Kannaḍa.

J.F. Fleet (1847-1917)

J.F. Fleet was born in Chiswick in 1847 to George Fleet and Esther. He passed the Indian Civil Serice examination at the age of 18 and was appointed as the Revenue Officer in Bombay. He rose to higher positions by his efficiency and honesty. His contemporary, B.L. Rice was an Educational Officer in the South Divison (1872) of Karnataka. He served in Kolhapur as a Junior Collector, Magistrate and Political Agent, Senior Collector and Customs Commissioner and died in England in 1917.

Though a Revenue Officer, he took great interest in the study of History. He did in north Karnataka what Mr. Rice did in the south. He collected historical inscriptions and studied them scientifically. He was proficient in Pāli, Prākṛt, Kannaḍa, Sanskrit and Marāṭhī languages. His articles dealing with the ancient life and civilization and the royal dynasties were published in the *Royal Asiatic Society* (Bombay Branch) and the *Indian Antiquary Paper*. He was good at the study of inscriptions and knew History, Geography and Linguistics well. His book entitled *The Gupta Kings and their Successors* has become quite famous. *The Kannada Royal Dynasties in Bombay Province* is his another publication.

In England, he was interested in the study of History even after retirement. He wrote many articles to *Epigraphia Indica* and the *Imperial Gazetteer* and brought out many folk songs. He enriched the Kannaḍa language with yeoman's service.

Bibliography

Published Original Sources

Narasimhachari, R., *Epigraphica Carnatica, Inscriptions at Sravanbelgola,* vol. II (Mysore Govt. Press, Bangalore, 1923).

Panchamukhi, R.S., *Karnataka Inscription,* vol. I (Dharwar, 1941).

Rice, B.L., *Inscriptions at Sravanbelgola,* vol. II (Bangalore, 1889).

Sewell, Robert, *Historical Inscriptions of Southern India* (Madras, 1965).

Sastri, H.K., *South Indian Inscription,* Archaeological Survey of India, New Series, vol. X (Madras, 1891-1917).

Sastri, N.P., *Epigraphica Indica* (Delhi, 1935).

Shamsastri, R., *South Indian Inscription,* vol. IX (Madras, 1939).

———, *Epigraphica Carnatica, Inscriptions in the Kadur District,* vol. VI (Bangalore, 1901).

———, *Epigraphica Carnatica, Inscriptions in the Shimoga District,* vol. VII (Bangalore, 1902).

———, *Epigraphica Carnatica, Inscriptions in the Shimoga District,* vol, VIII (Bangalore, 1904).

———, *Epigraphica Carnatica,* Mysore District, Part I, vol. IV (Bangalore, 1894).

———, *Epigraphica Carnatica,* vol. II, Revised Edition (Bangalore, 1823).

———, *Karnataka Inscription,* vol. III (Dharwar, 1953).

———, *Mysore and Coorg, From the Inscriptions* (London, 1909).

Archaeological Sources

Annual Progress Report of Archaeological Survey of Southern India, Madras, 1920-21, 1922.

Annual Report of the Archaeological Survey of India, Calcutta, 1917-18, 1920-22, 1924.

Annual Report of the Archaeological Survey of Mysore, (ASM) 1903-04-Bangalore, 1904.

ASM AR, 1905-06, Bangalore, 1906.
ASM AR, 1906-07, Bangalore, 1907.
ASM AR, 1907-08, Bangalore, 1908.
ASM AR, 1908-09, Bangalore, 1909.
ASM AR, 1909-10, Bangalore, 1910.
ASM AR, 1910-11, Bangalore, 1911.
ASM AR, 1911-12, Bangalore, 1912.
ASM AR, 1912-13, Bangalore, 1913.
ASM AR, 1913-14, Bangalore, 1914.
ASM AR, 1914-15, Bangalore, 1915.
ASM AR, 1915-16, Bangalore, 1916.
ASM AR, 1916-17, Bangalore, 1917.
ASM AR, 1917-18, Bangalore, 1918.
ASM AR, 1918-19, Bangalore, 1919.
ASM AR, 1919-20, Bangalore, 1920.
ASM AR, 1920-21, Bangalore, 1921.
ASM AR, 1921-22, Bangalore, 1922.
ASM AR, 1922-23, Bangalore, 1923.
ASM AR, 1923-24, Bangalore, 1924.

Annual Report of the Mysore Archaeological Department for the year (*ARMAD*), Bangalore, 1925.
ARMAD, Bangalore, 1926.
ARMAD, Bangalore, 1927.
ARMAD, Bangalore, 1928-29.
ARMAD, Bangalore, 1929-31.
ARMAD, Bangalore, 1932.
ARMAD, Bangalore, 1931-35.
ARMAD, Bangalore, 1934.
ARMAD, Bangalore, 1935.
ARMAD, Bangalore, 1936.
ARMAD, Bangalore, 1938-40.
ARMAD, Bangalore, 1939.
ARMAD, Bangalore, 1940.
ARMAD, Mysore, 1941.
ARMAD, Mysore, 1941-42.

ARMAD, Mysore, 1942-43.

ARMAD, Mysore, 1944-45.

Secondary Sources

Aiyangar, K. and S. Rao, *Studies in South Indian Jainism* (Madras, 1922).

Aiyangar, S.K., *Some Contributions of South India to Indian Culture* (Delhi, 1980).

———, *Ancient India and South Indian History and Culture*, vol. I, II (Poona, 1914).

Ali, A.Y., *Medieval India* (London, 132).

Altekar, A.S., *The Rastrakutas and their Times* (Poona, 1934).

Altekar, R.S., *Jainism in the Deccan under the Rastrakutas*, Arrah, 1949.

———, *Prachin Bharatiya Shikshan Paddhati* (Marāṭhī) (Nagpur, 1935).

Balabhal, V., *Feudatories of South India, 800-1070 AD* (Madras, 1978).

Barodia, U.N., *History and Literature of Jainism* (Bombay, 1909).

Basavaraja, K.R., *History and Culture of Karnataka* (Dharwar, 1984).

Basham, A.L., *The Wonder that was India* (Sidgwick and Jackson, London, 1954).

Benerji, R.D., *The Age of Imperial Gupta* (Banaras, 1933).

Bhandarkar, R.G., *Early History of the Deccan* (Poona, 1927).

Bhargava, P.L., *Chandragupta Maurya* (New Delhi, 1996).

Bhattacharya, B.C., *Jain Iconography* (Lahore, 1939).

Bhattacharya, N.N., *Jain Philosophy: Historical Outline* (Delhi, 1976).

Bhattacharya, T., *Handbook of Ancient Indian History* (Patna, 1027).

Brown, Percy, *Indian Architecture, Buddhist and Hindu Periods*, Second edition (Bombay, 1965).

Burgess, Jas, *Digambara Jain Iconography* (Bombay, 1904).

Chakravarti, Haripada, *Asceticism in Ancient India* (Calcutta, 1973).

Chakravati, A., *The Contribution of Jainism to World Culture* (Arrah, 1943).

Chand, Bool, *Jainism in Indian History* (Varanasi, 1951).

———, *Historical Jainism, A History of the Jain Church* (Delhi, 1951).

Chatterjee, A.K., *Comprehensive History of Jainism, up to 1000 AD* (Calcutta, 1978).

Prof. Chakravartinayanar, A., *Panchastikayasara, Kumar Devendra Prasada*, The Central Publishing House, Arrah (India, 1920).

Das, Benarsi, *A Lecture on Jainism* (Agra, 1962).

Deo, S.B., *History of Jain Monarchism from Inscriptions and Literature* (Poona, 1956).

Derrectt, J.D.M., *The Hoyasalas: A Medieval Indian Royal Family* (Oxford University Press, Madras, 1957).

Desai, P.B., *Jainism in South India and some Jain Epigraphs* (Jain Sanskriti Samarakshak Sangha, Solapur, 1957).

Dhaky, M.A., *Santara Sculpture, Journal of the Indian Society of Oriental Art*, vol. IV (Calcutta, 1971-72).

———, *Santara Architecture, Aspects of Jain Art and Architecture*, (Ahmedabad, 1975).

Dikshitar, V.R., *Early History of Jainism in South Jndia* (A.I.O.C. Session, VIII), 1935.

Diwakar, R.R., *Karnataka Through the Ages* (Mysore, 1968).

Diwakar, S.C., *Religion and Peace* (Mathura, 1957).

———, *A Jain Scripture of the Sixth Century* BC (Gauhati, 1965).

Fergusson, James, *History of Indian and Eastern Architecture*, vol. I, II (London, 1910).

Fischer, Klaus, *Caves and Temples of the Jains* (World Jain Mission, Aliganj, 1957).

Fleet, J.F., *Dynasties of Kanarese Districts* (BG, vol I, Pt. 2).

Ganguly, O.C., *The Art of the Rastrakutas* (Calcutta, 1958).

Ghosh, A.G., *Jain Art and Architecture*, vols. I, II, III (Delhi, 1974, 1975).

Ghoshal, S.C., *The Sacred Books of the Jains* (Arrah).

Gopal, B.R., *The Chalukyas of Kalyana and the Kalachuris* (Dharwar, 1981).

Hampa, Nagarajaiah, *Jina Parsva Temples in Karnataka* (Bangalore, 1999).

———, *Sachitra Hombuja*, Bangalore, 1997.

Hasting, James, *Encyclopedia of Religion and Ethics*, vol. II, Hymns-Liberty (London, 1914, 1950, 1955, 1959).

Heras, Henry, *The Araviau Dynasty of the Vijayanagara* (Madras, 1927).

Hiralal, M., *Ancient History of the Jain Literature* (Jamnagar, 1902).

Hukkerikerkar, R.S. (ed.), *Karnataka Darsana* (Bombay, 1955).

Hultzsch, E., *Die Digambaras, Von Mysore* (Mysore, 1914).

———, *Reports on Sanskrit Monuments in Southern India* (Madras, 1905).

Hunter, W.W., *The Imperial Gazetteer of India* (London, 1886-87).

Hunter, W.W., *The Imperial Gazetteer of India*, vol. V (London, 1885-87).

Jacobi, H., *Studies in Jainism* (Ahmedabad, 1946).

———, *Jain Sutras*, Pt. I, SBE, vol. XXIII, Oxford, 1884.

———, *Some Aspects of Jainism* (Calcutta, 1914).

Jain A.K., *Lord Mahavira in the Eyes of Foreigners* (Meena Bharata, New Delhi, 1975).

Jain, C.R., *The Practical Path,* The Central Jain Publishing House (Arrah, 1917).

Jain, Chhotelal, *Jain Bibliography* (Calcutta, 1945).

Jain, J.L., *Outline of Jainism* (Oxford, 1940).

Jain, J.P., *Jainism* (Banaras, 1916).

Jain, J.P., *Pramukha Aitihāsika Jain Puruṣa aur Mahilāyen* (Hindi) (New Delhi, 1975).

———, *Religion and Culture of the Jains,* second edn. (New Delhi, 1977).

———, *The Jain sources of the History of Ancient India, 100 BC-900 AD* (Munshiram, Delhi, 1964).

Jain, J.P., *Remaking of Jain History* (Arrah, 1957).

———, *Jainism* (Calcutta, 1937-38).

———, *Some Historical Jain Kings and Heroes* (Delhi, 1941).

Jain, K.C., *Lord Mahavira and his Times* (Delhi, 1974).

Jain, Muni Uttam Kamal, *Jain Sects and Schools* (Delhi, 1975).

Jain, R.K., *Śravaṇbeḷagoḷa aur Dakṣiṇa ke Ahya Jain Tīrtha* (Hindi).

Jain, Rajamala and Laxmichandra Jain, *Bharat ke Digambara Jain Tīrtha* (Hindi), vol. V, Karnataka (Bombay, 1988).

Jain, S., *Some Common Elements in the Jain and Hindu Pantheon: Yakshas and Yakshinis* (Arrah, 1952).

Jawaharalal, G., *Jainism in Andhra as Depicted in Inscriptions* (Hyderabad, 1994).

Joharapurkar, V., *Bhaṭṭāraka Sampradāya* (Hidni) (Solapur, 1958).

Kalghatgi, T.G. (ed.), *Gommatesvara Commemoration Volume, AD 981-1981* (Sravanbelgola, 1981).

———, *Jainism — A Study* (University of Mysore, 1976).

———, *Some Problems in Jain Psychology* (Dharwar, 1961).

Kane, P.V., *History of Dharma Shastras,* vol. II. Part II, (Poona, 1941).

Kannoomal, *The Study of Jainism* (Agra, 1962).

Kapadia, H.R., *Jain Religion and Literature,* vol. I (Lahore, 1944).

———, *Women in Jainism* (Lahore, 1933).

Karmarkar, A.D., *Cultural Heritage of Karnataka* (Dharwar, 1947).

Karmarkar, D.P., *Cultural Aspects of Medieval Karnataka* (Bangalore, 1944).

———, *Vijayanagara Smaraka Grantha* (Poona, 1936-37).

Krishnan, K.G., *Studies in South Indian History and Epigraph*, vol. I (Madras, 1981).

Krishna, Rao, M.A., *Jainism in Gangavadi* (Bangalore, 1933).

Krishnarao, M.V., *Gangas of Talakada* (Madras, 1936).

Latthe, A.B., *An Introduction to Jainism* (Bombay, 1965).

Luniya, B.N., *Life and Culture in Ancient India, From the Earliest Times to 1000* AD (Agra, 1978).

Mackennzie, C., *Account of Jains* (Calcutta, 1809).

Mackennzie, S.F., *Sravanbelgola* (Bombay, 1873).

———, *The Struggle for Empire*, vol. V (Bombay, 1957).

Madan, A.P., *The History of the Rastrakutas* (Harman Publishing House, New Delhi, 1990).

Mahalingam, T.V., *Readings in South Indian History* (Delhi, 1977).

———, *Administration and Social Life Under Vijayanagar*, Part, II, Social Life (Madras, Univ., Madras, 1975).

Majumdar, R.C., *The Age of Imperial Unity*, vol. II (Bharatiya Vidyabhavan, Bombay, 1951).

———, *Ancient India* (Banaras, 1952).

Mehta, M.L., *Jain Culture* (Varanasi, 1969).

Michal, W. Meister and Dhaky, M.A., *Encyclopedia of Indian Temple Architecture: South India*, Upper Dravidadesa, Early Phase (Univ. of Pennsylvania Press, 1986).

Moraes, G.M., *The Kadamba Kula: A History of Ancient and Mediaeval Karnataka* (Bombay, 1931).

Mugali, R.S., *The Heritage of Karnataka* (Bangalore, 1940).

Murari, K., *Chalukyas of Kalyani, from c. 973* AD *to 1200* AD (New Delhi, 1977).

Murty, H.V.S. and R. Ramkrishna, *A History of Karnataka* (New Delhi, 1966).

Murty, H.V.S., *A History of Karanataka: From the Earliest Times to the Present Day* (New Delhi, 1977).

Nagaraj, H.L. and N.H.L. Nagaraj, *Jain Temples and Tourist Places of Karnataka* (Bangalore, 1993).

Nagaraj, Nalini, *Sravanbelgola* (Bangalore, 1980).

———, *Development of Religion in South India* (Madras, 1963).

Nandi, R.N., *Religious Institutions and Cults in the Deccan* (Motilal Banarsidass, Delhi, 1973).

Nilkantha Sastri, K.A., *A History of South India* (Oxford, 1966).

———, *Comprehensive History of India*, vol. II; *The Mauryas and Satavahanas, 325 BC-AD 300* (Bombay, 1957).

———, *A Guide of Sravanbelgola*, (Govt. Textbook Press, Mysore, 1981).

Parsons, C.E., *A Town in the Mysore State* (Mysore, 1931).

Patil, B.B., *Dakshina Bharata, Jain and Jain-Dharma* (Marathi) (Sangli, 1938).

Phaltane, L.A., *Ancient Jain Books Shed any Light on Ancient History* (Arrah, 1920).

Prasad, Beni, *World Problems and Jain Ethics* (Lahore, 1945).

Prasad, Ishwari, *History of Medieval India* (Allahabad, 1928).

Premi, N.R., *Jain Sahitya aur Itihas*, second edition (Hindi) (Bombay, 1956).

Puttaswamy, D., *Karkala, A Jain Centre* (Karkala, 1961).

Rajasekhara, S., *Karnataka Architecture* (Dharwar, 1985).

Ramachandran Rao, S.K., *Jainism in South India* (Madras, 1970).

Ramachandran, T.N., *Harappa and Jainism* (New Delhi, 1980).

———, *Jain Monuments and Places of First Class Importance* (Calcutta, 1944).

Ramanaya, N.V., *Essay on the Origin of the South Indian temples* (New Delhi, 1980).

Ramappa, K., *The Essentials of Jainism* (Ahmedabad, 1982).

Ramaswami, Ayyangar, *Studies in South Indian Jainism* (Madras, 1922).

Ramesh, K.V. and M.V. Kitti, "The Origin and Early History of the Santaras of Santaliage 1000," *The Quarterly Journal of the Mythic Society* (Bangalore, 1966-67).

Ramesh, K.V., *History of South Kanara* (*From the Earliest Times to the Fall*) (Karnataka University, Dharwar, 1970).

Rao, D.S.A., *The Early Wodeyar of Mysore: Their Cultural Traditions* (Bangalore, 1956).

Rao, Hayavadana, C., *Mysore Gazetteer*, Descriptive, vol. I, New edition (Bangalore, 1927).

———, *Mysore Gazetteer*, Historical, New edition (Bangalore, 1930).

———, *Primitive Religion in Mysore* (Bangalore, 1922).

Rao, N.L., *Eminent Women of Karnataka* (Bangalore, 1954).

Rao, N.S., *Two Centuries of Wodeyar Rule in Mysore (1565-1761)*, (Bangalore, 1932).

Rao, S.B., *New Studies in Jainism* (Arrah, 1937).

Rao, V.R., *The Kadambas of Banvase* (*Q.J.M.S.* vol. II) (Bangalore, 1931).

Raychoudhary, H.C., *Studies in Indian Antiquary* (Calcutta, 1932).

Rice, B.L., *Mysore and Coorg*, vol. II (Bangalore, 1876).

———, *Mysore*, vol. II (Bangalore, 1877).

Saletore, B.A., *Medieval Jainism*, Karnataka Publishing House (Bombay, 1938).

———, *Social and Political Life in the Vijayanagara Empire* (Karnataka, 1346-1646).

———, *Ancient Karnataka*, vol. I, History of Tuluva (Poona, 1936).

Sangave, V.A., *Jain Community, A Social Survey* (Bombay, 1959).

———, *The Sacred Sravanbelgola: A Social Religious Study* (New Delhi, 1982).

Sastri, K.A.N., *A History of South India* (London, 1958).

Sastri, N.A., *A History of South India from Prehistoric Times to the Fall of Vijayanagara* (Madras, 1953).

———, *A History of South India*, (Madras, 1955).

Sastri, S.S., *Devaraya II* (*Indian Ant.*, vol. VII) (Bombay, 1928).

———, *Narasimha II* (N.I.A. vol. 4) (1941-42).

Sastri, S.S., *Some Jain Gurus in Kannada Inscriptions* (Arrah, 1943).

———, *Sources of Karnataka History* (Mysore, 1940).

———, *Early Gangas of Talakad*, 1952.

Setter, S., *The Classical Karnataka Literature and the Digambara Jain Iconography, Aspects of Jain Art and Architecture* (Ahmedabad, 1975).

———, *Sravanbelgola* (Bangalore, 1981).

Shah, C.J., *Jainism in North India* (Bombay, 1932).

Shah, U.P. and Dhaky, M.A., *Aspects of Jain Art and Architecture* (Gujarat State, 1975).

Sharma, S.R., *Jainism and Karnataka Culture* (Dharwar, 1940).

Sheik Ali, B., *Hoyasala Dynasty* (Mysore, 1972).

———, *History of Western Gangas* (Mysore, 1976).

Sherwani, H.K. and P.M. Joshi, *History of Medieval Deccan* (vol. I, 1973 and vol. II, 1974, Hyderabad).

Sheshagiri, B. and M.S. Ramaswamy, *Studies in South Indian Jainism* (Madras, 1922).

Shripal, Surendranath, *Colossus of Sravanbelgola and other Shrines of Deccan* (Bombay, 1953).

Singh, Ramabhushan Prasad, *Jainism in Early Medieval Karnataka* (Delhi, 1975).

Srikantaiya, S., *Life in the Hoyasala Period* (1918, *Q.J.M.S.*).

Sripati Joyess, B.D., *Aithishaya Kshetra Hombuja* (Hombuja, 1977).

Stein, B., *South Indian Temples* (New Delhi, 1978).

Stevenson, Sin-Clair., *The Heart of Jainism* (Oxford, 1915).

Swell, Robert, *A Sketch of the Dynasties of Southern India* (Madras, 1983).

Tripathi, R.S., *History of Ancient India* (Delhi, 1942).

Thompson, E.M., *Religion in the Mysore State* (*Q.J.M.S.* Mysore, 1911).

Upadhye, A.N., *Jains and Jainism* (Poona, 1950).

———, *The Ethics of the Jains* (Delhi, 1956).

Venkatasubbiah, A., *When was the Gommata Image at Sravanbelgola set up?* (*I.H.Q.*) vol. VI, 1930.

Vidyabhusana, S.C., *History of Indian Logic* (Calcutta, 1921).

Yazdani, G., *The Early History of the Deccan,* vol. I-IV (London, 1960).

Journals

Indian Antiquary, vol. II (New Delhi, 1873).

Indian Antiquary, vol. XXXII (Bombay, 1903).

Journal of Indian History, vol. XXX (Trivandrum, 1952).

Journal of Indian History, vol. XXXI (Trivandrum, 1953).

Journal of Indian History, vol. XXXIX (Trivandrum, 1961).

Encyclopedia of Religion and Ethics, J. Hastings.

New Indian Antiquary (Bombay).

The Quarterly Journal of the Mythic Society (Bangalore).

Jain Siddhanta Bhaskara, Hindi Journal (Arrah).

Jinamanjari: Contemporary Jain Reflection, vol. I (U.S.A. 1990).

Jinamanjari: Contemporary Jain Reflection, vol. V (U.S.A. 1992).

Jinamanjari: International Journal of Contemporary Jain Reflections (U.S.A. 1996).

The Jain Antiquary, vol. I (Arrah, June, 1935).

The Jain Antiquary, vol. I (Arrah, June, 1936).

The Jain Antiquary, vol. IV (Arrah, June, 1938).

The Jain Antiquary, vol. XV (Arrah, June, 1949).

The Jain Antiquary, vol. XIV (Arrah, June, 1949).

The Jain Antiquary, vol. XVIII (Arrah, June, 1952).

1. Sule basadi, Humcha.

2. Side view of Pārśvanātha temple, Humcha.

3. Tribhuvan chudamani basadi at Karkala.

4. Inscriptions at Śravaṇbeḷagoḷa on Chandragiri.

5. Inscription at Śravaṇbeḷagoḷa on Chandragiri.

6. Image of Bāhubali at Karkala.

7. Jagadguru Karmayogi Swastishree Charukeerty Bhattarak Swamiji, Śravaṇbeḷagoḷa Maṭh.

8. Devendrakeerti Bhattarak Swamiji, Humcha.

9. Charukkeerti Bhattarak Swamiji of Moodbidri.

10. Chāmuṇḍarāya Basadi at Śravaṇbeḷagoḷa on Chandragiri.

11. Bhadrabāhu cave at Śravaṇbeḷagoḷa on Chandragiri.

12. Side view of inscription near the foot of lord Bāhubali

13. Inscriptions present at Pañcakūṭī Basadi, Humcha.

14. Clear view of inscription present at Pañcakūṭī Basadi, Humcha.

15. Interior design, art, and architecture of
Pañcakūṭī Basadi, Humcha.

16. Birds eye-view of Chandragiri, Śravaṇbeḷagoḷa.

17. Image of lord Bāhubali at Śravaṇbeḷagoḷa.

18. Monuments of Goudad Basadi, Humcha.

19.a. Mahāmastakābhiṣeka of lord Bāhubali.

19.b. Mahāmastakābhiṣeka of lord Bāhubali.

Index